VOICES FOR THE CULTURE OF PEACE

Voices *for* the Culture *of* Peace

Compendium of the
SGI-USA Culture of Peace
Distinguished Speaker Series

VOLUME 2

Culture of Peace Press

Published by Culture of Peace Press

An imprint of the SGI-USA

606 Wilshire Blvd., Santa Monica, CA 90401

© 2013 SGI-USA

ISBN 978-0-9844050-4-6

Printed in the United States of America

Cover and interior design by VJB/Scribe

LIBRARY OF CONGRESS CATALOGING-IN-PUBLICATION DATA
Voices for a culture of peace: compendium of the SGI-USA Culture of Peace
distinguished speaker series.
    v. <1-> ; cm.
Includes bibliographical references and index.
ISBN 978-0-9844050-4-6 (alk. paper)
1. Peace. 2. Peace-building. 3. Peace—Religious aspects—Buddhism. I. Soka
Gakkai International-USA. II. Title.
JZ5538.V65 2013
303.6'6—dc22

2013091074

10 9 8 7 6 5 4 3 2 1

Contents

Foreword

I t's up to us: Together we must take on the mission to change history. The good news is that we *can* do it; we do not have to wait for the politicians. We are lucky enough to be living in an age when we have the capacities, technologies and tools to do absolutely wonderful things as individuals and as a global community.

The world today is interconnected in fundamental ways. Our connections are becoming more and more immediate, and the possibility of a truly global community, mobilized for peace, exists now more than ever before.

That's why I am pleased to write this introduction to the second volume of *Voices for the Culture of Peace*, a collection of lectures from the SGI-USA Culture of Peace Distinguished Speaker Lecture Series, essays imbued with the wisdom and determination of those who are already leading the way.

I am always reminded of the optimism and the sense of purpose that great leaders have. In my view, John Kennedy was one of the greatest. At another time of great pessimism about the Cold War and the possibility of spiraling into an outright hot war with the Soviet Union, President Kennedy gave a speech that I regard as one of the greatest speeches of modern history, and which resonates for us today. It is known as his "Peace Speech," the commencement address at American University in June 1963.

Kennedy said:

> First: let us examine our attitude toward peace itself. Too many
> of us think it is impossible. Too many think it unreal. But that is
> a dangerous, defeatist belief. It leads to the conclusion that war is
> inevitable, that mankind is doomed, that we are gripped by forces
> we cannot control.

We need not accept that view. Our problems are manmade –
therefore, they can be solved by man. And man can be as big as
he wants. No problem of human destiny is beyond human beings.
Man's reason and spirit have often solved the seemingly unsolv-
able – and we believe they can do it again.

I am not referring to the absolute, infinite concept of peace
and good will, of which some fantasies and fanatics dream. I do
not deny the value of hopes and dreams but we merely invite dis-
couragement and incredulity by making that our only and immediate goal.

Let us focus instead on a practical, more attainable peace
– based not on a sudden revolution in human nature but on a
gradual evolution in human institutions – on a series of concrete
actions and effective agreements, which are in the interest of all
concerned. There is no single, simple key to this peace – no grand
or magic formula to be adopted by one or two powers. Genuine
peace must be the product of many nations, the sum of many acts.
It must be dynamic, not static, changing to meet the challenge
of each new generation. For peace is a process, a way of solving
problems.[1]

What I love about this speech is how President Kennedy talks at length
to Americans about their *own views*, rather than "dictating" terms to the
other side. In the middle of the Cold War, in the middle of so much attack
and vilification of the Soviet Union, Kennedy's speech was about what
Americans should believe and how Americans should be looking inward
at their own attitudes toward peace. He went on to give massive praise to
the Russian people. He says, "As Americans, we find communism profoundly repugnant as a negation of personal freedom, but we can still hail
the Russian people for their many achievements in science and space and
economic and industrial growth and culture and in acts of courage."[2] He
repeatedly calls on Americans to think about how they can set a path for
others to find peace with them.

---

1. Vito N. Silvestri, *Becoming JFK: A Profile in Communication* (Westport, Conn.:
2000), p. 224.
2. Ibid.

The outcome of this particular speech was absolutely startling. Nikita Khrushchev (then USSR premier) heard it and immediately declared that it was the finest speech of any American leader in modern times. He called the American diplomat Averrel Harriman, former US ambassador to the Soviet Union, and said, "I want to make peace with this man." Six weeks later, the first partial nuclear test ban treaty was signed. Six weeks after the speech. That is what can come from reaching out to find a constructive connection with others. It is a demonstration of what is possible and practical when we overcome fear and search for the true human connection.

Today, many people believe that solutions to our problems are impossible; that poverty cannot be solved, that climate change cannot be addressed, and that the future will be worse for our children. As John Kennedy said about those who said that war is inevitable, "That is a dangerous, defeatist belief." He was right—such pessimism leads to the conclusion that we are doomed.

None of the problems we face are beyond solution if we overcome the fear, which is the greatest obstacle of all, and understand the nature of the challenges, the power of the technologies that we have, and the practicality of potential solutions.

I believe we are capable of ending poverty and changing the world. I have no doubt that by doing so, we can make the most important connection of all, across every racial divide, religious divide, linguistic divide and any other divide, including between the rich and poor. Human-to-human contact is the essence and the path to peace on the planet. The essays in this collection show the path ahead—how we can overcome the fissures that divide us and build a global culture of peace and cooperation.

~ Jeffrey D. Sachs
Director, The Earth Institute, and Quetelet Professor of
Sustainable Development at Columbia University

Preface

SGI-USA is very happy to be publishing this second volume of *Voices for the Culture of Peace* featuring talks delivered in our Distinguished Speaker Series. The focus of each of the lectures in this series continues to center on one or more of the eight action areas defined in the 1999 *United Nations Declaration and Programme of Action on a Culture of Peace*, namely: (1) Fostering a culture of peace through education, (2) Promoting sustainable economic and social development, (3) Promoting respect for all human rights, (4) Ensuring equality between women and men, (5) Fostering democratic participation, (6) Advancing understanding, tolerance and solidarity, (7) Supporting participatory communication and the free flow of information and knowledge and (8) Promoting international peace and security.

We feel fortunate to introduce another series of stimulating and thoughtful talks in this volume. They demonstrate the variety of disciplines and perspectives that touch on the culture of peace and represent the wider dialogue about building the culture of peace we hope to foster.

The SGI-USA does not necessarily endorse all of the ideas or views expressed by each speaker in this series. We simply hope they awaken the peace builder within each person who hears or reads them, inspiring a realization that a true culture of peace requires the active engagement of all citizens, all organizations and all institutions.

On behalf of the SGI-USA, I want to express appreciation to former United Nations Under-Secretary-General Anwarul K. Chowdhury for his ongoing support of both this series of publications as well as the speaker series. Further, we are indebted to the president of the Soka Gakkai International, Daisaku Ikeda, for his decades of leadership and example as an individual working to fulfill humankind's shared desire for the global culture of peace.

~ Ian McIlraith
Director, SGI-USA Peace and Community Relations

Introduction

Peace That Is Sustainable

Ambassador Anwarul K. Chowdhury

Ambassador Anwarul K. Chowdhury has devoted many years as an inspirational champion for sustainable peace and development, ardently advancing the cause of the global movement for the culture of peace that has energized civil society all over the world.

As a career diplomat, Permanent Representative to the United Nations, President of the UN Security Council, President of the UNICEF Board, UN Under-Secretary-General, and recipient of the U Thant Peace Award, UNESCO Gandhi Gold Medal for Culture of Peace, Spirit of the UN Award and University of Massachusetts Boston Chancellor's Medal for Global Leadership for Peace, Ambassador Chowdhury has a wealth of experience in the critical issues of our time — peace, sustainable development, and human rights. He served as the Senior Special Advisor to the President of the 66th session (2011–12) of the UN General Assembly.

Ambassador Chowdhury's legacy and leadership are boldly imprinted in his pioneering initiatives at the UN General Assembly in 1999 to adopt the landmark Declaration and Programme of Action on a Culture of Peace and, in 1998, the proclamation of the International Decade for Culture of Peace and Nonviolence for the Children of the World (2001–2010).

Equally pioneering is his initiative in March 2000 as the President of the Security Council for the political and conceptual breakthrough leading to the adoption of UN Security Council Resolution 1325, recognizing for the first time the role and contribution of women in peace and security.

He served as Ambassador and Permanent Representative of Bangladesh to the United Nations from 1996 to 2001 and as the Under-Secretary-General and High Representative of the United Nations, responsible for the most vulnerable countries of the world, from 2002 to 2007.

In March 2003, Soka University of Japan conferred on Ambassador Chowdhury an honorary doctorate for his work on women's issues, child rights and culture of peace as well as for strengthening the United Nations. In May 2012, he received a Doctor of Humane Letters honoris causa degree from Saint Peters University in the United States. He has been decorated by the Government of Burkina Faso in West Africa with the country's highest honor, L'Ordre Nacionale, in 2007 for his championship of the most vulnerable countries.

Dr. Chowdhury has structured curricula and taught courses on the culture of peace at Soka University of America and the City University of New York. He is the honorary chair of the International Day of Peace NGO Committee at the United Nations since 2008. He is a part of the twelve-member Wisdom Council of the Summer of Peace 2013, a worldwide initiative to advance the culture of peace. He is among the five-member Board of Trustees of the New York City Peace Museum initiative and a member of the Advisory Council of the National Peace Academy in the United States.

I had the pleasure of launching the SGI-USA's Culture of Peace Distinguished Speaker Series in July 2007 in New York. Now this series is also held regularly in Los Angeles, New York and Washington, D.C. Occasional lectures as a part of this series are also held in Honolulu and Chicago. Five SGI-USA Culture of Peace Resource Centers, as well as a sixth that opened in February 2013 in San Francisco, contribute in a significant way to spread the essential message of the culture of peace and to empower people toward self-transformation – individually and collectively – to embrace peace and nonviolence as part of their existence.

I extend my heartfelt recognition of the tremendous success of the series and its role in raising awareness of the multidimensional perspective of the culture of peace. The activities of each center also deserve our wholehearted commendation. I believe this lecture series will become a very important landmark in the history of the SGI-USA's efforts in promoting the culture of peace, far beyond just being a number of lectures by eminent personalities.

I believe the culture of peace transcends boundaries. It transcends differences in age and differences in culture or background. It is the most universal thing that one can internalize. My heartfelt, sincere appreciation goes to the Soka Gakkai International in particular for giving this special profile to the global movement for the culture of peace. I believe humanity as a whole owes the SGI and its president, Daisaku Ikeda, a great deal for championing this cause of global peace and human empowerment.

Tracing back to my initiation to the United Nations in 1972 – when I worked for Bangladesh's membership to the world body immediately after the country's independence – the decade that I served the United Nations and as the ambassador for Bangladesh to the United Nations gave me a once-in-a-life-time opportunity to make my humble contribution for the good of humanity.

On July 31, 1997, as the Bangladesh ambassador, I wrote to United Nations Secretary-General Kofi Annan, asking him to circulate my request for a separate agenda item on the culture of peace for the plenary sessions of the UN General Assembly. That very letter has mushroomed in a big way to today's global movement for the culture of peace. Last year's first-ever High Level Forum on the Culture of Peace convened by the President of the UN General Assembly is a much-heralded testimony to that.

"Toward a culture of peace" as an issue was debated for a number of years at the behest of UNESCO before it became a separate agenda item of the most universal and apex global deliberative body – the General Assembly Plenary – in 1997 at my proposal. That year, the UNGA adopted a resolution declaring the year 2000, the millennium year, as the International Year for the Culture of Peace. In 1998, the United Nations adopted a significant and promising resolution to declare the years 2001 to 2010 as the International Decade for the Culture of Peace and Non-violence for the Children of the World. These were all our initiatives.

The high point in this process came in 1999, when the United Nations adopted by consensus the Declaration and Programme of Action on a Culture of Peace. This action by the United Nations was a watershed event in the post-Cold War world. It was an honor for me to chair the nine-month-long negotiations that led to the adoption of this historic, norm-setting document that is considered to be one of the most significant legacies of the United Nations that would endure generations.

Peace is integral to human existence – in everything we do, in everything we say and in every thought we have, there is a place for peace. Absence of peace makes our challenges, our struggles, much more difficult. I believe that is why it is very important that we keep our focus on creating the culture of peace in our lives.

The quest for peace is as old as human history. The prehistoric cave-man was also looking for peace, and we are here today talking about peace, trying to see how best to achieve an enduring culture of peace. I say that it is the longest human endeavor or quest going on, but it runs alongside many of the things that we do on a daily basis.

This I have seen firsthand, as my work took me to the farthest corners of the world. What I have seen has outraged me but also has given me hope and encouragement that there are forces determined to turn our planet into a livable place for all. From Sierra Leone to Sri Lanka, from Mongolia to Mauritius, from Paraguay to the Philippines, from Kosovo to Kazakhstan, from Bhutan to the Bahamas to Burkina Faso, I have seen time and again how people—even the humblest and the weakest—have contributed to building the culture of peace in their personal lives, in their families, in their communities and in their countries. And that ultimately is contributing to build a new and better tomorrow for humanity and to the global movement for the culture of peace.

One lesson I have learned from this is that to prevent our history of war and conflict from repeating itself, the values of nonviolence, tolerance and democracy will have to be inculcated in every woman and man—children and adults alike. Another message comes out loud and clear—we should never forget that when women, who comprise half of world's seven billion people, are marginalized, there is no chance for our world to gain sustainable peace in the real sense.

Sometimes we see peace as the opposite of war. That is not at all what the culture of peace means. The absence of war or the absence of violence is not peace. It may halt violence, it may bring cessation of hostilities, but it is not peace in its totality. Certainly it is not sustainable peace.

The most important thing to realize is that the absence of peace takes away the opportunities that we need to better ourselves, to prepare ourselves, to empower ourselves to face the challenges of the world. Absence of peace takes away that opportunity and that is why peace is essential in our lives.

Do not isolate peace as something separate. It is part of our very existence. Anything that we do or say or how we interact with one another is important. We should know how to relate to one another without being angry, without being violent, without being disrespectful, without neglect, without prejudice. Once we are able to do that, we can take the next step in advancing the global movement for the culture of peace. Let us start with ourselves.

For that, all of you reading and enjoying this second volume of the collection of lectures from the Culture of Peace Distinguished Speaker Series and taking actions in your lives, in your own spheres of influence to create the culture of peace, deserve a big "thank you" from all of us!

Working Locally, Thinking Globally

Community Approaches to Media Activism and Literacy

Paolo Davanzo

Founder, Human Rights Film Festival
Executive Director, Echo Park Film Center, Los Angeles

Paolo Davanzo is the founder and executive director of the Echo Park Film Center in Los Angeles, California. He was born in Italy and immigrated to the United States with his family at age seven. He started EPFC in honor of his parents, social justice activists who passed away early in his life. An associate professor in the Film & Video Department of College of the Canyons, Paolo holds a bachelor's degree in visual arts and political science from the University of California, San Diego and a master's in film from Humboldt State University. He is the founder and programmer of the Human Rights Film Festival, the EPFC Youth Film Festival and the Polyester Prince Road Show. The goal of the Human Rights Film Festival is to highlight social justice issues often ignored by the mainstream media. Every year, the festival presents an engaging variety of documentary and experimental films that explore themes of home and community. Basic human rights, including the right to peacefully assemble, the right to religious freedom, the right of political sovereignty and the right to life and liberty, are often taken for granted in Western industrialized nations. In the post-9/11 landscape, issues of human rights are increasingly crucial and closer to home than ever before, and these films are vehicles to promote thought, discussion, debate and action.

Paolo Davanzo's work addresses many of the eight action areas in the 1999 United Nations Declaration and Programme of Action on a Culture of Peace, most notably the seventh: supporting participatory communication and the free flow of information and knowledge. As Mr. Davanzo says: "Our students examined, talked to historians, talked to activists, looked at work, and once again politicized themselves, making themselves aware of the importance of water rights and water in the city and access to that water—many, many testimonials, many beautiful stories."

Today's lecture is called "Working Locally, Thinking Globally: Community Approaches to Media Activism and Literacy." I am obviously borrowing that expression from one made popular by David Brower in 1969 with the Friends of the Earth organization, something that was co-opted by progressives, you know, thinking globally, acting locally. So I just changed it a bit to "Working Locally," finding ways within your community, not to just act and be political but to create change through your good deeds and through your work.

A lot of what I am talking about has to do with that. I also think I was initially brought here because of my work with the Human Rights Film Festival, which I continue to do. It's something that we began in Orange County at the University of California, Irvine, and since have moved to the Echo Park Film Center, which I will talk about later.

The Human Rights Film Festival is a powerful event because people become politicized, if they aren't already politicized, through films, predominantly through documentaries. At the Echo Park Film Center, we recently showed a film called *Vietnam, American Holocaust*, which was made by a filmmaker in Santa Monica, Clay Claiborne. It was a diverse crowd, and here was a young man, I think probably not more than nineteen years of age, and he talked about how he grew up in a progressive household. His mom was always against the Vietnam War and protested against it, and he knew it was a bad thing, but he didn't really understand why. This film drew parallels between our current administration and the war in Iraq and things in Vietnam. It opened his eyes, and he could now articulate his thoughts and draw comparisons between what happened in Vietnam and what is happening currently.

For me, the power of film to change us, to politicize us, to make us act, to make us want to act, is a very powerful vehicle. And that's what I want to talk about today. For years, I felt that filmmaking was one of the most democratic art forms for the consumer, meaning we can all turn on a television, we can watch a film, for the most part, right? But to make work that is socially relevant or to even have access to that work is still difficult. We talk about the media revolution, where computers cost less and cameras cost less, but they still cost money, and you still need the resources.

With that in mind, I started the Human Rights Film Festival in 2001, and an organization called the Echo Park Film Center in 2002.

It's not a story of my life, but I think my life is relevant to explain why we're here.

Back to my mother and father. Being raised in a progressive household, I was working to create change from a very early age. My father was someone who talked the revolution. He was from Italy, he was gregarious and had a big, booming voice, but I think Mama was the one who was really working for change. Papa fancied himself a revolutionary, but Mama was working for the United Nations Association and homeless shelters and public education and libraries and was always doing good deeds.

I think, growing up, my brother and I were instilled with these values. My mama often said, "You've been given so much, you need to give back to the system, replenish the system." Working in soup kitchens and working in the UNICEF store as a kid and selling things from all over the world, where all the money went to UNICEF, I think it became part of my life. When you live the dream, the progressive ideology, it's through your actions, it's through your deeds, and this is the culture of peace we're talking about, trying to promote that as an ideology, as a way to live our lives.

We're all touched by people who shape our lives. When my father passed away in 1997, I was devastated. I was working in the film industry as a filmmaker, and I was politically active, but it wasn't the way I was living my life. So I quit my job and lived in my van for two months.

It is sad that this town is all about filmmaking but not at all about filmmaking. It's largely about the product, really the commerce of film as opposed to the storytelling and the community of film.

I had to get out of Hollywood. I was working a job I didn't love, and I decided I had to drop out of society. For two months, I drifted around the United States and showed my films. I brought a little gas-powered generator and in campgrounds, on the side of buildings, sometimes chased by the police, sometimes encouraged by the police, whatever the case was, I was showing films and creating a dialogue with people. It was a way to deal with the loss of my father.

And it was magical. If I were in a campground, with ten retirees in RVs, maybe they'd say, "Paolo, I don't get it, but I love your spirit," or someone else would say: "I love it! I understand what you're trying to do," and demystify the world of filmmaking. We all have ideas, we just need access. We need to be able to tell our stories, and this is what led me to start the Echo Park Film Center.

> ⧉ *The power of film to change us, to politicize us, to make us act, to make us want to act, is a very powerful vehicle.*

When my mother passed away two years later, that's when things kind of skidded, and I said, "I need to be more proactive about creating this change." In her memory, we started the Human Rights Film Festival in Orange County. It began at the University of California, Irvine, and was cosponsored by the United Nations Association.

It was a spectacular, wonderful event. Hundreds of people came, we had lectures, we had speakers, but eventually it became too big and unmanageable. I stole it back, and I don't mean this with any disparaging terms. I said, "I'm taking this film festival back, and I'm going to reinvent it." The next year, I started the Echo Park Film Center.

And that's the heart of this lecture, along with the United Nations' Programme of Action on a Culture of Peace. I'm going to talk about some of the ways we work toward a culture of peace, some of which are through education. Another one is through access to tools and knowledge and the dissemination of information. These are key things that we sometimes take for granted in this country, but things that are relevant throughout the world.

The premise of the Echo Park Film Center was simple: to create a public access center that was a safe haven for the community of Echo Park. Echo Park is in the east side of Los Angeles, a world away from Santa Monica, but I had been living there for a number of years, and so I was drawn back to Echo Park.

Echo Park resonated with me—the culture of Catholicism and people coming together and walking down the streets and being in the park and celebrating community and being part of an extended family and not driving to a place and locking themselves indoors. It seemed like the most appropriate place to open the center.

From day one, we did certain things. Now, after six years, going on our seventh year, I hope we are doing them well. We do free film and video-making classes for youth and for seniors. We've taught more than four hundred kids in the last six years, and about eighty seniors.

It's a volunteer endeavor, one of those things for which we felt there was a need. There was a need for access, a need for storytelling. A group of us who were activists, who were filmmakers, who were educators, said, "Let's create this safe haven." We're not the first to do it, but our model is unique because—besides the school, which is free for young and those in the twilight of their life, whatever the term we like to use—we also offer very low-cost classes, $40 to $50, for adults. Once again, it's about access, right? Whether you're selling fruit on the side of the road or you work as an insurance broker, we all have ideas for films. We just need the access and the tutelage and the encouragement and the passion to say, "I can do it!"

We've taught hundreds of adults who have gone on to make films, many of them very progressive—anti-war films, films about affordable housing, about getting on your bike and riding down the street instead of driving your car, and other films that are maybe more playful. The school is a big part of it.

We also created a sixty-seat cinema where we hang a big sheet, and we show films that are underrepresented. You can go on any corner of this town and watch a two-hour narrative starring Brad Pitt and Angelina Jolie, right? So we're showing anything except a two-hour narrative. We show human rights films, short films, films in Spanish, gay and lesbian cinema. Whoever approaches us with an idea, we say: "We're a resource. Let's show the films here, and let's talk about them." With the multiplex [theatres], it's disheartening as we pay the $14, and it's air-conditioned, and we don't commune with our neighbors. We watch the film and we go home.

At the film center, we always have a dialogue afterwards. The majority of the time, we encourage the filmmaker to come and present the work, which is wonderful. Some of us played in bands growing up, and we kind of stole this do-it-yourself ethic, for example, if you tour the country, we'll give you all the money you make at the door, we'll feed you, and you'll sleep on my couch. It's really this encompassing, treating the artist as someone important and disseminating this information. So, if you have films, use our resources. Come to this center, show your work, learn how to make films.

We've also created a co-op, meaning that if you need a camera, you need a tripod, you become a member, it's $30 a year, and you get access to all our equipment. You can borrow the light that you need, borrow those other things, and, finding a way that you—all of you in this room— can tell your stories.

That's the basis of the film center, and the reason I'm excited about it. That, and really politicizing a lot of our youth.

Some examples of the films we've done: We made a film called *Red Hill*. Some of you who are lifelong Angelinos, you know that Echo Park was notorious in the '50s. It was called Red Gulch or Red Hill, because it was a renowned haven for leftists and progressives. We interviewed, it's kind of a funny term, the "red diaper babies," the children of the residents who lived in the era, who are still alive and now in their sixties and seventies, and they told stories of having to hide people in their home from the FBI, and, "Mom, why was that guy always in our attic?" and these stories that are so compelling. We used those stories, very real stories, to politicize our own children. I sound like a surrogate father, which I feel like, but our students are our children. The filmmakers used that example of these early progressives to once again study issues of affordable housing, immigration, and politicize themselves where maybe they weren't already politicized.

We just did a piece called *This Is the LA River*. It's fascinating, if you ask Angelinos, "Where is the LA River?" a lot don't know, and some respond, "You mean the big cement thing that kind of goes through the city?" But when you talk about the origins of the Los Angeles River, you're talking about where the Tongva-Gabrielino Tribe first settled, and where the original pueblo of Los Angeles was built. Now, sadly, the river is kind of a wash for which no one has any passion.

Our students examined, talked to historians, talked to activists, looked at work, and once again politicized themselves, making themselves aware of the importance of water rights and water in the city and access to that water—many, many testimonials, many beautiful stories.

I thought the best way to share these stories with you is to show you some of the work that the students have made. They're short films, each is about five or six minutes long. I thought we'd watch two or three of them, I could talk a little bit about them, and then we can talk about how it affects you and how we can perpetuate this culture of peace through media literacy, through disseminating information and through the work of our young people.

EDITOR'S NOTE:

> Dodger Blues *by Gabriel Perez tells the story of Chavez Ravine, which was a thriving community comprising three neighborhoods: Bishop, Palo Verde and La Loma, which were torn down to make way for the building of Dodger Stadium in 1962. The residents were told an affordable housing complex would be built on the site and that the people who sold their homes to the city would get first pick when the new buildings were completed. The people who sold their homes to the city were paid only half of what their property was worth, and those who refused were evicted and their homes destroyed. Perez interviews several Dodger fans, some of whom had never heard of Chavez Ravine. Perez says many Angelinos saw Chavez Ravine as a dump or wasteland, but he says it was a community in which people took care of one another. Perez describes himself as a Dodger fan, but says Dodger Stadium's dark past troubles him. He quotes a former resident who says, "I came back to the*

ravine in 1997, and I feel like people were dancing on my grave."
Perez says he can relate to that feeling because he had to leave Echo
Park in 2002 when rents became too high for his family to afford,
and it was hard for him to leave the neighborhood in which he had
grown up. He wonders what lies in store for Echo Park as it becomes
more gentrified and draws a comparison to the question of what the
Dodgers will become, because Baseball seems more concerned with
profits and less concerned with the fans. Perez ends on a positive
note, stating that no matter what he loves the Dodgers.

This film is interesting because it raises issues that are going through
Los Angeles, including issues of affordable housing. To politicize young
people is not easy, to talk about issues of genocide and international relations when our kids are just getting by day to day. We asked Gabriel, "Do
you know the history of Dodger Stadium?" He said, "No, I don't." So we
sent him to the library, and he researches and he talks to people who lived
in Chavez Ravine and lost their homes, and he becomes politicized, and
that's a catalyst for him to create change. In some ways, the film is rough,
but the heart is powerful, and to read the story from a man of sixteen years
helps us to talk more about the issues at Echo Park using this film as a
vehicle.

EDITOR'S NOTE:

The second film, Not in the War, *was made by Ava Hess. She inter-*
viewed some of her relatives, women who had been born in Iran and
were now living in America, about how they feel about the war in
their home country, what they think the war is truly about, how the
war affects them, and how their daily lives affect the war.

It is a very powerful thing, sharing these stories.

Questions and Answers

AUDIENCE MEMBER 1: Most of the youth are involved in the Internet
community. How are you embracing that?

DAVANZO: That's a great question. I started the lecture with this notion
of access. When I first started making films fifteen years ago, it was

cost prohibitive. There was no digital revolution yet. Today, it's getting more affordable but still not totally accessible for people. Also, the notion of uploading to the Internet is making a difference, including YouTube and other ways to get things out there. We promote the work. And we're only open ten months out of the year, because, as an educator and also as a filmmaker, my first love is traveling with my own work, as I alluded to with my father's story. So we close in January and July, and we travel with the students' work. We've done tours through Mexico, through Japan, through Europe, showing this work to other cultures. For example showing a film made by a thirteen-year-old in Mexico or in Italy creates a dialogue between cultures.

I'm a big proponent of the Internet and getting work out there. With it, however, there's an oversaturation of content. I think it's sometimes a problem and makes it hard to find the most relevant work. But I love the notion that you can be anywhere and click and see a movie that inspires you.

I don't know if I answered the question appropriately, but I think it's a vehicle for change. And I guess the caveat is that still not a lot of people have access to the Internet, especially internationally. The notion of the itinerate cinema caravan was prolific in Mexico and India and a lot of cultures in the 1920s and '30s, where you would physically take films to a town. We always do free shows. It kind of embraces that community. So we take it on the road as often as possible.

AUDIENCE MEMBER 2: You said it's run by volunteers, but how many people work there? How does that work? How many people did it take to start?

DAVANZO: I'm the cofounder of the center. I teach filmmaking at a junior college. And there's actually a sweet story. One of my students took my class ten years ago. He grew up in the Midwest and could fix anything, like his Trans Am, his fridge, and so on. He heard that I wanted to open a cinema in a school.

I was lecturing at the college, up this sloped area. There was a little window, and I saw Ken banging on it. He's a mild-mannered man, you know, very passive, very calm. And he had said after taking my class that he had learned to fix cameras. He became obsessed with film cameras. So with my vision of having the school and the cinema, he brought a business perspective to it, where we did camera repairs. We did rental of cameras. It was great because a lot of nonprofits, it's always a struggle for funding. We had a very successful business model that helped to pay the rent, buy new equipment, buy new cameras. That's how the two of us started. I've recently met a woman with whom I fell madly in love, who was a volunteer. Now she is also one of the core elements of the film center. When I say "volunteer," for the first five years and nine months, we were volunteer, absolutely. We worked fifty, sixty hours a week. Just recently we got a grant to pay staff, but pennies on the dollar. If I told you what I was getting paid, you would laugh. We are starting to pay some of the teachers for teaching the kids. Our goal is to be sustainable. We're trying to get to that level, so it'll take a few more years. Hundreds of volunteers come in, some maybe just mentor a kid or come to a screening. I think 5,000 people came to the film center last year, be it for an event or to see a film or to borrow a camera. We taught hundreds, like I've mentioned. It really is a community resource.

AUDIENCE MEMBER 2 (CONTINUING): How does it work exactly? Are the students coming after regular school hours? Can you tell us a little bit more about the program?

DAVANZO: It's a twelve-week course. The children like the routine, and it's successful in teaching them. They have to come once a week for a lecture, or tutorial. We show films. We talk about filmmaking. After twelve weeks, they can come any time they want, any time we're open.

    I spend most of my time teaching filmmaking. I spend a large amount of my time counseling youth about situations in the neighborhood that all youth deal with. That's a big part of it. And I enjoy that part of it. But they have to commit to a class, and we call it "tough love." The first day of the course, the parents or a guardian have to come. We instill this kind of trust.

    As I said, we've had more than four hundred kids, but only one camera broken and one camera stolen. That is amazing, because we give the kids the cameras. They take them home. A lot of youth film media programs, students make the film in one hour, in the classroom. But that's not real filmmaking. It's important to trust these kids. By meeting the parents and establishing this trust, we've been fortunate. Once kids have taken a class, they can come in any time they want. It's open. They can borrow equipment. They get a certificate, and they become part of the film center. Same thing with adults. On any given day you'll have an eighty-year-old grandmother making a film about her grandson next to someone making a resume to get into college. It's this kind of energy, community energy, that you would feel at other community centers. I encourage you to visit.

AUDIENCE MEMBER 3: I was wondering what it means for you to politicize someone or for someone to become politicized. I was wondering if you could talk about it in terms of what you've envisioned or specific examples of what you've seen.

DAVANZO: It's a good question. It's a catch phrase that sounds good, but how is it relevant to what people are doing? The Los Angeles River piece was one specific example, right? A lot of the kids would just throw their trash into the storm drain or think, "Why should I ride my bicycle when I can drive to the store that's two blocks away," right? So by politicizing them—making them aware there's a river in Los Angeles and it deserves to be green and healthy again—instilling these environmental issues, they turn around and start talking to their own families about issues like recycling and other things. When I said *politicize*, sometimes it's as subtle as that. People start to think, "Maybe I will recycle this tin instead of throwing it in the storm drain." Other times, the kids are making passionate antiwar films or are involved in other actions concerning, for example, affordable housing or immigration. So, politicizing, for me, is taking kids who are oblivious in many ways to what's going on and helping them find their voice: "I'm a young person. I deserve to be heard." That's what I mean by when I say *politicize*.

I think not every child is politicized, and I think maybe this is a buzzword that I may have misused or misrepresented. For me, it's about trust and it's about community; that's the core of it, right? When a child takes a class for twelve weeks, that student may never make a film again. That's not the most important thing. For those twelve weeks, we've given that child humanity, we've given love, we've given compassion, right? So obviously we think about change, an immediate change for those twelve weeks. Maybe that child wasn't loved at home, or believed. For me, it starts at a very basic level.

If we're making films like these that are more profound and maybe touch issues that are dealing with society, then great. Then we've taken it up another level.

AUDIENCE MEMBER 4: What does the Echo Park Film Center offer people with disabilities?

DAVANZO: We've never targeted that group as a group, but many people in wheelchairs, deaf students, whatever disability is ailing them, have come and taken classes. And we've had interpreters working with people as they take computer-editing classes.

So accessibility is all "yes." As far as doing projects, I'm open to any suggestions.

We never commit to a project unless we can do it well. And we work within our means. We have a volunteer whose brother is autistic and he's offered to teach a class for autistic youth. We said: "Great, let's find funding for it. Let's find a way we can do it." The worst thing you can do is to promise and not deliver. We would never do that.

I'm accessible. And I'm sticking around. We are a community access center.

~ February 16, 2008
SGI-USA Santa Monica Culture of Peace Resource Center

Gandhi in Palestine

Lessons Learned on Enhancing Cultures of Peace in Ongoing Conflicts

Farshad Rastegar

President and Chief Executive Officer, Relief International

Dr. Rastegar is founder and has been the chief executive officer of Relief International since its inception in 1990. He has a doctorate in comparative and international education from UCLA and has served on the faculty of UCLA's Graduate School of Education, in the Sociology and Political Science departments. His research and program interests include the impact of displacement on political marginalization and radicalism, minority-majority relations, Islamist political movements, and organizational learning behavior. His academic work includes the study of the ideology and organization of the Afghan mujahedin organizations. Since founding Relief International, he has designed and overseen innovative approaches in transitional programming from relief to development and from centralized to market economies including integrated multi-sectoral approaches in active conflict areas such as Afghanistan, Albania, Azerbaijan, Burundi, Georgia, Kosovo and Tajikistan.

Farshad Rastegar's work most notably addresses the sixth of the eight action areas of the United Nations Declaration and Programme of Action on a Culture of Peace: advancing understanding, tolerance and solidarity. As Mr. Rastegar says: "In youth group after youth group, this idea of engagement and taking responsibility is part of building solidarity, building community, building hope, building dignity and belief in one's own power to influence one's environment. When you empower young people to take responsibility for their lives, it doesn't mean ignoring the wider political dimensions of the problem."

W hat I will try to do in this short speech is to take you through the implementation of a project about peace.

About four years ago (in 2004), the chairman of Relief International, a gentleman named Kamran Elahian, a venture capitalist in Northern California, was visiting some of our projects in Palestine. We have Internet Learning Centers in schools, a project of Schools Online, the education division of Relief International. We thus provide Internet access and connect youth in Bangladesh, Afghanistan, Palestine, India and elsewhere, bringing youth together to work on common projects and develop a global understanding of how their lives are connected. That's one dimension of this work.

In visiting these centers, he spoke with the youth, suggesting, "Instead of throwing stones, why don't you use the Gandhi method?"

Their response was: "Who? What are you talking about?"

Not that they didn't have any orientation to peaceful resistance and indigenous movements, but the limitations of time and space and life in Palestine are such that easy access to other sources or experiences of other nations—South Africa, the U.S. civil rights movement, the Gandhi movement and so on—are not readily available and not so readily discussed.

The chairman himself was a Che Guevara enthusiast in his youth until he saw the movie *Gandhi* and recognized another approach. He became a Gandhi fan and started reading more books.

After this trip to Palestine, he visited his good friend, Jeff Skoll, eBay's first president and now founder and president of Participant Media. He told him about his visit to Palestine and urged Jeff to take action. He kept on going and going, very excited, and at some point Jeff said, "Stop for a second and just look behind you on the wall." There was a picture of Gandhi on the wall. Jeff shared the same belief in Gandhi's principles.

In other words, the instigation of the project came from these two people saying, "Let's show the movie *Gandhi*." Through them, we contacted Sony, got the rights to show the movie, and then we built on that idea, starting by engaging these two men in a dialogue, saying: "Look, showing the movie is not enough. It may have worked for you personally, because you had other resources, but in this context, we need to look at the complete Gandhi philosophy of economic self-reliance, open communication and so on." It's a longer process, particularly in the context of an ongoing conflict, to come in and tell people there's another method. It takes a little bit more effort to use the movie *Gandhi* as a catalyst for discussion in order to mobilize people and create a movement.

Keep in mind that in countries like Palestine, perhaps 50 percent or more of the population is youth. That's a big wave. If you want to create change, you have to work with youth, not just because they may be more amenable to change, and not just because you don't want them to strap bombs to themselves, but because that's the big wave that's coming, and it's getting younger by the day.

This project started on both the West Bank and the Gaza Strip, but the overwhelming focus right now is in the West Bank. In different towns and regions throughout the West Bank, we started organizing communities by showing *Gandhi*. We dubbed the movie into Arabic so it would resonate, and all the voiceover actors were Palestinian, so even the accent was really Palestinian.

> *Once you see that you have some control over your environment, you're not just a passive victim, you begin to grow. It could be dealing with the trash in your neighborhood to overcoming the war, whatever shape that takes in your life.*

We also engaged Ben Kingsley (who portrayed Gandhi in the film) and Jake Ebers, the producer, and Jeff and others to come to Palestine for a grand opening.

Of course, we had to lay some groundwork with local communities. We did up to seven hundred screenings over three years — in refugee camps, in schools, in NGO centers.

We divided the project into three phases. The first was to show the film and use that as a catalyst to get the idea out there and also to work with the indigenous groups.

Phase two is a bit more difficult to explain. Again, if you look at the Gandhi movement or any civil rights movement, there's a dimension of people coming together and actually wanting to work together, which is a very difficult process to achieve. We focused on youth to make that transition. It's a psychological transition, because you have to have a bit of hope to look at the world differently and to work together.

Last, we focused on the issue of economic self-reliance. If you remember Gandhi and the Salt March,[1] it broke the colonials' economic system. People need economic self-reliance to get food on the table.

One thing that we'll come to at the end is this idea of communication. We have always talked about doing some media work, and this time it was the kids at these centers and our actors saying, "We want video cameras and musical instruments, because that's how we need to document and communicate." This was great, because instead of throwing stones and bombs, they want to create videos to tell the story.

At some point, people were lined up for a screening of Gandhi when the police beat them, but they continued to stay in line. There's a critical side note to that scene, because if we don't pay attention, we're not going to remember. A New York Times correspondent observed this and ran to the phone to call in the story. That's the communication.

The point is that people need to be able to tell their story, to mobilize resources.

Lots of screenings led to a lot of questions and answers. There are dimensions to this. Some people agreed with parts of the movie, and others expressed angry resistance, for example, accusing organizers of being Zionist agents. Every discussion needed to allow for such scenes.

---

1. In 1930, Mahatma Gandhi proposed a non-violent march protesting the British Salt Tax. The Salt Tax made it illegal to sell or produce salt, allowing a complete British monopoly. On March 12, 1930, Gandhi and 78 male *satyagrahis* (activists of truth and resolution) started their 23-day, 240-mile journey. On April 5, 1930, Gandhi and his *satyagrahis* reached the coast. A month later, Gandhi was arrested and thrown into prison. The Salt March started a series of protests, closing many British shops and British mills, and is considered a key event leading to India's eventual independence.

The film is three hours long, and it was a struggle for a lot of people to sit through it. But the discussions that followed would go on for three hours afterwards.

And so the process was to show the movie, followed each time by discussions and an open invitation for follow-on discussion. We used this format as a catalyst. There were dimensions to the movie that we could focus on, parts of the struggle that are shared, and people would resonate with that. For example, the scene where the great massacre happened. People identified with that. There were also dimensions to which they totally objected, like the scene where people are lining up to get beaten. Our audience really took offense at that. They felt we were telling them to be submissive.

These discussions became very heated. Some people may have left; others may have stood up and said, "Yes, this is exactly what we need." the great majority were somewhere in between, saying: "Some of this makes sense, some of it I'm not sure. Maybe these guys are Zionist agents. I don't know what they're here to do." They would tell us that as well, "You are a Zionist agent." But again, this is the process that we have to go through.

Eventually, things took off. The kids themselves said: "We're going to take this to the next stage. We hate the war." The seeds began to take root. A few people here, a few people there were saying, "Yes, this is something that we can collect around and through which we can express our political and nationalistic ideals."

And at some point, somebody came up again and asked to show the film on the wall, so there were a few nights of using the wall as a screen and people gathered and, in that way, the film itself became a mode of protest.

That was the first phase, screenings in different contexts — big theaters, small theaters, with students, with farmers, at refugee camps, in every context possible, we went there or made it available to local groups who wanted to show it. Sometimes the audience was a thousand, sometimes fifty, but always with a moderated discussion group to follow, as well as an invitation for follow-on discussions. That resulted in, at the time, sixteen youth Gandhi clubs. I could never have thought about a Gandhi club before this, but enough people wanted to form a club around this and take it to the next stage.

The next effort for us was to figure out how to institutionalize this process and support this budding movement. We coalesced around a model of modern social entrepreneurship and activism, and we eventually created seventeen youth centers.

Somebody recently asked, "What is the definition of a social entrepreneur?"

I said: "Well, I think some people see a problem and say, 'Oh, somebody else will do something about this trash.' And other people see a problem and say, 'Oh, I'm going to do something about that.'" That's social entrepreneurship—where you see the problem and you say, "I'm gong to do something about that." That's the effort—the mind shift, if you would —that we're trying to achieve by getting young people to adopt a problem as their own and not play victim. As long as you see yourself as just a victim, you become passive, you become hopeless, there's no future, there's nothing.

On the other hand, once you see that you have some control over your environment, you're not just a passive victim, you begin to grow. It could be dealing with the trash in your neighborhood to overcoming the war, whatever shape that takes in your life.

It's not an easy process. When I visited a month ago (2004), I was just blown away by the light in the kids' eyes that I had never seen before. I went to one of the youth centers, and the kids were organized. I felt like I'd entered into a meeting with a labor union somewhere here in the United States. Their requests were very logical, not confrontational. For example, the center had one guitar. They pointed out that, if they had more instruments, they could form a band. They also asked for video cameras to make documentaries and even record weddings to generate income for the center.

I asked myself: "When did this shift happen? How did they make that shift?" There was no magic bullet. It was the process of listening to the kids and involving them and enabling them to take on projects that are closer to them. They learned they can work together and make things happen, like a soccer field. Gradually that took on a wider range, like art projects and creating a library in the youth center.

Let me take a step back and talk about this heuristic shift, because it's not an easy thing to do. I grew up in Iran; I came to the United States when I was fourteen and in high school. It wasn't until my first or second year as an undergrad that I took a sociology or political science course in which game theory was discussed. The professor mentioned a non-zero sum game. It took me a few days to digest it, because I figured if I gain something, the other side would lose. I saw no way that two sides could play something and both win. That concept is foreign to our experience.

I was attending an experimental school and tried to adopt all kinds of innovative things. But if you corrected a teacher, you would get reprimanded, as I did a few times. I learned, don't criticize, don't think creatively. It's a big cultural shift and change in mindset to think that, if we work together collectively, both sides can grow; it's not a competition for finite resources.

That's difficult to talk about in the midst of an ongoing conflict where, maybe on a daily basis, resources are being encroached. But it is possible to do that, it is possible to get people to see that, despite the victimization, we each have control over the garbage in our neighborhood. We do have control over creating a sports program.

We can plant that seed in the context of evidence to the contrary. Once that happens and that engine begins to move gradually, then it can get bigger and bigger and stronger and stronger.

Not every scenario is zero sum, but where you want to see a shift, where you are seeking, you are creating non-zero sum scenarios. That takes a bit of values, knowledge of the people and some skill sets to get there, and the program has worked to make that happen. It's not as though we simply hand a package to the students or the community and then watch a shift happen. We must build trust, build those relationships.

After working together to establish these sports and youth activities that are very fun and of immediate value, the next step was to go to the community, to the village or a refugee camp, which we'd never done before, and talk to the elders of the community and see what were their problems and where we might be able to do something.

Palestinians, much like any other society, are divided into elite, middle and lower classes. The refugee camp falls into this last category. Why go to the refugee camp if you don't have to?

Many of these kids and their parents had never gone to the refugee camp, which is maybe a mile a way. Now, for the first time, they acknowledged that it was part of their society. They wanted to take responsibility for it, to help do something about it. They were ready to go there and find out, and that's what they did.

They started paying attention to their communities' needs, actually seeing it, something they may not have done otherwise, and taking responsibility for what they could by working to understand it. For example, they created posters—about upcoming holiday celebrations and so forth—on their own and posted them around town to ask for donations of money or toys or whatever. They raised thousands of dollars, not from rich people in Beverly Hills but from the community in which they lived, in Palestine itself. They raised money and bought things for kids in a different neighborhood, including the refugee camp. The results they experienced were the same joy and satisfaction that I get from this work. They saw from that process the joy in the faces of other kids, and they felt empowered for having done something to improve somebody else's life.

Again, that's where the wheel begins to move faster, and that's the answer to my question, "How did you achieve this shift?" *Because I was always positively blown away by the shine in the eyes of these kids I met in these centers.* For example, last month (February 2008), I went to another youth center, a newer center, and when I spoke with young people about coming to the center, I got the same response I had gotten three years earlier: The kind of disbelief and noninterest you might get from any youth who is asked to participate in something that adults have organized. These kids expressed the wider dimension of "The Israelis are attacking me, and it's somebody else's fault. I'm the victim, why should I do something about it?" It's a much more difficult challenge.

In youth group after youth group, this idea of engagement and taking responsibility is part of building solidarity, building community, building hope, building dignity and belief in one's own power to influence one's environment. When you empower young people to take responsibility for their lives, it doesn't mean ignoring the wider political dimensions of the problem. The whole idea is to get to a point where people can say: "I'm invested in the process, and I have the power to sit across the table and communicate with the supposed enemy. I can reach across and communicate." That takes a sense of dignity and empowerment. It is the people who don't feel empowered who may blow themselves and other innocent people up just to make a point, but the real point they're making is, "I've given up; it's hopeless."

How do you overcome that? We feel that it's totally doable.

If you saw the joy in the faces of the kids who provided the gifts, the kids who received the gifts, you would see the connection they are building. These guys were able to experience the satisfaction of having engaged other people and feel useful, feel that they can make a difference in the lives of other people in their own community. This is another phase of this community—building solidarity and belief in one's empowerment.

Another phase that we focused on is economic empowerment. We saw that 70 percent of the population of Palestine consists of farmers who don't have a whole lot of money. We struck on this idea of helping farmers, looking at their issues and the possibilities of microcredit, a way of empowering people rather than giving handouts. We especially focused on women farmers.

To kick off the project, we invited and paid for farmers who wanted to come to Ramala for four or five days, free hotel and everything, and asked them to share their issues and concerns. We also showed them the movie *Gandhi*, if they wanted to see it, and explained the larger project, to help people recognize their role in creating peace. Of the key issues that came up, one was access to markets, and another was access to capital. There were others, but these were two that we felt we could influence.

One example that I would like to refer to is Mona, and she's a farmer. She's the breadwinner in her family—three sons and a husband. She told us that she didn't want to be a farmer at first—she had to do that out of necessity—but she loves her land and she loves farming now more than anything else in her life.

However, the wall cuts through her farm, and so far she has lost one third of her farm. In addition, the military has also started a factory that is increasingly encroaching on her land. But she says, "My way of resistance is to farm, and I am just going to farm more and more, and better and better, and I will farm till the day that I die." She tells how a bulldozer was brought in, and her husband stood in front of the bulldozer. After a few warnings to the husband, the driver just started piling dirt on him until he was buried to the neck, and at that point she started shouting and screaming, and the bulldozer left.

This is a daily reality that these people face, but the desire for peace, the desire for a peaceful life, is inherent in everyone, including Mona and her family.

Part of the project now is to provide microcredit to people like Mona. We are starting with only $200,000, and we are also creating local events to which producers can bring their products, because those facilities don't exist in the country.

What we've done is to have the youth that we talked about engage in the microcredit loan process. More than half of these farmers are illiterate, so they cannot come up with a business plan or fill out applications. The youth in these centers help the farmers design their market analyses and answer questions such as how much they should take as a loan, how long it will take to pay the loan back, what they need to make it to the market, and so on. The youth help the farmers through the application process, so that they can be successful. That's tremendously empowering to the kids as well, because they're seeing now that it's not just a charitable act of buying and distributing something, it's that exponential power of giving a loan and watching it grow. They begin to see the wider dimensions of sustainable change.

We're focusing on expanding the youth centers, expanding the economic self-reliance program. Also, as I said, we're working on this new plan to create small media centers with maybe one video camera. We just ordered the first one. We can only do so much: one video camera per youth center, plus maybe a couple of still cameras, software for editing and local resources to get things going. These are modest beginnings but doable.

We also provide training in using computers and the Internet and so on. I have not been there for two years since we started the project, but I can see the excitement, the ownership and the dynamism of these kids as they take on responsibility and see the results. It's not just a project any longer, it's really their lives.

Finally, we must never forget the reality that these youth live in and the challenges that they have to overcome. We have now, if I am not mistaken, just less than two thousand kids who are active participants of the Gandhi Project in about seventeen centers. We believe that peace is not a short-term process, much as it wasn't for Gandhi. He wasn't always successful.

He got kicked out of South Africa; South Africa struggled many more decades to come to resolution.

We have obtained the rights from Sony to show the film on the Israeli side, and we hope to start sometime soon. The dimensions are different; there are legitimate points of view and legitimate concerns from both sides. We've worked in enough conflicts to realize that nothing is one-sided, but at some point you need to overcome those issues and see the madness of conflict, especially armed conflict, and the benefits of peaceful resistance. One point we emphasize with the community is that peaceful, non-violent resistance is not just "Love thy neighbor and forget your problems," it's a validation of the problem and talking or seeking or creating ways of solving it that are not self destructive.

Questions and Answers

AUDIENCE MEMBER 1: What were some of the immediate results of showing the film *Gandhi* in Palestine?

RASTEGAR: Once we started showing the film and campaigning—because it was a real campaign with billboards all over Palestine promoting the Gandhi Project website and stating "be the change" in Arabic.

Suddenly there was a demand for Gandhi. So the Palestinian national TV station, for the first time, showed the English-language film *Gandhi* (a significant number of people speak English).

As part of the IT program in these youth centers, we also encourage youth to communicate with schools in the United States. We have a program linking schools in the United States to schools in Palestine and other regions. They collaborate on problem-solving projects. Thus, a school in Tajikistan works with a school in Detroit to address youth gang violence and the school in Detroit works with the school in Tajikistan to address ethnic conflict. They share these sorts of issues. A good number of students speak or strive to use English, but the core of the program is in Arabic in order to reach as many people as possible, particularly in the most deprived communities that may not have access to language training.

AUDIENCE MEMBER 2: Have you considered bringing similar projects to other places, such as Mexico? Does Relief International take a stand on the wall constructed to separate Israel and Palestine, or the wall proposed between the United States and Mexico?

RASTEGAR: We're not currently in Mexico. In general, we don't see ourselves as an advocacy organization. We're what we call an *implementing organization*. There's a significant difference.

If an advocacy organization were to go to Darfur and research or document something, they'd be kicked out. On the other hand, we are in Darfur, where we may engage the government directly and criticize them about this and that—for example, about the number of rapes. But if we go on the radio and television and talk about the number of rape cases we've seen in our clinics, we'd be kicked out.

We see a value, what we call "protection by presence"—in those places where we are present, that kind of violence doesn't happen. That's the driving force behind an implementing organization.

Just this week, an advocacy organization gave us some money for our work in Darfur. They sent a representative to Darfur to meet with us, but unbeknownst to us he also met with some of the human rights organizations. He was arrested at the airport and his laptop confiscated. On the laptop, they found the name of our organization, Relief International, so right now we're going through a crisis, trying to not get kicked out of the country because of this association. These things are real.

In response to the wall itself, we're not in a position to say to the Israelis that they should or should not build a wall. I'm Jewish and I have family in Israel. I understand that people on each side of a conflict have real or perceived notions of what protects or doesn't protect.

What I believe can work with the Palestinians is a wall that goes through their territory. If the wall blocks off one-third of a farmer's land, then we have a legitimate role to work with that farmer, to employ protection by presence, as I've described before. If our presence is not protecting the farmer from that encroachment, then something is wrong.

Similarly in Darfur, if we were in Darfur and we didn't see a reduction in rape or violence as a result of our presence, then why are we there? In most scenarios, such a presence, an international presence that may include cameras, videos and so on, does prevent that kind of violation.

Regarding Mexico, do I like it personally? No. But as long as it's on the international border I think that's something between the two countries' legislators and executive branches to resolve. That doesn't mean society cannot be engaged, but Relief International, I think, is not going to take a position on it.

AUDIENCE MEMBER 3: Are you aware of indigenous movements in countries in which Relief International is present? Why did you choose to work in Palestine before Israel?

RASTEGAR: Let me backtrack for just a second. I said that, in an anecdotal context, our chairman found there was a lack of knowledge about Gandhi. At the same time, I said that there are indigenous movements. It is not that, as a whole, people in Palestine are not aware of Gandhi or there are no indigenous movements. In fact, we take extreme care to be very sensitive. If we went in as outsiders and said that we want to talk about *non-violence*, red flags would go up. You just cannot use the word *non-violent*.

Great care has gone into working with local organizations that are doing that kind of work. But to bring it to a new level, bring support and make it more of a cultural movement rather than a political movement on the side. If you want to be more political, there are organizations that are better equipped. But our intention was to make it more of a cultural, ground-up movement, using media and related resources in the process.

But the question of why not Israel also has much to do with at least the perception among some Hasideans that if we did it in Israel at the same time, it would be seen as a Zionist movement. Whether that's true or false, I don't know. Also, we *are* working to carry out this project in Israel as well, but, again, with the understanding that the dimensions there will be totally different.

I worked with fifty-five NGOs before we chose four with whom to work. Their advice was that this needs to be owned by Palestinians. It needs to be seen as a Palestinian initiative before it's taken to Israel.

The OneVoice campaign is a good example of something that was started on both sides, although it's stalled a little. But our advice was that our project needed to be a movement "owned" by Palestinians first and then taken into Israel.

But it was an issue that we really struggled with, debated, went back and forth. Some of us were opposed to it, but at the end of the day, the Palestinian voice in our group won.

I want to come back again to the issue of communication. I mentioned the example of the New York Times reporter who gave the Indian movement, Gandhi's movement, a higher level of world attention and credibility. That dimension (of international media attention) is even more paramount today than seventy years ago. That's because we live in a more globalized world, a media-driven world, and a world where every time an Israel spokesperson, is on TV, he is nicely shaven, wearing a tie, speaking perfect English with American idioms if talking to an American audience or French idioms if talking to a French audience or whatever.

That image just doesn't have a counterpart on the Palestinian side or the Iranian side or for much of the Middle East. There's a savvy quality to the media relationship.

The next phase includes creating these media centers for youth so that they can explore ways to get their message out. Not to forget their own idioms, because they need to make films and videos for their own community as well, but to make videos that have the Western sort of storytelling. It's a different style of communication.

The idea is to empower these youth, as I mentioned earlier, this communication is a key part of this peaceful resistance—to communicate your message in a way that your counterpart understands it, and the huge audience in the middle that can be swayed can also understand and resonate with your message.

I don't think we necessarily have the ultimate answer to creating a peaceful resolution, but I believe through the media project we'll at least address that challenge.

AUDIENCE MEMBER 4: Would you say the main point of your project is to become more media savvy?

RASTEGAR: I think the goal of this project was not to teach Palestinians about non-violence. What we tried to do was empower them to take that struggle to new dimensions. And, yes, I think that, obviously, we Americans should do something. I hope we'll vote for a different sort of future for ourselves and the world. But I think as long as we see images that portray Palestinians as aggressors, which is basically what happens when a bus blows up on our television screens, that doesn't help the farmer in Iowa to understand the situation or what he can do to change it. I think again it goes back to this issue of communication and media.

How do Palestinians engage with the world so they can tell their story in a way that humanizes them, in a way that we don't dehumanize people.

For example, there are more Muslims in the United States than there are Jews. It's a question of the Muslim community, for example, speaking out in the United States. Also, there's no difference between how a Palestinian Christian suffers versus a Muslim. They suffer equally. And they're both equally nationalistic.

But in terms of politics, the numbers are on the side of the Middle Easterners, if you will. It's a question of organizing. It's a question of crafting your message in a way that resonates with your intended audience. That's my belief.

I think that's where the peace movement of the Middle East has lost the battle, because we have not been able to craft a message in a way that resonates with the majority of the American public.

AUDIENCE MEMBER 5: Where does your funding come from?

RASTEGAR: This project, the Gandhi Project, was funded by our chairman and Jeff Skoll. Skoll, I mentioned earlier, was the first president at eBay and now runs Participant Media. He happens to be Jewish. Our chairman is not. But they both share this passion about Gandhi and peace in the Middle East. They each put up $250,000 and said, "Make this happen."

Overall, funding for our projects comes from the United Nations, from USAID (the United States Agency for International Development), from the British government, from corporate contributions and from public donations. A video camera costs about a thousand dollars, and we have other projects where people can contribute a book in a library, which costs a dollar. There are projects that are government driven and others that we design ourselves, like the Libraries Programs.

With US government money, we build schools in Afghanistan. That's great. But schooling, as I remember it, is what happens within the four walls, not building the four walls. When you go to these schools, at best they have textbooks they're sharing, five or six children to each textbook. But there's nothing else to read. In the village, what happens is the mullah has the Qur'an, which is in Arabic. The kids can't read that either. So it comes down to the mullah's interpretation, and in many cases, he is limited in his own education. He learned from his father or his grandfather. And so the children get the same black-and-white version of history.

I grew up reading books. We had a little library in our home, and a library at the school. I was very lucky, and I read books from A to Z as much as I could. I was a bookworm.

I wouldn't be the person I am today if I hadn't read from many sources—children's books, novels, Steinbeck and so on. I loved that stuff when I was a kid. But these people just don't have access to that. Imagine if a library were there, and kids actually read from many authors. These are the kinds of projects that we push ourselves.

About taking media action, as I've said, we are not an advocacy organization. That's not our role. We see our role as empowering—the Palestinians on one side and the Israeli peace activists on the other, or in Darfur to empower people to tell their story in the way that they need to and want to.

That doesn't mean to say that advocacy organizations shouldn't do that. But I think within the gamut of international NGOs, there's that divide. It's a healthy divide, I think, because that way we're not choosing the fight. We're empowering people at the grassroots to express their concerns. I may disagree with some of the things that my Palestinian friends or colleagues say, but it shouldn't be up to me to filter their perspective. If they are empowered to voice their concerns and their opinions, then the majority in the middle can filter that and decide what makes sense.

We praise and support advocacy organizations that do what they do, for example, bringing Darfur to the forefront.

Our focus as an implementing organization, what might be considered a civic society movement, was not alive, was not there seventy years ago. The model was that governments did everything. Since the 1960s and the activism of that decade, people started out active, protesting and then organizing. It's a group of people who have come together and said let's do something, much like the Soka Gakkai International. That's in line with the definition of social entrepreneurship. That didn't exist sixty or seventy years ago, but now it does. That's where we are today.

~ March 29, 2008
  SGI-USA Santa Monica Culture of Peace Resource Center

Religion and Peacemaking

Daniel L. Smith-Christopher

Director of Peace Studies, Department of Theology
Loyola Marymount University

Dr. Smith-Christopher is the author of several books, including *Jonah, Jesus, and Other Good Coyotes: Speaking Peace to Power in the Bible*, *A Biblical Theology of Exile* and *Introduction to the Old Testament: Our Invitation to Faith and Justice*, a text for secondary school courses in Old Testament. Dr. Smith-Christopher is also the author of "The Books of Ezra-Nehemiah" in *The Oxford Bible Commentary*, and "Daniel" in the *New Interpreter's Bible Commentary*. Dr. Smith-Christopher is the editor of and a contributor to the text, *Subverting Hatred: The Challenge of Religious Nonviolence*.

Dr. Smith-Christopher has taught and spoken on topics in scripture, particularly of the Exilic and Persian periods, and on issues of peace, justice and non-violence and the role of scripture in African-American Gospel and Blues musical and lyrical traditions. Dr. Smith-Christopher has also consulted on many television and multi-media projects in these areas.

Dr. Smith-Christopher addresses many of the eight action areas in the 1999 United Nations Declaration and Programme of Action on a Culture of Peace, most notably the sixth: advancing understanding, tolerance and solidarity. As he says: "All of us have a place in the world where we feel at home, even if it is in the imagination and not where we actually live. Sometimes it can be the focus of our hope for the future, a home where we are safe, where we are loved, where we are among friends. If we want to understand passions of the Middle East, think on these things. There are profoundly moving emotions connected to this place for Jews, Christians and Muslims."

I was very privileged to work with the Soka Gakkai International in producing *Subverting Hatred*. The idea of this book was that each of us who wrote in it would speak from our tradition, be willing to criticize our own tradition and also to speak about the resources that may be drawn from our various traditions. In other words, rather than criticizing another, we looked for those resources for peacemaking that are to be found within our tradition.

I speak, of course, out of the Christian tradition. I have been teaching the Bible at Loyola Marymount University for nearly twenty years (as of 2008). Because of my interest in the three religious traditions of Judaism, Christianity and Islam, and because of my own experience there for a couple years, I have a keen interest in the Middle East as a kind of laboratory for at least these three religious traditions and how they struggle to find a way of coexistence.

There is a famous joke that visitors to the Middle East hear very quickly after they arrive: A scorpion wanted to cross a river but could not swim. He asked a frog to ferry him across on his back.

"Certainly not!" said the frog. "If I take you on my back, you'll sting me!"

"No, I won't," said the scorpion, "because if I do, we'll both drown."

The frog saw the logic in this, so he let the scorpion hop on and struck out across the water. Halfway across, the frog felt a terrible pain. The scorpion had stung him.

As the two of them sank below the ripples, the frog asked the scorpion, "Why on earth did you do that? Now we both die."

Replied the drowning scorpion, "Welcome to the Middle East."

Not very funny, of course. But then, the Middle East, like many parts of our world, is not a particularly funny place these days. Unless you're interested in irony and dark humor.

Thinking again about the Middle East as an experimental place where these three religions struggle to coexist, I think also of another interesting story that was told about the Sesame Street Gang, which was trying to organize light entertainment for children in this part of the world. Producers of the beloved American children's program were planning to launch an Israeli version that would promote mutual understanding between young Palestinians and Jews. The idea was to have a Palestinian and a Jewish puppet appear on the same show, chatting amiably, using a limited vocabulary of words that sound very similar in Hebrew and Arabic.

Alas, Palestinian puppeteers didn't want their puppets to live on the same street as the Jewish puppets. When the Americans tried to act as mediators and suggested, if they didn't live on the same street, perhaps there could be a park where they could play together. Both sides asked, "Who owns the park?"

Such questions can be multiplied in a number of places around the world. We think of Sri Lanka. We think of Nepal. We think of indigenous peoples in many of the traditional immigrant countries—Australia, New Zealand, Canada, the United States. Conflicts among local residents, it seems, are particularly compelling and disturbing for us, because religion seems to be a significant and inflaming part of these conflicts.

Again, think about three major traditions clashing in the Middle East. Judaism is informed by its ancient Hebrew tradition that sees this land promised to their patriarch Abraham, where Moses also brought slaves who were freed from Egyptian bondage. Thus, for Jews, the land represents God's care and God's liberation. For a people who have experienced minority existence, frequent persecutions and finally a horrendous attempt to annihilate them in Europe, the hope of a land that represents God's blessing, God's gift and God's compassion has obvious importance. To live there is to be reminded of both identity and faith. Even if you aren't particularly religious, it is a tradition that is a part of who you are in the world. The land means that you are not rootless, and you are not merely a barely tolerated minority. Religion gives comfort and identity.

Christianity sees this land as the birthplace of the one that God sent, whom most Christians believe was more than just a man. In some profound sense, this one is a part of God in a way that no other human ever was. The Christian tradition says that God became incarnated, that God's spirit materialized in a person from that land. If Jesus the man represents the meeting place between the spiritual and the material worlds, then the place where this takes place is considered important to Christians, too. Making pilgrimages to that land just to see it, to feel closer to Jesus, has ancient roots in the Christian tradition. Religion gives comfort and identity.

Finally, Islam believes that God clarified God's instructions for human life based on previous traditions rooted in this land. The holy message of God that is the Qur'an was delivered through Mohammed the Prophet, Mohammed the Messenger. Part of his experience of God involved this same land. Once, Muslims prayed facing Jerusalem before the tradition changed to Mecca. Faithful Muslims believe that Mohammed miraculously ascended into Heaven from Jerusalem. To this day in Islam, Jerusalem is considered the third holy site in their tradition after Mecca and Medina. Again, religion gives comfort and identity.

The passion of faith that is illustrated in these three traditions in this place in the world shows us that the idea that there is a God who cares for us and has expressed part of his message through a special involvement with a unique place on earth is obviously a very powerful idea.

The idea of a home, the idea of a place where we belong, brings a powerful feeling. It combines familiarity with the setting with the love of family and friends. All of us have a place in the world where we feel at home, even if it is in the imagination and not where we actually live. Sometimes it can be the focus of our hope for the future, a home where we are safe, where we are loved, where we are among friends. If we want to understand passions of the Middle East, think on these things. There are profoundly moving emotions connected to this place for Jews, Christians and Muslims.

But emotions can fuel many kinds of actions and attitudes. Emotions can fuel hatred and violence as well as love and compassion. Religion also has to do with passions. Colonel Harry G. Summers, who once taught at the U.S. Army War College in the United States, writes that war is rooted in the passions of people. Violence is rooted in the passions of people. If that is the case—and clearly I think he is correct—then for those of us who care deeply for peace and coexistence, these must also be rooted in the passions of the people or it is not real. Peace must come from whom we are. As I am a Christian, I speak out of that tradition.

Now, I am one who disagrees with the general tendency, especially in twenty-first-century American society, to blame religion for violence. I accept, however, that we can lay some blame on the wrong religion. The

wrong religion is the religion of the State. The wrong religion is the religion of the Nation. For that religion, I call on us all to practice atheism, in
reference to the State, in reference to the Nation, in reference to the false
hope that a particular boundary, a particular border is for us God's place.

I invite us to think about being two things as people of faith, of many
different faith traditions: think about being atheists and about being border runners. Contrary to what we normally hear, especially those of us
in Southern California, I want to talk about the importance of violating
borders. Indeed, I'll go much further than that. I would like to suggest,
especially as a Christian speaking out of the biblical tradition, that it is a
biblical mandate in the modern world that we must learn to be border runners. I would argue, in fact, that the Bible calls on those who treasure those
writings to flagrantly violate borders in the name of peace and justice, and
that any authentic theology built on those scriptures should be true to the
radicalism of that book that calls on us to treat borders with suspicion in
the best case and with open contempt in the worst.

As I said, living in Southern California, we are especially interested in
borders. It seems to me an interesting set of images for us to be thinking
about. So, what about that image of being atheist? Let's begin with borders again. We have heard so much about the border between the United
States and Mexico that some have suggested it has become more than
merely a border; It has become a symbol—of privilege, of what we have
and others don't have, of keeping what is ours, of keeping out people with
the wrong skin color.

Notice that very few volunteers today are carefully patrolling the borders of Canada. I would argue that the U.S.-Mexico border has become
so powerful a symbol that it has become virtually a shrine, an idol. And
when it comes to the gods that are represented by that idol, I proclaim
myself an atheist. When it comes to the religion represented by that border, I proclaim myself an atheist.

So what kind of atheist am I? Quite simply, I do not believe in the
gods of the Nation State, as if that is what is all-important for us today.
What kinds of gods are worshiped at the border shrine? The border gods
would have us believe that we have inherent rights over the resources of
the earth, especially over poorer peoples and nations. The border gods
would have us believe that we are allowed to dictate to others what we

would never accept for ourselves. When it comes to these kinds of gods, I am an atheist.

I am not particularly original using that image. It turns out that the first Christians were called atheists by the Romans, because they refused to worship the gods of the Roman state. So what I am calling for is a resurrection of early radical Christian atheism.

This kind of atheism, however, must be combined with a radical faith. I am not talking about the U.S.-Mexico border particularly. What I am thinking about are all those borders that separate humanity from one another, that encourage nationalism, that encourage hatred, that encourage separation, and, of course, ultimately, war.

I recognize that sometimes borders can be a useful fiction. In the best sense, they can indicate differences between peoples and cultures and faiths that we respect and, in fact, that we enjoy. In the best cases, borders are friendly recognitions of differences in place, and we can honor those differences.

However, borders—these imaginary lines that are drawn between people—have a nasty habit of becoming excuses for bigotry, conflict and ultimately for war. When this happens, I would argue that people of good will, people of good faith from many different traditions, could benefit from reminding themselves that there are lessons from many of our traditions, and there are certainly lessons from the Bible, that suggest that somebody needs to be willing to intentionally violate the borders that separate us. I would argue as a Christian that the Bible teaches that that somebody is us. We are called to violate borders.

What are the signs that borders are becoming dangerous? Danger signs are evident when people use borders to speak about the goodness of everyone on "our side" and the suspicions of everyone "over there." Patriotism, for example, has tended in recent years to become a corrupted and self-righteous arrogance toward people outside our borders. I believe it's time for people of good will, and, I would argue, especially for those who treasure the Bible, to become suspicious of all this talk of protecting our borders when it is spoken with violent hatred of others, those on the other side of the lines that we have invented in our minds. You see, if we feel bad about our group, we can always point to others and try to make them look worse. The other can be any kind of group, a nation with whom we are preparing to go to war, a radical group within our nation, a religious group within our nation. Notice how borders can easily be manipulated and changed. Instead of enjoying the differences among groups and the joyful discovery of new ideas, new traditions, new experiences, we set up borders. It is a human tendency to separate, to worship borders, to worship lines that separate us. If those lines get mixed up in business interests – in other words, if somebody's making money from negative attitudes about "those others," then there is serious potential for somebody getting hurt.

For example, take oil money, defense contractors, political power and differences of religion, mix them all together and add liberally some serious worry about our borders, and we have an explosive and horrendous mixture. Usually we don't like to talk about the anger or admit the injustices that our borders create, and our basic human response is to try to return to feeling good about "my border" by avoiding or dehumanizing "those others" or denying "their" history as well.

Consequently, borders become locations of trouble. The shouting continues, the anger builds. How do we get back to joyful coexistence? How do we return to learning from one another and enjoying our differences without feeling threatened?

I would suggest that somebody needs to start demonstrating the value of violating the borders that separate us, those cruel separations, and perhaps by our being willing to violate borders that separate us we can suggest a different way of existing together. War, of course, is the ultimate expression of resentment across borders, and the huge efforts and horrendous sacrifices necessary for warfare conjure up those bad feelings about "those others." History teaches us, sadly, that many religious and political leaders often find that their power, their wealth and their authority is actually strengthened by feeding this mistrust of "those others," by advocating strong borders, using words like "our way of life," and especially by shouting, "Our borders are in danger!" To strengthen power is to dehumanize "the other," and talk about them as if they are people we can *never* trust.

Another effective leadership tactic by those who are hungry for power is to try to make themselves appear to be the leaders of the majority, the "normal people," by using the language of infection to dehumanize people within our border. Clearly this kind of language can build until it is used to justify horrendous genocidal violence – the destruction of Muslim

Bosnians, Tutsi Rwandans, Jewish Germans, Turkish Armenians, Native Americans. The list sadly goes on.

Is it important for us, as people who seek peace, to study the creation and maintenance of these border conflicts? I would suggest very much so. That we live in a country where virtually every conflict in which this nation has engaged has involved massive expenditures by our government, not just on the weaponry, not just on the hardware of warfare, but massive expenditures on convincing the general population that the conflict is necessary and that the enemy is only worthy of being destroyed.

I believe that people of good will have deeply important reasons for being suspicious of any attempt to encourage us to dehumanize another human. As the Old Testament frequently reminds the Israelites, "Remember, you were once slaves in Egypt." In other words, you were once "the other" in the eyes of a hostile majority. So, always be suspicious of the language of hate and separation, the language of building up borders. Being part of a tradition, part of a religious faith, can be deeply rewarding, fulfilling and meaningful, but what do we do when group loyalties, those innocent borders of membership and participation, start turning into the borders of separation and hatred?

As a teacher of the Bible, I suggest that the Bible has some interesting suggestions for us. I believe that the Bible says that we should learn to start running those borders, that we should violate those borders that separate us. Someone has to have the courage to cross the border, to be willing to listen, to overcome the desire to make borders tighter and more secure whenever we feel criticized.

In a book called *Reading the Bible With the Damned* (published in 2005), Pastor Bob Ekblad describes what he has learned by working with immigrant and migrant workers in Washington State. One image that he uses in that book struck me deeply. He said that he had worked a lot with illegal border crossers from Mexico, and he was unprepared for something that he heard about coyotes (people who smuggle people across borders). On television and in film and in newspapers, we are familiar with the image of the coyote. The coyote is the one who helps people cross the borders, usually taking money to do so. And we are used to many, many stories of unscrupulous men and women who exploit the poverty of Latin Americans who are desperate to find work in the United States. And, of

Somebody needs to start demonstrating the value of violating the borders that separate us, those cruel separations, and perhaps by our being willing to violate borders that separate us we can suggest a different way of existing together.

course, this is often true. There are hundreds of horror stories of bad coyotes mistreating poor immigrants who only want to find a better life.

What surprised Pastor Ekblad, however, was that many of the immigrants with whom he worked had stories of good coyotes. These were the people who used the money they were paid to make sure that the people crossing the border were fed, that they were cared for, that they had safe passage.

I was so surprised to hear Pastor Ekblad say that some people spoke of good coyotes that I tried to find evidence of this for myself. In hardly a very liberal publication known as *USA Today*, I found the following suggestion: In this December 1, 2003, article, the writer interviewed many immigrants and said that migrants don't see them all as the bad guys in the movies. Many call them heroes because they got them and their families across the border. If you ask these immigrants, they would say: "Thanks to the [coyote], I am in the United States. Thanks to the [coyote], my mother, my children, my grandfather are in the United States."

Pastor Ekblad wondered, "Gosh, is there really such a thing as a good coyote?" And then he made a fascinating observation. As a Christian pastor working in the prisons and among migrant workers in Washington, he said it suddenly dawned on him that Jesus is a good coyote. Jesus, he said, asks us to cross borders.

I considered this idea of Jesus as someone in my Christian tradition who might be calling on me to violate borders in the name of peace. What an interesting thought! A very controversial one for a Californian. And as I was thinking about this, suddenly images came back to me.

I thought about the sanctuary movement along the Mexican border in the 1980s that was staffed by many of my fellow Quakers. The sanctuary movement, of course, intentionally violated US border laws in order to provide asylum for Latin Americans who were escaping torture in countries that had official ties with the United States. The Reagan administration, as some of you remember, refused to classify these people as refugees. Therefore, they were not allowed in the United States because we had official ties to their regime. Yet, Jim Corbett, the Quaker organizer and one of the leaders of this movement, is, I have to say, a model "good coyote." Even further back in American history—forgive me if I am proud—some of my Quaker forebears in the nineteenth century I consider to be good coyotes who ran the Underground Railroad that took many African Americans from the South in slavery to the North and into Canada and freedom.

Harriet Tubman, the famous Black Moses, who led more than three hundred slaves to the north and freedom, is another good coyote. There's a great Willie Nelson song that says, "My heroes have always been cowboys." As I thought about that song I realized that my heroes have always been coyotes.

I think, for example, of John Howard Griffin, a deeply devoted Catholic layman, who in 1959 colored his skin black and then lived in the South. He could only handle it for three months! Then he wrote his famous book, *Black Like Me*. That book has been criticized, sometimes fairly, but *Black Like Me* taught two generations of white Americans some of the realities of racism in the South. John Howard Griffin was quite a coyote. He crossed the color border to try to learn what the realities were.

I think, for example of Uri Avnery, an Israeli activist who persisted in meeting with Yasser Arafat when it was illegal to meet with the enemy. I think of Isam Sartawi, the Palestinian doctor who once organized military resistance to Israel but then came to believe in peaceful negotiation. He was killed by hard-liners because of his willingness to meet with Israelis to discuss peace. I think of Taner Akcam, who openly and compassionately writes about truth of the Armenian massacre. He has infuriated fellow Turks, who still deny that it ever took place. There's a good coyote.

I think of Dr. Ronald Grigor Suny, the Armenian historian who has accepted every invitation to go to Turkey to speak on the genocide, and he regularly engages in dialogues with Turks whenever he can. I think of Mahmoud Taha, who was known as the African Gandhi. He was a Muslim teacher who defended equal rights for Christians and non-Christians in the southern Sudan and was a fearless advocate of equal rights for women. I think of the brave critics of the Crusades, such as William of Tyre. And finally, I think of John Woolman, the American Quaker who refused to wear dyed cloth, because in his day dyed cloth, he discovered, was all produced by slave labor.

So I am sympathetic to the need to sometimes violate borders in the name of peace and justice. Recently, I've come to understand that this holy border running is a deeply biblical idea. Therefore, I'd like to mention two examples of this. In ancient Israel, in what is today the country of Jordan, were a number of small entities, small countries we might say, although that's a little strong—they were really tribal associations. Two of them were known as Ammon, in the area where the capital of Jordan, Amman, now is, and the people were known as Ammonites. Farther south, closer to the Dead Sea, were people known as Edomites.

As you read through the Hebrew scriptures, you will find considerable hatred in many places expressed toward the Ammonites and the Edomites. You will find many angry denunciations of both groups. Yet, there are other voices. For example, in the Book of Genesis is a famous story with which I'm sure many of you are familiar. It's the story of two brothers, Jacob and Esau, sons of Isaac, who was blind. Esau was the firstborn, a great hunter and apparently a big, burly man. Jacob was the herdsman and agricultural worker. He was considered a bit smaller.

The time came when Isaac was to deliver the great blessing to the first-born child. Well, Jacob wanted that blessing. He wanted the advantages that came from that. His mother, who sided with him—your classic mama's boy, I suppose—dressed up Jacob and put on skins so that when Isaac reached out to feel his son, he would feel what he thought was the hairiness of son Esau.

When Isaac puts the blessing on Jacob, it was apparently not something he could revoke. Once spoken, it was done. So Jacob, of course, receives the blessing, and then escapes, because immediately it says that when his brother, Esau, found out, he said he would kill Jacob for taking the blessing from him.

According to tradition, Jacob has to work for fourteen years for a rather corrupt herdsman by the name of Laban, and at the end of the fourteenth

year, he must return to the homeland. In order to go back to the homeland, according to tradition, he must pass through the land of Esau, his
estranged brother. Now, the story gets quite powerful. Jacob begins to send
gifts ahead of him to Esau. There's a particular Hebrew word for the gifts
he's sending: *minha*. The last thing Jacob sends out ahead of him is the
berakah, the blessing, the same word as the blessing that he stole from his
brother.

Then Jacob sheepishly sends his family and he comes along afterwards,
thinking, "Well, if he attacks and kills me, at least my family will live."

The Bible sets the story up rather powerfully. It says that Esau shows up
to meet his brother with four hundred men. In the Bible, whenever it talks
about four hundred men, it always means an army. We get the point. Esau
is going to do in his brother. Justice will be served. There is a powerful
moment in the story where Jacob, having given back the blessing, cowers
before his brother, and his brother runs up and embraces him and kisses
him—an incredible moment of reconciliation between Jacob and Esau.

Why is this so important? Because an ancient biblical writer put a little phrase in that story: "Esau is Edom." That ancient writer, slipping that
phrase into the story, is saying, "We can reconcile with Edom just as Jacob
reconciled with Esau." That little phrase changed everything. It offered
hope; it offered another voice, another possibility. Someone is saying,
"Violate the border! Dash across! Make peace! If Jacob and Esau can do
it, we can, too."

Similarly with the Moabites, my friends. One of the most intense issues
in the Hebrew scriptures is intermarriage with Moabites: "Don't do it!
That's 'them'! We don't associate with 'them'!" Along comes a storyteller
who tells a little story about an Israelite woman with two sons. They flee to
Moab to escape famine, and the two sons marry two Moabite girls. When
the two sons die, the elder woman gathers her Moabite daughters-in-law
and says: "My daughters, stay with your people. I must go home." One of
the Moabite girls says: "Nice knowing you, Mom. I'm staying here." The
other one surprises the ancient as well as the modern reader by saying,
"No, please, I will go with you."

This woman, her name is Ruth, goes on to be the hero of the story. In
fact, it's Ruth who marries Naomi back into the tribe so that Naomi can
be cared for. The point is, a Moabite woman is the hero of the story. In

the midst of this mistrust, in the midst of the tradition that says, "Maintain the borders! Don't cross! Don't associate with *them*!" other voices are bubbling up, saying, "What about Ruth? What about Jacob and Esau?" Border running.

I suggest, my friends, that in many of our traditions, oftentimes within our religious traditions, there are those voices. They are loud, they are clear. They are the voices that say: "Maintain the borders! It's us and them! Loyalty means keep the difference, respect the borders, patrol them!"

But there are always other voices, aren't there? Other hopeful suggestions: "Go over there. Find out what they're like. Meet them. Get to know them. Maybe things aren't so bad. Maybe, like Jacob and Esau, maybe Esau can be Edom. Maybe Ruth can be Moab. Maybe there's hope."

I suggest, my friends, that we have a task as people of good will from our various religious traditions. We were talking about the importance of learning from other religious traditions. Yes, that's true, and that is very important, but also, I think it's equally important to look within our traditions, to find those voices of hope, those voices that say: "Don't respect that border, run it! Violate it! Go meet with those other people. Find out if they're really what you're being told." Be an atheist when it comes to being told to believe in hatred. Be a border runner when it comes to being told to respect the differences and don't associate. So, my friends, I leave you with those two invitations. In the name of radical faith, be atheists to hatred. In the name of radical faith, run borders that separate us.

Questions and Answers

AUDIENCE MEMBER 1: It is difficult to be here and run a border in the Middle East. I don't know how to do the great, great, idea that you put forth.

SMITH-CHRISTOPHER: Those bigger borders have smaller versions, and the smaller versions of those borders are among us here even in Los Angeles. I think that we can train to be good border runners by running the local borders that separate us, by perhaps setting up a meeting. Let's try to get some folks together to talk who don't normally meet one another and don't speak with one another.

Here is some warning. It takes a little bit of thought and training to be a border runner. Why? Because there are some things that will start happening to border runners. Number one, you will start being treated as someone who is betraying your group. Where are you going? You are going to meet them? They are unreasonable, you can't talk to those people. You are going to have to face some heat.

The other thing you need to be prepared to face is that, when you cross that border, you're not going to be paraded as a hero. At first, they might think you're a spy. You might be trying to change them. Even worse, the real temptation for a border runner is to be treated like a hero. Why? Because that makes you unusual, special. You might expect them to think: "Wow! You're a hero for coming over here and talking to us! You're not like your other people." Then, suddenly the whole purpose of border running is defeated because the only reason you have run the border is show that you're unusual.

Remember, you are running a border to try to build a bridge, not to be a hero. Don't get suckered on that one.

So, border runners have to be a little careful. But as I say, that can be done locally as well as internationally.

AUDIENCE MEMBER 2: Recently, Jimmy Carter met with the Hamas leader (Feb. 5, 2009). Already there is tremendous controversy about the actions he has taken as an American, as a Nobel Peace Prize winner, and already people are taking sides. How do you see this going forward?

SMITH-CHRISTOPHER: What a great question! I support talking with any-body. I think what he is doing is the right thing. I think we should talk to anybody. I am not in favor of the "we'll only talk when" approach. It seems to me that you talk in order to get to "when." My father was a pharmacist who ran a small neighborhood drugstore. He was held at gunpoint a number of times, robbed and so on – the life of a small cor-ner drug store owner, right? The stupidest thing in the world would have been for him to say, "I am not talking to you until you put that gun down." No, I would be talking the whole time! I would be doing as much talking as I could, because when you are talking, you are not shooting.

So this business of laying terms to talking instead of talking to get to terms, that's part of that rejection you might feel as a border runner. I hope Carter's trip is the first of many that people take to talk with folks. It doesn't mean Carter endorses the bad things any more than I do. That's a great question.

AUDIENCE MEMBER 3: It seems to me that the call to run borders is directed at us middle-class folk who have no real substantial influence over the course of events, but you are suggesting that border running could be suitable for national or social leaders, too, is that not so?

SMITH-CHRISTOPHER: On one level, I agree with you—it's hard not to despair about what we can do when we're not in particularly politically powerful positions. Except that while I was living in Israel and Palestine, one of the things that I came away with was a profound sense of the importance of average folk meeting and maintaining friendships.

There was one organization of women—their whole organization consisted of about twenty-four women, twelve of whom were Israeli Jews and the other twelve Palestinian Arabs. Their purpose was to stay friends, no matter what happened. The director was an Eastern European survivor. She told me that there were times when they would just sit together watching the television and holding one another's hands, refusing to let the events they were watching separate them from one another.

Perhaps that's not the prime minister meeting with another prime minister, and it may have limited impact, except that starts happening more and more, and eventually empowers the leaders to meet. That is how we can help create the atmosphere.

There is a lot to be said for the fact that when Menachem Begin left to meet with Anwar al-Sadat, Shalom Achshav (Peace Now, the Israeli peace organization) flooded the airport in Tel Aviv. Their message to Begin before he left was essentially "Don't come back without an agreement." Tens of thousands of people were at the airport to say, "We are demanding and empowering you to make peace." I think that we have a role in empowering leaders, including those who may not agree with us, by finding ways to tell them they have a constituency behind peace. There are some Christians who unfortunately believe that unless one is confessionally Christian, one is in error. Other

Christians, however, believe that is not the case, that Christianity is one way of relating to God, but there are others. I happen to be of the latter, and I think that I have pretty strong backing from none other than Paul himself, in the second chapter of Romans. That is a debate I would love to get into with my fundamentalist Christian brothers and sisters, bless them.

I don't agree with the idea that Christianity is invariably and inevitably an exclusive religious devotion. Nor do I believe that it is a bad thing to incorporate the profound insights from other religious traditions into one's Christian faith, as long as one does that carefully and not exploitively. I am not going to start to beat on Native American drums and things like that without the permission of the tribal peoples from whom I am borrowing that tradition. We sometimes exploit people's traditions, without the respect of asking for permission and to learn how to properly incorporate that tradition into our spiritual life. Nine times out of ten, people are happy to say, "Yes, I would be happy to teach you."

AUDIENCE MEMBER 4: After having lived beside and amongst ultra-orthodox Jews for many years now, I can draw no other conclusion but that they are a people who really don't want to cause anybody any harm. At the same time, they intentionally, perhaps along religious lines, do not mix and are very much separate from me and other gentiles in the neighborhood. How do you maintain a healthy attitude toward somebody who is so spiritually and culturally distinct from myself, and be peaceful?

SMITH-CHRISTOPHER: I can only make friendly suggestions. One would be to inform yourself of the history of ultra-orthodox Judaism, because invariably that is a healthy process to understand those about whom you have some gut feelings. That's the first thing. The second thing is that most of these groups have members who are designated in some way to be the public face. I would simply seek that person out. Usually someone will say there is an office or a storefront. Take baby steps.

I think for some groups there is a long process of building trust, a long process of identifying yourself as someone who is not the typical threat. For many groups, and for very good reasons, they have a history of surviving by not trusting, and those are difficult circumstances. Be very patient and take small steps. Even in that circumstance. I think it is possible. Furthermore, there are amazing discoveries in the jewels of ultra orthodoxy.

AUDIENCE MEMBER 5: I grew up in the 1970s. I was a teenager in London when the IRA was setting out a lot of bombs. I was not political, but I remember thinking why can't they talk to each other. It seemed like the only logical, sensible answer. Thirty or so years later, they are not only talking together, they are laughing together. It's a symbol of great hope.

My question is why it took that long. I suspect world leaders are learning that talking does create positive benefits. I wonder if somebody somewhere very high up is trying to speak to [Osama] bin Laden. I suspect somebody is. Do you think that is the case?

SMITH-CHRISTOPHER: One hopes that people are talking about peace, because when they are talking about that they are not talking about making more bombs. Your lesson is a good one in the sense that impatience is a real danger in border crossing.

The interesting thing about the IRA situation is that it's much easier for the connections to be made outside of the actual place where the situation is the hottest. For the English and the Irish to meet each other in the United States and Canada was much easier and there were more opportunities there, so it seems to me that maybe one way we might exploit this is to go to the diasporas and get people to talk with each other. For example, if Turkish Americans and Armenian Americans begin to have a dialogue, some across-the-border dialogues may start happening.

I think that in peace work generally, we have tended not to pursue the small. The temptation is that we want it to be big and impressive and have our fundraiser. What we're talking about are just some cups of coffee where we can sit around a room and talk, and that can be a very important building block.

~ April 29, 2008
SGI-USA Santa Monica Culture of Peace Resource Center

Solutions at the Eleventh Hour

Leila Conners Petersen

Director, The 11th Hour;
Co-Founder and President, Tree Media Group

Leila Conners Petersen is co-founder and president of Tree Media Group, which creates media to support and sustain civil society. With a background in international politics, Leila set out to build a production company that tells stories about the pressing issues of our time. Tree Media works with groups and individuals, including the Council on Foreign Relations, NASA, RAND, Gorbachev's Green Cross International, Leonardo DiCaprio, PBS and Norman Lear.

Prior to Tree Media, Leila was associate editor of New Perspectives Quarterly, an international journal of social and political thought, and associate editor of Global Viewpoint of the Los Angeles Times Syndicate, an internationally distributed op-ed column that reaches two hundred papers. At NPQ, she interviewed thinkers and policy makers, including Kofi Annan, Nafis Sadik, Betty Friedan, Hans Bethe, Rigoberta Menchu Tum and Boutros Boutros-Ghali, among others. She is now editor-at-large for NPQ.

Leila is a life member of the Council on Foreign Relations and the Pacific Council on International Policy. She is a member of the Writers Guild of America. She was also a speaker at the Bioneers conference in October 2005.

Ms. Petersen touches on many of the eight action areas in the 1999 United Nations Declaration and Programme of Action on a Culture of Peace, most notably the second, promoting sustainable economic and social development. As she says: "The power to heal comes from understanding that the world we see is how we feel about ourselves, and how we respect all life is how we respect ourselves. To respect ourselves is to understand that we are a holistic system on a planet that is connected—we are all one."

I'd like to take the time we have together to ponder the only place humans can live, which is Planet Earth. Yes, maybe two people can live on Mars, but that doesn't really matter, so let's talk about Planet Earth.

When we look around the world today, we see a lot of beautiful things and we also see a lot of terrifying things. In an earlier discussion today with youth, which I really enjoyed, what we came to as a group was understanding that, on this planet, the only place where we can live, we've created both heaven and hell.

Sometimes when you look at the news, you're seeing the imbalances, the war, the strife, famine, the degradation. It seems like it might be overtaking us. When you look at sustainability, at the environment, the state of the ecosystems, that is true. The truth of the matter is that we are living in a time when every single life support system on this planet is in decline, and those systems give us life. So you wonder, *If the earth is our only home, why do we treat it the way we do?* It's a fundamental question, and that question is what drove me, my sister Nadia and Leonardo DiCaprio to make a movie about this. We thought, yes, there's climate change; yes, there's soil degradation; and there's all these things that are occurring, but why?

We asked about seventy thinkers, scientists, humanists and philosophers the same set of questions—Where do we come from? Who are we? What are people like? What do we want? What is the state of the world? What's your opinion of the state of the world? What do you think is going to happen? Where are we headed? What's the chance of our survival? One thing we found, to my shock, was that we are on a path to extinction. I didn't come in with, "I'm going to make an extinction movie." I thought I was going to make a film about the state of the world, and the little things we can do here and here, and fix it, and we're all going to be fine.

What came through these seventy people who were deeply committed to their work, to their lives, was that they were deeply in love with what they were doing, with the planet. They were saddened by what they knew, which was that we're going extinct. The earth has been around for four billion-ish years, and life has been evolving for billions of years. The human species as we know it today has been around for 200,000 to 150,000 years. In that time, we have basically taken all of creation and sent it toward the trash can. The question becomes, *What in us is doing this?* And what we're finding is, it's really the human brain and how it functions and how it disconnects us from the feedback loops of life.

The feedback loops of life include our souls and our higher selves and our connection to the divine. In fact, what we found was that the only way out of our dilemma—and this message today will be one of hope and of bravery and of courage—is that we have to connect to our higher selves, to a deeper place in order to get through the dilemma we've created for ourselves.

The exciting thing is that we know how to do this. We've done it before. In connecting to ourselves, we create a world that is at peace, that is in balance, that does have fairness, that does have healthy ecosystems. In that connection lies a beautiful future.

The work starts within ourselves and then our awareness moves outside ourselves and creates this connection in our community.

Summary of a 20-minute segment from the film *The 11th Hour*:[1]

> *The excerpt begins with Stephen Hawking talking about global changes created by the human race and explaining that we are at a critical point: There is no room for more poison and pollution and no more land to use up. Leonardo DiCaprio, Stuart Pimm, Joseph Tainter, David Orr, Mikhail Gorbachev, Thom Hartmann and several others discuss whether they believe we are headed for*

---

1. *The 11th Hour* describes the last moment when change is possible. The film explores how humanity has arrived at this moment—how we live, how we impact the earth's ecosystems, and what we can do to change our course.

The film features dialogues with experts from all over the world, including Gorbachev, Hawking, former head of the CIA R. James Woolsey and sustainable design experts William McDonough and Bruce Mau in addition to more than fifty leading scientists, thinkers and leaders who present the facts and discuss the most important issues that face our planet.

Narrated by Leonardo DiCaprio, *The 11th Hour* was produced by Leonardo DiCaprio, Leila Conners Petersen, Chuck Castleberry and Brian Gerbe. It is written and directed by Leila Conners Petersen and Nadia Conners and was released in 2007.

extinction and that, because of us, at least fifty thousand species become extinct every year, leading to speculation we will take the whole planet down with us. They discuss possible solutions, including saving "the caring capacity" and bringing science and the world into harmony.

There's a lot before what you just saw, which really proves why we're in such deep trouble. I just want to touch on that. I believe the debate in this country about climate change is doing a deep disservice to the survival of humanity, and I think that most of the rest of the world understands that we are changing our climate. Rather than debate that, let's debate how to solve the problem, because we need a lot of work just doing that. Let's get about the business, as David Orr says, I love that statement. Everyone is needed. All hands on deck time.

I want to diagnose the problem a little better, because the problem isn't about carbon dioxide, the problem isn't about chemicals, it's about the way we think. And the way we think is based on our evolution in that we are a short-term-thinking species. We don't see the distant future, and a person who doesn't see the big picture can't understand it.

We tend to focus on our day-to-day survival. How much does it cost to fill up my car with gas? What's my salary? How do I feed my children and myself? I am not downplaying these very real concerns, but in getting these needs met, we are unable to see the bigger picture.

This has always occurred in human development, but in the last hundred years, the tools that we use for survival have become much more powerful, and that's a problem. In our early history, we had fire, we had wood, brass, iron, things like that. Now we have rockets, nuclear power, nanotechnology. The speed of development has increased to such a degree that we don't know how to integrate them into a balance with the world. In effect, we are creating an accelerated destruction of the planet. As the change in our thinking accelerated the number of tools that we had, the more nature became a resource rather than an integrated element in our lives.

In *The Industrial Revolution*, Bruce Mau says we started to cut things up into pieces, so, for example, trees became tables. They were no longer recognized as being imbued with the spirit, they were no longer the patron saints that protected and provided food, shelter, shade, habitat, water cachement. Suddenly, trees became tables and chairs. I'm not arguing that they shouldn't become tables and chairs, but we need to understand that they have other purposes as well, and that we need to integrate back into our thinking this idea of the long term and that the world is more holistic than little isolated pieces.

Part of the problem really is the short-term thinking, which has led to all these other problems, excess pollution, excess carbon dioxide, and all those other issues. And part of what has happened in the over-intellectualizing of our world is this disconnection to our environment, but mostly from ourselves, from our higher selves.

Our connection to our soul has been severed in a modern culture that rejects things we cannot see. It rejects things that we cannot prove. Because we can't see it and we can't prove it, it doesn't exist. Because it doesn't exist, it has no value, and because it has no value, then what fills the void are things we can make ourselves, things that we can see ourselves. Consequently, we've created a world that has material things and a materialist view of the world. That materialist view on fossil fuels, on oil, on all of these wonderful energy sources, has been at the service of very good things—for example, the medical community has done an incredible job with oil resources.

We have created a spectrum of new objects in our lives that don't consider the invisible world, that don't consider the soul, the higher self, the life force that lives in all of nature. They don't consider nature's rights or how it all fits together, because we're short-term thinking, and everything is disconnected in pieces. That vision is killing us.

Part of the problem also is that, in this material world, which we acknowledge we need to exist, material items are important. The question is, how much more happy are you with five blankets, ten blankets, three houses? Where does that end? What we have come home to in a time where every ecosystem is in decline is that nothing has improved. There isn't a single paper in the past twenty years issued by the scientific community that has said that an ecosystem has improved. Our soil, our air, our water, the amount of fish in the ocean, the amount of pollution in the ocean, the amount of toxins in our air, water, food, everything has gotten worse. Even knowing that it's getting worse, we can't stop ourselves, we can't prevent it from getting worse.

How do we heal this? How do we solve this? One of the quotes in *The 11th Hour* that you didn't get to see is from Wes Jackson. He's a farmer in Kansas who is president of The Land Institute. And he basically says, "Now to me the value that comes from the healing power that comes from getting, that it's not just global warming, it's not just fossil fuel dependency, it's not just soil erosion, it's not just chemical contamination of our land and water, it's not just the population problem, and it's not just all of those, the deterioration of the environment, of our planet, is an outward mirror of an inner condition. Like inside, like outside, and that is part of the great work."

The power to heal comes from understanding that the world we see is how we feel about ourselves, and how we respect all life is how we respect ourselves. To respect ourselves is to understand that we are a holistic system on a planet that is connected—we are all one. I was told by a friend that there is a Buddhist concept, the oneness of self and environment, that defines this connection.

If you're going to cure this disconnected mind, this short-term-thinking person or species, how would you address that? Reconnection and a healing process of understanding. This is what Leonardo DiCaprio describes at the end of the film as "a conscious evolution of our species." In other words, we connect to ourselves and others, we connect to all of life, and we start designing our world to take that into account.

Many of you have heard American indigenous people referring to "the seventh unborn generation." When you create something, it must contribute not only to the current generation but to seven generations down the line. We need to incorporate that into our thinking again.

If you respect yourself and respect life, you understand that when you throw something away it's not going anywhere. Plastic bottles, 25 million of them, are thrown away every hour in this country. Where are they all going? Eventually to the ocean. What happens to them? They dissolve. Seventy percent of all oxygen on this planet is generated by phytoplankton, small little planktons floating in the ocean. The ratio of dissolved plastic to phytoplankton is 6:1. What do you think will happen if we crowd out the space for that life form to live? So, plastic bottles—eliminate them. If you understand that "waste" does not mean "away," then you start looking at nature the way described by Janine Benyus, American natural sciences writer.[2]

What does nature do with things it doesn't need? Well, someone else eats it, essentially. John Todd developed an incredible thing called the living machine. He started by looking at nature and then at a factory giving off waste, in this case a chocolate factory. And he asked what eats the first thing that comes out of this factory? He found it was fish that like to eat the waste, plus some bacteria. He built a big tank, put the fish and the bacteria in the tank, and they ate what was coming out of the factory. The tank started filling up with the waste from those animals, so he created another tank with plant life that ate the waste from these fish and bacteria. And so it goes. Todd ended up in this case creating a living machine system with twelve tanks, and by the end of the last tank, what came out? Fresh drinking water. No chemicals, no energy to clean it up.

If you've ever lived in New York, all the waste goes to the Bronx. It gets inundated with chemicals and put in little pellets, and then they try to find who will take all of these pellets. But instead you can create a living machine in a house where none of your sewage goes anywhere. It gets turned into water that can go back into the water supply perfectly safe. It's about understanding and respecting all life and how to position ourselves within life.

I think, honestly, what gave me hope in all of this was biomimicry. It's what you call a game changer. It's stuff I'd never heard about. For example, the lotus leaf is constructed in such a way that water never adheres, nor does dirt. The question is, why? Well, if you look at the nanostructure of the lotus leaf, it's positioned so that nothing can adhere because it has a certain shape. A paint company wondered what would it be like if they mimicked the lotus leaf technology and made a paint that behaved like the lotus leaf? And now we have paint that, when you put it on a building or a car, you have a self-cleaning car or a building that never gets dirty. In addition, you never have to use water to clean your car or your building.

---

2. Janine Benyus: American natural sciences writer and innovation consultant; she has authored six books on biomimicry, including Biomimicry: Innovation Inspired by Nature, in which she outlines the basic thesis that human beings should consciously emulate nature's genius in design.

Just look to nature, see what it does, copy it. That's what we're starting to do. It's really advanced chemistry. Like Janine Benyus said, and I want to reiterate what she was saying—in our industrial process, because everything was cut into pieces and isolated, we came up with very smart solutions, but they didn't take into consideration all of life. When you start to consider all of life, suddenly the use of sulfuric acid makes no sense, or heating something up to 1500 degrees makes no sense, because you have to burn gallons of oil just to get there. It's highly wasteful. Basically you're going to start hearing things like "gecko technology." For example, adhesives are hard to make and chemically destructive. Researchers looked at a gecko's "fingers" and it's fascinating—their sticky effectiveness is not due to the shape, it's really at the quantum level that the gecko is playing with energies of electrons and photons and can actually stick upside down because of the weak forces in the quantum level of reality. Shocking, right? They've actually made a Spiderman suit where a person can crawl all over the place using the weak force at the quantum level because of the structure of the materials of this suit.

There are a lot of reasons why renewable energy is debated. Remember that fossil fuel energy is subsidized in the billions of dollars. If we apply those subsidies to renewable energy, it will be very competitive very fast. We know that we're not going back to a dollar or less for a gallon of gasoline. Never again. So, let's get to renewables. Let's get there quickly. Imagine if we took all our attention and all our resources and started to pay real attention to this problem, there would be a lot more that we could do.

I want to talk a little bit more about intention and attention. People often ask me how long we have, and I say, "It all depends on whom you ask." You know, Lovelock, who created the Gaia theory, says it's too late, it's over. There are other people who say that we have five to fifteen years to change. Other people say we're going be just fine. I don't know the correct answer. I love this quote from Paul Hawken (in *The 11th Hour*): "If you look at the data, you get depressed, but if you look at the human heart, you know everything's going to be OK." My purpose in making the film and the reason I'm here is to call on all of us to recognize that we came to this planet at this time for a specific reason. That reason is twofold: One is to have the bravery to witness the hell we've created on this planet, without running away, without shutting down, without pretending it's not there, without sitting in denial. We have to sit there, look it straight in the eye, and have the courage to say, "We've really made a mess of this place, and this is the reason why. But we're going to try to make a change." I don't care what age we are, we have to make the change, and that means starting to look, first of all, within.

The second point is to start looking at your life and really looking at the local place and loving your home, loving yourself enough to say: "I'm not going to have chemicals in my life anymore because they're killing me. I'm not going to have chemicals for my friends. I'm not going to hire a gardener who uses a leaf blower because it's polluting my neighbor."

> *The power to heal comes from understanding that the world we see is how we feel about ourselves, and how we respect all life is how we respect ourselves. To respect ourselves is to understand that we are a holistic system on a planet that is connected—we are all one.*

Love where your water comes from, love the source of your food. If you love where your water comes from, you quickly get the chemicals out; you quickly try to find sustainable ways to catch the rainwater that comes into the city. Love how you eat. Love the farmer who is growing your food, buy organic. These are the things that you have to look at. These are the small acts of bravery that are important to get us from the destructive place we are now to the restorative place we need to be. And a lot of it is scary. A lot of people look at me and say: "You know you're really bumming me out. I wish you wouldn't talk like that." But it's not my fault. When you open your eyes, this is what you will see.

How do you stay positive in a world that's falling apart? You have to stick together, stick with your community, create a world that is beautiful around you. That's a great start. We also talk a lot about networking the local, meaning looking around your own local place and finding out what's happening.

We're doing that with the 11th Hour Action (http://11thhouraction. com/). It's a movement to help people take local action. Yes, we need to work on the federal level; yes, we need to take action on the Kyoto Protocol and climate change and all of those things, but while presidents and prime ministers are acting or not acting, we can make major changes at home. There is much power in that. Let's recycle, but we need to do more than that. I'm realizing that I myself am not doing enough. How do we take it up a notch? We need to get over our laziness, get over our own inertia, and keep it going, keep it persistent, keep it truthful. Without this action, we are not going to leave the world a better place. Without this feeling of urgency coupled with hope and love, we're not going to make it. That's what I'm calling on with myself and others—to be aware of what's happening, don't let it take you down, and work together, love yourself, love your community, and start making real changes. That's the message of our film.

Questions and Answers

AUDIENCE MEMBER 1: How do we make the organizations with the most power make channels for people to connect and change lifestyles?

PETERSEN: Inner work is first. We keep coming back to the understanding that small groups of people are very important to mutually reinforce change. For example, the Soka Gakkai International is a global organization, and through this organization this group of people is sitting here today. When people sit together and start drawing up plans and things to do and actionable items, this is not just thinking anymore, it's real action on the ground, a physical manifestation of change. Then you can network that idea throughout your organization. So let's say you figure out how to cheaply install solar energy or cheaply do composting, you network that knowledge throughout your organization. It's about execution, and that's the daunting thing. That's why I keep saying, after the film, how can we help people make change? It's really about joining in small local groups, because that's how changes happen. As the groups start networking, they become more powerful and they can enforce change at a bigger level.

AUDIENCE MEMBER 2: I was very impressed that you focus on solutions. Can you tell us what the website is?

PETERSEN: I really want everyone to understand that talking about bad news isn't adversarial, it's just truth. You talk about the bad news and you say okay, well the environmentalists are always bumming everyone out because they are talking about all this bad stuff that's going on, but you know, it's kind of what's going on. So, can we be okay with that and realize that it's not about the environment, it's a human issue. We should do away with the word *environmentalism* and just say it's a human issue, because the planet is where we live, it's a human home. Forget about the word *environmentalism*, it's really about humans and how to behave correctly and in a healthy manner. We have two websites: the action website (www.11thhouraction.com) where we are networking the local and the website on *The 11th Hour* film (www.11thhourfilm.com).

AUDIENCE MEMBER 3: You appear to have an amazing amount of tolerance and also an amazing amount of insight into how to pace yourself. I would like to know how you do that. How do you maintain that mind set?

PETERSEN: It is so hard, even with all the awareness in the world, to stick to your guns and make your commitments real. Ironically, before today's talk, I was drinking out of a plastic bottle because I didn't fill up my personal container.

The word I would use is *forgiveness*. It's about forgiving yourself and about understanding that you can't do it alone. You must create a support group, knowing that mistakes will be made.

It's the same thing with bigger companies. Big Fortune 500 companies now are making zero carbon goals and zero waste goals—they call it climbing the mount of sustainability. It is one step at a time. You are climbing a very steep mountain, and you are going to make mistakes, but that's part of it. If you can come from that place, then I think it's more tolerable.

AUDIENCE MEMBER 4: Is cutting our consumption really the best thing
for us to do for the environment?

PETERSEN: It's about how it's done. The problem with food in general is
that we have more than 6 billion people on the planet, and the only
reason we have that many people is because we have taken fossil fuel
and turned it into human biomass. I am paraphrasing that from Wes
Jackson in the film. He is saying that the only reason we can feed all
these people is because we have turbines and tractors and we can
plow gigantic fields and transport food to far away. That has enabled
us to grow our numbers. Industrialized food production is destructive
whether it is beef or corn or soy. Can we change the process of food
production to more organic, local-based food production, which definitely includes less meat. It doesn't mean no meat, because if you look
at perma-culture, it includes meat—it's just a more sustainable, holistic
system upon which people eat and nurture their food supply.

I will say a plug for the oceans: Don't eat Orange Roughy, it is a
species of fish that has existed for 150 years. Fish in general are old.
Big fish like tunas are twenty years old, other fish are fifty to eighty
years old.

People are asking, what's a sustainable fish? The answer is catfish
and tilapia. They grow in a year. By the way, there was no salmon run
this year. We have to back off on fish, even though I really love, love,
love fish.

Paul Stamets in Washington State is doing incredible research
on the strains of mushrooms that can decontaminate chemical weapons. Mushrooms have evolved for millions of years. Their root system
uses all these chemicals to defend against protozoa, bacteria, animals,
worms, whatever. Over millions of years, mushrooms have collected
all these chemical defenses.

There is a mushroom that can actually eat VX gas, a nerve agent
and weapon of war, and turn it into a nonlethal substance in which
you can grow tomatoes and eat them. In other words, you can decontaminate chemical weapons with mushrooms. Think about the power
of that. Meanwhile, people are building incinerators in Russia to burn
this stuff. Surrounding communities are starting to voice concern,
because no one knows what will happen with all this VX gas exhaust.

The other thing mushrooms can do is, in your body, it starts chelating and disassembling toxic molecules—that means mercury poisoning, bird flu, perhaps even AIDS. Mushrooms disassemble viruses and detoxify our body of illnesses. One of my favorite things is that Paul Stamets says he found a mushroom that is active against pox viruses. These strains of mushroom are being challenged by the National Institutes of Health and the Pentagon.

One particular mushroom only grows in 2 percent of the old growth forests left in northern Washington State. It grows nowhere else on the planet. Paul Stamets says we should protect national old growth forests as a matter of national defense because there is no other place this mushroom grows, much less everything else you can find in the forest. You will hear more about mushrooms as the years go on. There are suggestions to put mushroom centers in communities.

AUDIENCE MEMBER 5: I am wondering if you had anybody on the panel who was a spiritual leader, like Native American shamans and people who are connected with the land.

PETERSEN: We did talk to some of those people. We talked to an Oua Shaman, we talked to Oren Lyons, we talked to Rabbi Nemmom. The next film is specifically dedicated to this question of the spiritual response to this crisis.

~ May 31, 2008
SGI-USA Santa Monica Culture of Peace Resource Center

Because We Must

Women As Peacebuilders

Dee Aker

Deputy Director, Joan B. Kroc Institute for Peace & Justice
University of San Diego

Dee Aker is a psychological anthropologist and conflict-resolution professional with more than thirty years of experience working with international communities and individuals in transition. At the University of San Diego's Joan B. Kroc Institute for Peace & Justice, where she is the deputy director, Aker created and directs the Women PeaceMakers Program, the Nepal Peacebuilding Initiative, and the WorldLink—Connecting Youth to Global Affairs program.

Before coming to the IPJ, Aker worked with Carl Rogers at the Center for Studies of the Person and the Carl Rogers Institute for Peace on special conflict-transformation efforts in Europe and Central America.

Aker has extensive international experience in higher education, including administration, curriculum development and teaching. For more than a decade, she worked as a TV host, columnist and freelance journalist covering women and gender concerns, including the production of 234 thirty-minute interviews with women leaders, pioneers and survivors from around the world.

Aker was the 2007 Phillips Brooks House Association Fellow at Harvard University, selected to "share a distinguished public service career" with students and staff at the PBHA and Center for Public Interest at Harvard.

Dr. Aker covers many of the eight action areas in the 1999 United Nations Declaration and Programme of Action on a Culture of Peace, including the fourth, ensuring equality between women and men. She says: "Women are finding new paths to peace and out of these cycles of violence, just as they must. Testimonies and actions of women in the toughest situations now expose and challenge the doublespeak and deceit that dwells in peace plans that ignore conflict victims and survivors."

Today, I bring you some stories of women peacemakers who are trying to create this world of peace, starting in their own lands. They need your help; they need your wisdom as members of the global community committed to strengthening resources for a culture of peace.

Some of what I share today exposes what must change in the world. I apologize in advance if some of what we discuss is discomforting, but this is the world of women peacemakers. It is also the world where the spirit of hope and recovery and change can reach our hearts. I invite you to listen to the wind carrying their wisdom and to see the horizon of their vision of peace as well as their hurt.

Sharing the words and stories of women confronting globally rampant abuse and gender-based violence, and working to change the direction of conflict in societies have been part of my personal journey to support those laboring to end the cycles of violence in their lives, in their homes, in their lands and on our shared planet.

The last six years have been especially rewarding for me. I was privileged to help create a very special program because of a gift from the late philanthropist for peace, Joan Kroc, widow of the McDonald's hamburger chain founder, Ray Kroc, at the University of San Diego.

Mrs. Kroc, who came from humble Midwestern beginnings, did not suffer personally from the violence that inspires many of those whom we will be talking about today. But she looked out on a struggling world in which she saw conflict and tension and unnecessary violence, and she began her quiet career as a philanthropist for peace and justice at home and abroad. Peace personal, peace cultural—she envisioned a place where people could come to explore and uncover paths to a more-peaceful world.

After working discreetly behind the scenes with her funds to open up opportunities for better relationships between the United States and the Soviets, the Contras and the Sandinistas in Nicaragua, and elsewhere, she supported "citizen diplomats." She gave funds to create the Institute for Peace & Justice, and more recently a school of peace studies, perhaps the first in the United States. Our IPJ mission is to foster peace, cultivate justice and create a safer world. Asked why she gave the money to do such things, she would say, "We must make peace, and not just talk peace."

We try to live up to her dream of being a space where people from the grass roots and those in policy leadership can sincerely seek understanding and reconciliation, to be a place where they can dialogue with one another. During its first eight years, IPJ has had the privilege to work with diverse people in many settings: We have been on the ground in Uganda and Nepal for conflict-resolution work. We've focused on connecting high school kids on both sides of our border with Mexico. We've had a chance also—and this is the most exciting part—to document women peacemaker stories from around the world, because they are not sufficiently heard. We won't know how to transform conflict unless we listen to them.

It's important to introduce those isolated by geography or by mindset to a greater understanding of what's happening in this world, as well as to give access and experience to those in communities needing visions that are alternatives to biased and manipulative media, and to ignorance. Our desire has been to open minds beyond labels and bring into focus the meaning of words like those of the Palestinian Dr. Hanan Ashrawi, who asserts that we need to redefine *security* as human, comprehensive, multifaceted, transnational and cultural—beyond any sovereignty. That's the way we'll build a new and sustainable peace.

The women peacemaker's program has allowed us to document the lives of women who are leaders in social justice, activism and resistance to violence. As a psychological anthropologist and a journalist, I want to magnify how women are transforming violent conflicts in spirit and in community. From the former UN High Commissioner of Human Rights and former president of Ireland, Mary Robinson, to the young ex-Maoist combatants that I have been working with in Nepal, I have seen the exact same powerful drive, not just to question why violence, abuse, and exclusion hold sway but also to change such realities into a non-violent and more inclusive world. It's essential that we see them, believe them, join them. Their success is our survival. We know that violence and war are easy—look at the world today. We know that peace and justice are difficult, but come with me on any mission and see that women can do the hard stuff.

As a young Peace Corps volunteer 45 years ago, in a remote village with the Guambiano Indians, I watched women bear children and bury them, work in the fields and cook the food, quell arguments and soothe the injured. They taught me about peace, acceptance and being a humbler person. They were the guardians of life and peace 10,000 feet up in the Andes. Now, unfortunately, these many years later, policies and conflicts they had no part in creating and no way of voicing their opposition to or stopping, are taking away some of the hope; and their children are being killed by the guns, drugs and warmongers they never had to face in the past. Like other women around the world, they must have their voices heard.

> ⇥ *Testimonies and actions of women in the toughest situations now expose and challenge the doublespeak and deceit that dwells in peace plans that ignore conflict victims and survivors.*

In Uganda, walking through fields of skulls and open graves at the end of a 20-year civil war, I found women facing wild pigs in order to gather coffee, rebuilding coffee factories on their own, tending to their raped selves and sometimes to the babies born of those rapes and to violated little girls. They were taking in the children of parents who had been slain. They were planting small roadside gardens while they slowly took back the land from the bush that had grown up during the violence. This land was so laden, as you walked through it, with broken families and the bones still scattered in the countryside. Those women had to stay during the wars. They had babies who cried, whom they couldn't run away from in those times; they had to care for them. Their men had scattered, either to join rebel forces of one stripe or another, or they had died. So, putting life back together was their task, as it has been women's work throughout the ages after wars and violence that the women did not start.

A woman's experience of suffering the brunt of the increasing impoverishment of her people, of knowing intimately the fragmenting of her community, of being targeted for sexual violence, gives her a right to have a voice in confronting the seemingly endless cycles of conflict. Women are finding new paths to peace and out of these cycles of violence, just as they must. Testimonies and actions of women in the toughest situations now expose and challenge the doublespeak and deceit that dwells in peace plans that ignore conflict victims and survivors.

Women must not—and often do not—accept that being consumed, commodified, devalued and destroyed are inevitable. Many of their stories are inspirational, giving both women and men the courage to move forward for human rights and for peace with justice. Today, I'll introduce you to four women responding to some common challenges in cultures moving away from conflict, or in its aftermath.

Through the eyes of these women, you'll see them beginning to try to solve the abuse problems and create a change in thinking that can bring peace, even for children caught in the conflict, and the psychological minefields left behind. You'll even see women confronting the guns left in the society after a conflict is over, and women standing up for fair elections. One woman you'll see in the film I'll screen today is from Zimbabwe, and if you've been following the news you know what's happened there. She is now in hiding, and several people in her election group at the time have since been injured. A woman still trying to move for bringing civil society after having succeeded in enacting a ceasefire through bringing men and women together.

EDITOR'S NOTE:

> A summary of the video follows. The video can be viewed in its entirety at www.peace.sandiego.edu.

> Today's film discusses the plight of the people harmed by the civil war in Uganda, by the unpardonable tactics of the government military forces and by the sadistic insurgents called the Lord's Resistance Army. As a result, the roads have been filled with some 40,000 children known as "night commuters."

> Sister Paulina Acayo works in northern Uganda's Gulu District to support peace efforts, the prevention of child abduction and the reintegration of formerly abducted children back into their homes

and communities. Sister Acayo says the children have to move every day, as much as six miles or more, to avoid abduction. They sleep in the sand. It is cold; they get sick. There is no money for health care, and they end up dying.

More than 60,000 children have been abducted in Gulu District alone. Children are taken violently and used as sex slaves, porters and soldiers, often forced to kill their own friends and family. Sister Acayo's reception center sees that the returned children undergo the traditional reconciliation cleansing ceremony, and after that, a community celebration. There are other pitfalls: As the children are reintegrated, they often meet up with people who are alcohol- and drug-addicted, making it more difficult to help them heal. The center tries to steer them off alcohol or drugs, and gets them involved in activities like team sports. The children are eventually trained in managing conflict in the community and in their families, and also to help others. A lot of women's groups are also being formed for the purpose of standing up for women's rights.

Thavory Huot's childhood instincts saved her from being slaughtered alongside an estimated 150,000 peasants during the 1969–73 secret bombardment of Cambodia by the United States. She also survived the Khmer Rouge genocide, the four-year "Killing Fields" atrocity in which some 2 million people were starved, overworked and killed, including most of Thavory's family. The Cambodian people are still picking up the pieces after three decades of war.

So many weapons were left behind by the war, and these weapons extended the violence far after the war was over. Thavory worked with a group that endeavors to awaken the people and stop them from using the weapons; they create posters to explain the consequences, to educate the communities and encourage them to hand over their weapons to local authorities, to educate the armed forces to understand their roles as holders of weapons.

Most weapon-holders are men. Armed violence has been used to facilitate rape and sexual assault of women and girls by military forces in battle, by security forces assigned guardianship, and by intimate partners at home. Thavory says a neighbor got angry with

*her and threatened her frequently with a gun and even sometimes
shot through her window. Today, Thavory, inspired by her children
and her personal freedom, embraces non-violence.*

*Emmaculeta Chiseya of Zimbabwe discussed the difficulties she is
facing while trying to create peace. As a project officer and monitor for the Zimbabwean Election Support Network, Emmaculeta
pushes for democratization of the electoral process, despite repressive
laws that make her work more and more difficult. She says people are
threatened into voting for a candidate, or bribed with things that will
never be done. She says they need to take their leadership to task.*

*Attorney Mary Ann Arnado is a peacemaker in Mindanao promot-
ing the role of women in the peace process between the Philippines
government and the Moral Islamic Liberation Front. She has organized a ceasefire monitoring team working directly in zones of conflict to educate warring factions on international humanitarian law
and human rights.*

*For evacuees, malnutrition and disease cause more death than bul-
lets. There is no medical treatment. Attempting to affect a ceasefire,
the evacuees tried standing on the side of the road with signs asking the fighters to go home. Three weeks later, the Liberation Front
declared a unilateral ceasefire, after which the government recipro-
cated. The women's demonstration contributed greatly to this victory. Since then they have moved forward with peacebuilding in the
community and helping the displaced to return home.*

It's a little bit hard to watch, but these are also things we have to know
because that's where some people have to start from to build this culture
of peace. To bring you up to date on the women in the film—Sister Pauline is still active in northern Uganda, working with children coming in
from the bush. That the night commuters have mostly gone home doesn't
mean there's peace in the north, but there's more peace than there has
been in the past.

Peace talks with Joseph Kony, head of the Lord's Resistance Army,
flounder; but, this week, he actually said he wants to return to the talks at
which he failed to show up in the past few months. This is a complicated

situation because he has killed his own superior officers in the bush, and the International Criminal Court has an indictment that hangs over his head. In the meantime, some people are coming home, children are getting treatment, more people are working in the north, and people like Sister Pauline are getting a lot of training in how to deal with the psychological trauma. Both culturally and from within, as she mentioned briefly in the film, we have them go through a process of coming to peace with themselves because of what they've been forced to do, and then trying to come to peace with the community, which is sometimes even harder.

Thavory Huot, from Cambodia, has created a series of educational books for schools called A *Culture of Peace*, and it is about the need to end the gun culture.

As for Emmaculeta Chiseya in Zimbabwe, I already mentioned that things are not going well there because of difficulties with Mugabe and the elections. We're hoping that she can join us in San Diego in the fall for a special conference on human security in an insecure world, in which we are bringing in people who deal with military levels and asking them how we are going to handle these kinds of things.

Finally, Mary Ann Arnado's work in the Philippines continues. She is a lawyer. She's done a lot. She's met with both the President and the head of the Moral Islamic Liberation Front. It's a complex situation involving indigenous rights, etc., in Mindanao, but she is still there on the front lines.

There's nothing simple. There are survivors and spokespersons who suggest that changing the bad habits of the world and reclaiming respect for the dignity of the person are possible even in these worst of times. To create a culture of peace, we must also understand what underlies violence against women in particular. Sexual violence continues to be a weapon of war and an impediment to peace. From Afghanistan to Zimbabwe, to the Democratic Republic of Congo and beyond, we hear and see the devastation writ large on women's bodies and spirits, in their families and in their shattered communities.

The 1949 Geneva Convention, the 1998 Rome Statute for the International Criminal Court, and the Rwanda and former Yugoslavia tribunals all tried to address this. But because war isolates, letting parties in conflict become more polarized, societal divisions deepen and sexual abuse intensifies. The violent nature of conflicts can be transformed, however, to provide constructive options and to let us know what options are out there. Things are happening. Women are often on the front lines of this effort to defy the atrocities and threats targeting them. Increasingly, at both the local and at international levels, women are playing a greater role.

In 1995, when 40,000 women came from around the world to Beijing for the 4th World Conference on Women, they reassured each other and the world that they had rights; that a global culture of peace was possible because they modeled it, and it became possible. At that moment in time, women from 170 countries – in their traditional dress and speaking their native languages – figured out how to share, how to listen with their hearts and how to find common threads.

People from the north and south of Sudan spent a week in a tent just learning how to actually talk to one another because they had been so separated. They did it, and they came back and made demands, and when peace talks took place later regarding northern and southern Sudan, the women, who couldn't get to the peace talks, figured out how to be effective. They created a sixth clan – because you had to be a clan member to be there, you had to have some kind of identification as having a role – and therefore, they could send their own representation, and that was very valuable.

We subsequently had a woman peacemaker from Sudan who was there in Beijing and then later on at the peace talks. When the men tried to walk out of the peace talks, when they continued down into Kenya, to Arusha, the women circled that group and would not let the men leave the talks until they had addressed some of the issues. In this particular case, this woman was asked to facilitate the warlords' discussion, because nobody wanted to give power to any particular warlord. This is a secret way, then, if people are vying for power, where someone can step in and take on the role of facilitator. This woman established rules, such as, "You can't talk longer than 10 minutes; you can't do this or that; and we can discuss such and such and move forward," which the men accepted. With these types of actions, there is a possibility for looking at things differently in the future.

I think that the demands for participation, and for decision making and creating machinery, provide opportunities where women can have access in government and in other world influences, like the World Bank. They have been somewhat successful, but it has been hard. People in power don't want to give it up. Historically, survivors and victims of the madness of war and those who don't carry guns or machetes have not been invited to the table. But women along with men sensitive to gender issues, at home and abroad, are making a difference.

On October 31, 2000, the Security Council Resolution 1325 was passed unanimously. There were actually cheers—you never hear cheers in the Security Council. The resolution declared that specifically women, because of war's impact upon them, should be contributing to conflict resolution. Women have a right to be at the peace tables, a right to make decisions about peacekeeping bodies, a right to participate in peacekeeping itself, and women should also have protection from gender-based violence, particularly rape and other forms of sexual abuse during conflict.

Resolution 1325 emphasizes that all states are supposed to do this. What we, along with the women peacemakers who have been coming to us, have been doing is going to governments, reading to them what's in 1325 and reminding them, "You signed this!" (Because all the governments signed it.) "You signed it. This was cheered on. You have to know what's going on." We need a whole community of people who know about these regulations and laws and resolutions, so that they can be moved forward; because the resolution also talks about other issues besides just getting to the table.

For instance, the issue of the refugee camps came up. Historically, women have not been involved. They've been in the refugee camps, but they've had no say regarding them, so there have been a lot of problems. Especially regarding things like sanitary napkins and other needs, for themselves and for their kids. We're just beginning to address those issues and to get people access.

Beyond 1325, there was a conference in Wilton Park [a U.K.-based organization that hosts conferences involved with problem solving and future policy shaping] this past May. It was organized by UNIFEM, the United Nations Development Fund for Women. The conference examined the role of military peacekeepers alongside other actors and NGOs. There were 70 participants only, but there were 27 military establishments from 40 different countries who attended. The message to the conference from UN Secretary-General Ban Ki-moon said specifically, "We know from grim experiences how sexual violence in conflict wreaks devastation on individuals, families, communities and entire societies ... Widespread and systematic sexual violence further heightens insecurity. There are consequences for recovery and reconciliation. When alleged perpetrators are not prosecuted and brought to justice, the rule of law is undermined and impunity reigns."

And Major General Patrick Cammaert, the former UN Deputy Force Commander, says "It is more dangerous to be a woman than to be a soldier (in the eastern Democratic Republic of Congo) right now."

There's a need for a more coherent, coordinated and robust approach to ending this kind of sexual violence.

Nine days ago, the UN Security Council again passed a resolution — 1820 — recognizing that there is this threat. While some of us who work in this field didn't want another resolution — we felt that 1325 was good enough — this allows us to go to the military organizations and those people participating in conflict and say: "Look, this has been signed, and you need to take action. We'll help you with training, we'll bring the women and men who can actually give you the experience needed so — even if yours is a cultural tradition where men have a lot of power and rights and women don't — you can deal with that and protect the community where you are brought in to serve." We need to ensure accountability, to ensure that women's participation in discussions on sexual violence, as well, is addressed. Exclusion of women from these fields has just been too traumatic.

Here are a few quick other stories, because I think they model what happens when women get involved.

Christiana Thorpe is a former nun and was a Mother Superior at a school. She had to go to the Pope in order to get dispensation to leave, because she wanted to be on the streets with the young girls in her country whom she was trying to protect, some 10,000 of them who were then in the capital. She had already been a Minister of Education. She is an amazing person. But most recently, because of her willingness to step up, she was selected the first woman election commissioner in Sierra Leone. About a year ago, Sierra Leone conducted the most corruption-free elections in all of Africa. Even though the people who appointed her didn't make it through, she stood up. She's standing up against death threats and is still there. She'll continue through the next round of elections for local people. She is there, and she can make a difference.

Luz Mendez is from Guatemala. She was a student rebel back in the

1970s. She was very much engaged and had to leave the country for her own safety and that of her children. She was a young mother at the time. She ended up working on the outside, on the Guatemalan peace accords, which initially had no women involved. She is a signatory to those accords. What's interesting about Luz and people like her—and the women that I know in this work—is that they bring in the people who aren't represented. Luz went out to the indigenous people and said: "What do you think should be in these peace accords? What else do you think we have to do?" Accordingly, she became the representative for a much larger community. That's often the case with women peacemakers. Historically, people just assume their own little square of power, but these women are making it much broader.

Hyun-Sook Lee is from Korea. She grew up during the separation, the Korean War. She had always wanted to get involved in peacemaking, but, at age 50, she decided she just had to do something. So, she became the person who created the first talks in the 1990s between North and South Korea. She started what we call the Sunshine Policy, in which food was given during a time of starvation in the North. She made sure that food got up there, and the first talks and exchange of people since the beginning of the Korean War took place. She is now working with the Korean Red Cross.

And finally, there is Zarina Salamat from Pakistan. Zarena is important because she, like Hyun-Sook, grew up at a particular time. She was 13 during the partition of India and Pakistan, so she also grew up when worlds were split. Being Pakistani and Muslim, she was part of the largest migration ever in the world. And she is also one who came to her activism at a later age. Zarina was 60 before she started working on the issues of conflict resolution. She started bringing people from Pakistan to India to talk to their counterparts, and then she got involved in the antinuclear movement. She protested when India tested its bomb back in the late 1990s and begged the Pakistani government not to engage. A few weeks later, Pakistan had its own test, as you may remember, and Zarina stood up in front of the press and was nearly killed by a mob of her own people for saying, "We don't want to test nuclear weapons here."

She later connected with the mayor of Hiroshima, and she has been taking young people from India and Pakistan—sometimes joined by youth from the United States—to Hiroshima to talk about what happened there.

These are just a few of the stories; there are many more online and available on DVD.

I thank you for your attention.

Questions and Answers

AUDIENCE MEMBER 1: Would you please go into more detail about the IPJ programs—the Woman PeaceMakers program, the Nepal Peace-building Initiative and the WorldLink program? And how can interested people get involved?

AKER: If you go to our website—www.peace.sandiego.edu—you'll see all the programs are there.

We have different Women PeaceMakers activities every year. This fall, we will be having peacemakers coming from four countries: the Democratic Republic of Congo, South Africa, Peru and Bangladesh. Among many events, we will have sessions where these women sit individually and tell their stories to small audiences interested in those particular places. We'll have another event where they all speak and give a history of what they are doing and how they do their work.

WorldLink is a program for high school students, connecting youth to global affairs. We bring students together from Mexico and the United States to look at global issues. We have been doing this for 12 years now. The students choose the topics; they run the program. What we do is get the speakers for them, whether they are from the State Department or the United Nations. Whatever they are interested in, we bring people there.

We restrict the speakers to giving a very short presentation about their work, and then the students get to question them. The students, who are bilingual, also produce their own newspaper; they are amazing. Better than our local newspaper, the students' paper really looks at and discusses the issues. It gives you various sides of the issues rather than just hyping a particular approach.

As for the Nepal initiative, we have been working in Nepal for eight years with leaders at the top level, both political leaders and those in civil society. The IPJ belief is that you cannot just deal with the people who carry the guns—the power brokers—you also have to prepare civil society to get involved.

Some 13,000 lives have been lost in their conflict. But two years ago, the public stood up and said: "That's enough! We're not going to do this anymore." A million people came out in the streets of Katmandu, and subsequently they forced their very tyrannical king to step down. On our most recent trip there, a republic was declared by a newly elected government. A constituent assembly is going to write a new constitution. I was there with the Carter Center (established by former US President Jimmy Carter) to help monitor elections in April, but by May they were already holding their first meeting of the people elected. It was considered free and fair.

AUDIENCE MEMBER 2: Have you interviewed any women from Palestine?

AKER: Yes. One of the peacemakers last year was the well-known Samia Fahmy. She had worked quite closely with Yasser Arafat, reminding him of what women's issues were. Samia has actually helped write the constitution that is in the waiting. Some of the women who come to us, like Samia, are devastated. They work alone a lot.

The advantage in what we do in bringing even four people together, even though the effort is so tiny, is that the participants suddenly discover that other people in the world are having similar difficulties. Palestinians, in particular, have been so isolated. It was so difficult for Samia to even get out of the country to come see us.

She started and is part of, a women's leadership council in which Palestinian and Israeli women meet. Because of recent difficulties, they can no longer go back and forth across the border. They used to meet in Jerusalem or Ramala or down in Gaza. Now, because things are so bad, when they do meet, they go to Italy or Spain or someplace else, but their meetings comprise twenty women from each side and twenty internationals from Europe and elsewhere. They sit as a council to figure out how they can influence what is going on. They have amazing stories, and I can't wait until hers comes out, it is very moving. She is very powerful.

One problem in doing a film is that we don't always have enough film stock, so it is difficult to produce updates. So, this year, we sent all the women home with their own video cameras. We weren't sure Samia would make it through all the checkpoints with her camera, but she did.

AUDIENCE MEMBER 3: Do people ever ask how you as an American can be promoting peace when your country has initiated war?

AKER: It's a good question. Certainly the attitude about the United States is the worse I have ever seen, after having traveled so many years. But, in my experience, it is mainly directed at the Administration. People love the work we do. We were just given an award, interestingly enough, in Nepal. Normally, we are quiet behind the scenes, but Prime Minister Prachanda, the Maoist leader, actually handed me an award for our work for the last eight years in Nepal.

I also had a workshop with Maoists as a group for the first time. At the end, we were dealing with some tough issues that they will have to face. All of a sudden, the sentiment came up that: "We don't like America, we don't want NGOs coming in here, this isn't a comfortable way to deal, etc." While it was very helpful to then get the award from their head person, that was an exception.

In Uganda and elsewhere, there is a lot of respect for our people, who are trying to do serious work. I do recommend, though, that we focus at home in some areas as much as we can, because it is not helpful just to send money or do something abroad. There is a new culture of corruption based on NGO realities that we have to pay attention to. It's not all pie in the sky.

We don't maintain permanent physical locations; we just work with local people wherever we go, unless we are merely conducting top-level negotiations. Otherwise, we are committed to dealing with local people, because they know how to do what they need to do and just need a little help sometimes, a little training. For example, we help them with the words they need in negotiation, with how to think about other people's interests and options, and with the process of how to begin to dialogue amid a new democratic process.

In one respect, war is easy, it works fast. You get a gun, you shoot somebody. Trying to establish peace and conduct dialogue, to come to a consensus, takes a lot more time as people need to get their minds around the idea, and that's what we help with.

AUDIENCE MEMBER 4: What about women who imitate men's violence, as in female gangs?

AKER: Everyone feels a need to belong. Cultures that have been steeped in violence, often as a reaction to mistreatment from the outside, have found out they look a little more impressive if they are violent. Women and young girls, too, want to be empowered in that way. It's a chance for them to have some recognition and to participate.

But it's not always the case. For instance, in Nepal's Maoist movement, a third of the rebel group were young women. When I interviewed certain individuals, I asked, "Why would you want to carry a gun around and do all this stuff?" They would say, "Because I am going to get a better education than the government was giving me before." So, there are a lot of reasons why women—young women in particular—get involved in violent situations.

Also, historically, women leaders have been combative, as we can see from examples such as Indira Gandhi, Maggie Thatcher and Golda Meir. It was not until Ireland President Mary Robinson, who later became the UN High Commissioner for Human Rights, said, "No, this isn't how we are going to do this," that a big model for change was presented.

We have to find out how we can create an environment where young women can get some other kind of attention that allows them to be something else. Maybe if we gave them 20 of these films, so they could look at many women who are dealing with these issues.

AUDIENCE MEMBER 5: I am curious about your own background. How did you get to where you are in terms of your career and your personal life?

AKER: Growing up in Hannibal, Missouri, I just always had this desire to do something. When John F. Kennedy talked about his vision and the Peace Corps, I joined. It was an amazing opportunity that allowed me to do a lot of things. Subsequently, I could draw upon that experience in my studies. Also, I did social work for four years, and I learned a lot from the people I was working with.

Once I was out of college—the first time; I did go back for two more degrees—I began learning from and visiting the world, staying for enough time in certain locations. But there was never one path. I was a psychologist for several years, I was a reporter for the *Chicago Tribune* and other papers. I did a lot of different things, but they all centered on what I do now, they really opened doors.

I worked for years for the very well-known psychologist Carl Rogers. That was really transformational. Carl and I worked in Poland when that nation was first dealing with the Solidarity movement, and he was an underground writer. Nobody was allowed to read his books. Subsequently, when we worked with President Arias in Costa Rica, that's when I first became aware of the help being offered behind the scenes by Joan Kroc.

I have this sort of "Forest Gump" life in which I get to hang out with a lot of good people who have enriched me and have been great mentors. I have a lot to draw on. I have a lot of friends, and I never really work alone. When we work in Nepal, I am as likely to bring a peacemaker or a woman who has been involved in the writing of Uganda's constitution as anybody else. I don't presume to have the answers, but I have a lot of friends who have a lot of good ones.

~ June 28, 2008
SGI-USA Santa Monica Culture of Peace Resource Center

Patriarchy, Pedagogy and Learning toward a Culture of Peace

Betty A. Reardon

Founding Director Emeritus,
International Institute on Peace Education

Betty Reardon, Founding Director Emeritus of the International Institute on Peace Education is internationally acknowledged as a founder of contemporary peace education. She is also a prolific author of peace, human-rights and gender-related materials since the mid 1960s and has been involved in peace education projects and publications with colleagues the world over.

Dr. Reardon covers many of the eight action areas in the 1999 United Nations Declaration and Programme of Action on a Culture of Peace, including the first: fostering a culture of peace through education; and the fourth: ensuring equality between women and men. As Dr. Reardon summarizes: "The achievement of a culture of peace requires confronting and transcending patriarchy; it requires social learning pursued through a pedagogy of critical engagement rooted in the values, visions and concepts, principles and standards of human rights as indicators of progress toward human equality and social justice. Achieving equality and social justice requires establishing a non-violent, disarmed and demilitarized, gender equal political order secured by the renunciation of war, weaponry and all forms of coercive violence. These are the essential elements of a transformed world order of mutually enhancing human relationships at all levels of human society, from interpersonal to global."

Tonight, I will speak about what I see as the most significant obstacle to a culture of peace, patriarchy. Some twenty-five years ago, I published a book called *Sexism and the War System* (Teachers College Press, 1985 and Syracuse University Press, 1995). When a friend asked me about the reactions I'd received to the publication, I said, "Apparently, it has a little something in it to offend everybody." So, I'm an equal opportunity offender. I fully recognize that when one speaks about patriarchy, about any gender issues, people are likely to have strong reactions. I apologize in advance, should I cause discomfort. But I won't change my mind on this long-held belief about the need for peace activists and peace educators to confront the patriarchal structures of inequality that impede social and economic justice and thereby prevent the achievement of a just and lasting peace.

For these reasons, I titled this lecture, "Patriarchy, Pedagogy and Learning toward a Culture of Peace." Those three themes—patriarchy, pedagogy and learning—are interrelated and inseparable in my view of the most potentially effective responses to the problematic of patriarchy as an obstacle to peace. A culture of peace depends on transformative, critical social learning. The pedagogy of peace must develop critical, creative and visionary capacities. The requisite transformation is both evolutionary, on going change in worldviews, relationships and behaviors; and revolutionary, radical changes in political, economic and social structures, changing from a culture of patriarchalism, an ideology that supports hierarchy over democracy to one of universal human dignity and equal human value of all persons. Because the devising of a culture of peace requires searching for new social and political possibilities, the effectiveness of these processes depend on the questions and queries we raise to guide the change process, to learn about *what is*, i.e., our present reality and, more important, about *what could be*, a preferred peaceful reality. Learning toward a culture of peace is an inquiry into the possible.

Toward the end of her marvelous novel, *The God of Small Things*, Arundhati Roy describes an incident in which two young children witness the lethal beating of a member of a lower caste, someone they love dearly, an incident that gives us deep insight into what is:

> The twins were too young to know that these were only history's henchmen. Sent to square the books and collect the dues from those who broke its laws. Impelled by feelings that were primal yet paradoxically wholly impersonal. Feelings of contempt born of inchoate, unacknowledged fear—civilization's fear of nature, men's fear of women, powers fear of powerlessness.
>
> Man's subliminal urge to destroy what he could neither subdue nor deify.
>
> Men's needs.
>
> What Esthappen and Rahel witnessed that morning, though they didn't know it then, was a clinical demonstration in controlled conditions (this was not war after all, or genocide) of human nature's pursuit of ascendancy. Structure. Order. Complete monopoly. It was human history, masquerading as God's Purpose.
>
> (Arundhati Roy, The God of Small Things
[New York: Random House, 2008], p. 245)

To me, that paragraph sums up the culture of violence and many manifestations of the negative aspects of patriarchy that comprises on present reality. But there is hope in a new world aborning. We begin to see glimmers of what could be, elements of a preferred reality. Such glimmers are glimpsed in the words of blogger Courtney E. Martin, a young feminist. She has an entry called "Generation Y Refuses Race Gender Dichotomy" in which she tells us: "My feminism is not just about gender equality in government, but also about racial justice, global security, community ethics … I'm grateful for being challenged to justify my choice … but only when it's initiated in the spirit of dialogue …" (http://www.alternet.org/activism/88472/generation_y_refuses_race-gender_dichotomy).

The dialogue she refers to is the political discourse around American empire. We want to call into question the whole idea of empire. The debate shouldn't center, as it seems to, on the quandary of how can we maintain our empire more effectively. Rather, it should focus on whether we want to be an empire in the first place. Since empires are essentially patriarchal structures, I think the question being asked by Ms. Martin is, "Do we want to continue to sustain patriarchy?" Well, I certainly don't. So the debate on empire might better serve us as a discourse of learning for a culture of peace, inquiring into what is and what could be. What is a culture of peace? What needs to be changed in order to achieve it? What needs to be learned in order to be able to achieve it?

Concepts of a culture of peace tend to be articulated in abstract value terms. Among those concepts, there are three that I find most revelatory. The first describes the culture of peace as shifts from a set of negative conditions to a set of positive conditions. It's offered by Evelin Lindner, founding president of Human Dignity and Humiliation Studies. "[A culture of peace] comprises the results of a shift from a culture of coercion to a culture of creativity; from adversarialism to complementarity; from hierarchy to equality; from separation and distinction to unity and diversity."

The second concept stipulates eight spheres of action advocated in the UN Declaration on a Culture of Peace: fostering a culture of peace through education; promoting sustainable economic and social development; promoting respect for all human rights; ensuring equality between women and men; fostering democratic participation; advancing understanding, tolerance and solidarity; supporting participatory communication and the free flow of information and knowledge; and promoting international peace and security. A tall task!

The third centering on learning requirements of a culture of peace is postulated in the statement of purpose of the Global Campaign for Peace Education. It asserts that a culture of peace will be the consequence of educating for peace. "A culture of peace will be achieved when citizens of the world understand global problems, have the skills to resolve conflict constructively, know and live by international standards of human rights, gender and racial equality, appreciate cultural diversity and respect the integrity of the earth. Such learning cannot be achieved without intentional, sustained and systematic education for peace." (www.peace-ed-campaign.org)

All three concepts provide some common general notions of what would comprise a culture of peace. There is a consistency of values among them all. Yet, most fail to indicate what a living, fully functioning culture of peace actually might be, what specific changes it would necessitate, why we need these changes and the practical measures to achieve the desired alternative culture.

So, too, all fall short of exposing the deeper roots of the culture of violence, of recognizing the depth of the radical transformation a culture of peace requires. None speak to the structural tasks that face us if we are really going to strive toward a culture of peace. None reflect, for example, such learning as that we should have derived decades ago from Alva Myrdal's assertion that world society was in the grip of a *weapons culture*, weapons being the tools applied to so many tasks of international relations and so integral to our ways of thinking and behaving that serious efforts for disarmament were not really being pursued (*War, Weapons and Everyday Violence*, Manchester University of New Hampshire, 1977). She suggested that most nations are addicted to weaponry; thus, anti-addiction education is necessary.

Neither did we learn from an earlier landmark in disarmament negotiations, achieved over forty years ago when the United Nations affirmed the McCloy-Zorin Agreements (1962) between the United States and the Soviet Union, acknowledging that the achievement of sustainable peace required general and complete disarmament and should be the ultimate purpose of all steps toward disarmament. For a short while we seemed to understand that we cannot achieve peace while we maintain vast arsenals of ever more destructive weapons, a learning that disarmament education seeks to revive.

Nor do any of these concepts adequately emphasize that other fundamental principle articulated in 1948 when the Universal Declaration of Human Rights asserted that recognition of human dignity and equality "is the foundation of freedom, justice and peace in the world." It called for nations to strive toward the fulfillment and realization of human rights "by teaching and education." *Realization*, i.e. to actually implement rights, not merely *respect* them, a very weak word when applied to universal rights or to the eight spheres of action for a culture of peace.

A culture of peace requires that the desired and advocated evolutionary shifts in worldviews and attitudes become manifest in the present culture. The requisite learning toward these shifts will involve skills of conflict processing, multiple perspective taking, the positing of alternative realities—all of the things that are constant themes in global peace education literature, and are widely acknowledged as basic requirements for a peaceful society, yet remain still peripheral to standard public education.

What we (both the general public and peace educators) have not yet adequately acknowledged is the need for revolutionary (i.e. explicit intention to bring out significant change in the distribution of power) confrontation of the structures that mediate the culture of violence and its institutional partner, the war system. Nor have we probed into the ancient and all-pervasive root of those structures, patriarchy. Transformation, as argued here includes evolution and revolution. It requires not only inner, evolutionary change within the individuals in terms of values, outlooks and attitudes, but also outer, revolutionary changes in the social structures, customs and habits that derive from those values and worldviews and attitudes. Our task is to build a new outside reality while developing a new inside reality. Overcoming patriarchy calls for an integrated and comprehensive inquiry into possibilities of transformation. A transformative inquiry would include truly probing queries. What constitutes patriarchy in this and other societies? How do we recognize it in its contemporary forms? What sustains it? How might we confront and change it?

For more effective responses to the query of what it is, I propose the application of three concepts or perspectives on patriarchy that hold the potential of providing deeper insight into its characteristics and functions. There are two with which we are already familiar, and one that I suggest as providing a perspective on change.

First is the classical and traditional concept of patriarchy as the rule of the fathers, wise old men who hold power over all, including ownership of women, children and slaves, holding them as their rightful property. It is imposed by the patriarchs' exclusive claim to power, control over weaponry and ownership of tools of production. It came to colonial America with the plantation system, classic model of patriarchy. Western patriarchy spread throughout the world with colonialism. Patriarchy was the foundation of the structures of colonialism.

The changes advanced in response to this traditional notion by those who would reform it have been movements for the abolition of slavery, wider political enfranchisement, voting and property rights for women, child-labor laws, and the rights of labor.

The second concept is what I will call the *transitional* and evolutionary patriarchy, largely the consequence of these reforms. It is evolving into other forms of the fundamental hierarchy. It acknowledges the mutability of gender, recognizing that gender roles change with times and cultures. Yet, it also acknowledges that we still live in a male-dominated culture, characterized by the continuation of oppression, exploitation and discrimination against women and all those on the lower levels of the hierarchy, generally imposed through socially prescribed roles and status, based largely on socioeconomic functions. Women's work and the work of the hands and body whether done by women or men are less valuable than the work of executing power and managing and controlling social and economic goods. High social value is placed on the role of the ruler, the warrior, the protector, the provider, the manager, the entrepreneur. While they are very few, some women also perform these power and management functions.

The response to this concept of patriarchy has been a movement for the full range of human rights for women, the overturning of rigid patriarchal gender roles and equal employment and education opportunities for all. It is certainly a somewhat less oppressive hierarchy, but one that is far from actual gender equality.

Considering Courtney Martin's reflections on potential change, I propose a third concept of patriarchy that in its self-awareness and declining intransigency is potentially transformative and diagnostic in seeking out its own dysfunctional nature. This third concept facilitates inquiry into what must be changed in social, economic and, especially in political gender roles, as well as, status in the patriarchal hierarchy, to make possible a transition toward human equality.

This third concept of a potentially transformative approach serves to reveal more fully the characteristics of patriarchy as "the rule of the worthy," the social order based upon the assumption of unequal value among all human beings; not just the unequal value of men and women, but unequal value across the entire spectrum of humanity, dividing it into categories of worthiness, even while leaders advocate equality. It cynically manifests the Orwellian vision of a society in which "some pigs are more equal."

This *transformative/diagnostic* concept of patriarchy benefitting from the emergence of masculinities studies enables us to examine patriarchy from the perspective of the mutability of gender roles, revealing the adaptability of the patriarchal paradigm even to the laws pronouncing equality. It demonstrates that the particular identity of "the worthy" changes with time and culture. However, the superior status of the worthy, the hierarchical structures upholding it that mediate what masculinity scholars now refer to as "the global gender order" (Connell, R.W. *Men and Masculinities*, vol. 1, nos. 1, 3–23, Sage Publications, 1998) remain very much as they are in traditional patriarchy. Gender, in this order, is determined by position and status in the hierarchy of wealth and power, and not by sex alone. At the highest level are the men (and perhaps a woman or two) of the most powerful economies. At the bottom are the poorest of the poor countries, primarily women and children. Today's patriarchs, the most powerful worthy are for the most part the CEOs of multinational and international enterprises, legal and illegal.

The major structural and psychosocial components that sustain this patriarchal gender order, the mechanisms that keep it going are violence and vulnerability. *Violence*, the threat or use of force to maintain the order, and *vulnerability*, the dependency on the hierarchy that makes certain groups constantly vulnerable to the decisions and policies of the worthy at the top of the hierarchy (current economic austerity policies are an example.) Both components are consequences of patriarchal belief systems, modes of thinking and the worthy's ready access to coercive force. Most crucial of the obstacles to a culture of peace among these elements sustaining patriarchy is war as a policy instrument, highly organized violence that society gives over to the hands of the state (essentially an agent of patriarchy,) ostensibly, to protect the vulnerable. More to the point, this "legitimate" violence serves to maintain the fundamental structures of power, keeping the vulnerable in their structurally dependent positions, their perpetual places within patriarchy's global gender order.

Armed force is re-enforced by the centuries old belief system of patriarchalism. Two of the main rationalizations imbedded in the belief system are especially noteworthy. The first holds that hierarchy is the fundamental, natural and necessary paradigm for social order. Without it, there would be the chaos of anarchy. Thus, all economic and political institutions should be structured more or less along these lines, replicating traditional patriarchy in one form or another.

Second, patriarchalism validates the superior human value and social worth of those at the top of the hierarchy. They hold this place because of purported greater wisdom (or what the media call "gravitas" i.e. they know more and make the best decisions.) They are the few endowed with the capacities to manage society and its institutions. Consequently public responsibility is assumed by the worthy who claim it, as did feudal lords, under the notion of *noblesse oblige* (their greater capacity obliges them to assume power) that helped to rationalize traditional patriarchy.

These rationalizations derived from patriarchalism infuse "the patriarchal paradigm," a category of human worth manifested in a framework of social organization built upon a pyramidal power structure that pervades virtually all of human social, economic and political institutions. The paradigm is also integral to most of the conceptual and normative frames within which we think. As such it becomes an issue that should be addressed within the core problematic with which peace education engages.

The paradigm has been perpetuated through time and across cultures by various forms of patriarchalism. The People's Movement for Human Rights Education has identified *patriarchalism* as an ideology of unequal human worth and social entitlement that gives rise to a broad range of abuses of human rights. (www.pdhre.org) An un-reflected mode of thinking, it influences our perceptions of and positions on most public issues and policies. It also affects social relationships and personal relationships, placing the most worthy with virtually unlimited entitlement to all the goods of society at the top; the somewhat less worthy with fewer entitlements in the middle; and the unworthy, without entitlements on the bottom. These three categories are, of course, gross simplifications of the multiple human and cultural variations at all levels below the very top of the hierarchy. Not all the arrangements of persons and groups in the *patriarchal power pyramid* are determined by sex *per se*, but also transnationally by race or the religious and cultural factors that rationalized colonialism. Within nations arrangements are usually by these categories, as well as, ethnicity, class, or age and other such indicators patriarchy has designated to determine human worth.

This pyramid is buttressed by militarized state security systems—the police and the military, collectively comprising what is referred to above

> ✎| *A culture of peace depends on transformative,*
> *critical social learning. The pedagogy of*
> *peace must develop critical, creative and*
> *visionary capacities.*

as *the war system* (See *Sexism and the War System*) This system assures that
the worthy continue to control and "secure" politics and the economy;
that is essentially what is meant by *national security*, i.e. protecting the
state that governs the political order and the economic interests of those
at the top who control the state.

How do we recognize patriarchy in our changing society and contemporary politics when gender roles are more fluid than in traditional,
and even more so in transitional patriarchy? The fluidity would seem to
indicate movement toward equality, yet the patriarchal power pyramid
remains the model of most socio-political organization, even in democracies. While power structures are in fact changeable, we have not been sufficiently aware of the gendered power order to make it the focus of change.
We haven't fully perceived it yet, primarily because we do not understand the complex functions of gender in contemporary patriarchy. But
we have ever more evidence of the longstanding distinction between and
among sex, traditional gender roles and the nature of the manifestations
of gendered power relations, from the Amazons to the Albanian tradition
of "sworn virgins," recently reported in The New York Times (June 2008.)

Apparently, there has been a long tradition in Albania among families
who have lost all their men to designate or allow a woman to live as the
man of the family, to carry the patriarchal responsibilities of manhood, as
well as to enjoy the privileges and powers thereof. Most interesting to me
is the rationale that the other women of the family needed a protector and
the family needed an avenger against those who may harm or dishonor
them —protector/avenger, the classical masculine role in the war system
that prevails even in peace time, even in less traditional societies. Failure to adequately perform these roles in recent armed conflicts has been

seen by both women and men in the conflicted societies as the cause for rapes and kidnapping of women and children to serve a force opposing the group to which the victims belong.

It was reported that most sworn virgins live very happy lives. In fact, some jumped at the chance to take the oath forswearing marriage and any sexual life. I don't know if it got to the point of fratricide to have the opportunity, but it seemed their perspective was, "I know who's got it better. That's the life I prefer to that of vulnerable-protected-subservient womanhood"

The quintessential political examples of this honorary manhood in 20th century democratic societies, demonstrating that it is not only sex that determines position in the patriarchal hierarchy are evident in the Six-Day War, the Falklands conflict and the State of Emergency declared in India in the 1970s; all presided over by women heads of state whose political status, in effect, made them honorary men. They foreswore the traditional gender role of dependency/vulnerability as they wielded the military power of the state. However, they remained in other respects, culturally women and traditionally feminine, Meir referring to herself and being referred to as mother of her nation – all three were actual mothers. Gandhi always wore a sari, considered by many cultures to be the most feminine of dress. Thatcher's hair was always elegantly coiffed. Yet all were as "macho" as any general in using force to "protect the security and national interests" of the nation states they governed.

In the Six-Day War, Golda Meir, the political sworn virgin prime minister came to perform the role of national savior/protector. At her funeral she was praised by being called "the greatest of men." In the Falklands conflict, the threatened military patriarchy of Argentina flexed its muscles to scare off some coming challenges to the dictatorship by seizing the islands. Another sworn political virgin, Margaret Thatcher, played the role protector/warrior in "the national interest" of the United Kingdom. Indira Gandhi imposed a tight grip on the Indian economy and forcefully put down Communist insurgents. All these undertakings purported to be acts of the greatest "patriotism."

The very word *patriotism* says volumes about the patriarchal nature of the nation state that is evident yet seemingly invisible even in the electoral politics of democratic states. The 2008 presidential primaries and campaigns showed this failure to truly perceive patriarchy in the discourse around race and gender issues. I believe that the two issues were much misinterpreted by both political parties. Racism and sexism were seen as separate forms of discrimination and oppression, rather than as particular but interrelated manifestations of an overall system of discrimination, a system that originates in the acceptance of the idea that people are of unequal value, that some people can be claimed as property. That idea is the root of sexism. It is the root of racism. And that is the essence of patriarchy as it is taken into consideration in the pedagogy of engagement, encouraging learners to reflect on such interrelationships and to take a system view of the problems manifest in this intersection of issues. Such reflections are sorely missing from electoral politics and all contemporary political discourse.

The media commented on Hillary Clinton's campaign tactics in terms of her proving her *bona fides* to be commander in chief. She had to prove she could be a warrior-protector. Barack Obama had to assure that he was not a civil order-threatening black activist. (This issue would have been raised even if the Reverend Wright controversy hadn't erupted.) Throughout their last-ditch competition for the nomination, both Clinton and Obama strove to convince the public that while they would fix the nation's problems, they would not challenge the fixed order. "If I am elected, the fundamental patriarchal structures will stay in place," they seemed to assure voters. The candidates, like the electorate, assumed the structures as a given, the only way to manage the society, the "natural" order of things.

Transformational inquiry into a challenge to the "only way" is what peace education as the pedagogy of engagement should be about. Raising core questions for an inquiry into the nature and function of patriarchy should be central to the learning required to cultivate the capacities to transform the present paradigm, leading us to ways of thinking that can produce an authentically democratic order based on the equal human worth of all. Such an inquiry would reveal what Arundhati Roy so vividly describes in her novel, but which most of us don't yet see as our present reality. It could enable us to plan and to realize the change in that reality to which Courtney Martin calls us in her blog entry defining her concept of feminism.

The beginning of such an inquiry informed a project initiated by the People's Movement for Human Rights Education (www.pdhre.org) with a series of questions designed to identify and explore the functions of patriarchy in our everyday lives. These questions demonstrate how the pedagogy of critical engagement might illuminate contemporary patriarchy so that we might both *apprehend* and *comprehend* it, i.e. *to see* it as a fundamental political reality that deeply affects both our private and our public lives; and *to understand* how it operates and why it is so entrenched, even in times when global human rights movements have become so assertive and effective. I would argue that these most precious and essential advances in human rights while at the center of what is needed to advance toward a culture of peace, have lulled us into ignoring the deeper structural and psychosocial roots of even the most visible social wrongs.

Digging into these roots should be facilitated by the pedagogy of critical engagement; a guided learning process that more fully illuminates the patriarchal reality, inspiring us to envision and strive toward a preferred peaceful and just alternative to the violence and the injustice of the global gender order. This critical inquiry would pose queries to inspire visions and images of alternatives. What would a gender-equal society be like? How might we describe such a society that includes not only equality between men and women, but among all the human groups who suffer discrimination and oppression? How might we achieve that preferred society? What are the mechanisms by which to realize all human rights so that they may actually become universal? How might we establish a demilitarized security system? How might we prepare ourselves to live in the institutions of a transformed nonviolent global gender order? Responding to such queries entails an extensive diagnosis of the obstacles to the universal realization of human rights, including assessing the symptoms, and a thorough excavation of the deeper roots so that the alternatives proposed might produce truly transformative change.

So, too, there is need to strategize for transition to a transformed reality, to make specific action plans for moving toward the goal. How do we move from here to there? What are the necessary and particular politics we will need to pursue to get the future we want? We don't see such transforming politics emerging, in spite of what politicians in power and candidates aspiring to public power may promise. We don't hear from them what I believe to be an essential statement of political purpose. They do not articulate a believable vision of a fair society that should inform all movement toward political and social change, toward a culture of peace. There is no politician offering us a strategy, not only to gain world-wide respect for human rights but to actually *live* by the principles of universal human dignity and equality on which all rights are based, to realize them in our daily lives so that they become the norm, the expected way of life that is the purpose of all the international human rights standards? While such a transition inquiry is not "political" within the current framework of standard patriarchal state politics, it is fundamentally political in its avowed purposes to learn our way into a process to transform that framework.

I find great hope and potential for change in the fact that the transformative process and the subject of the pedagogy of engagement often center on human rights as the basis of conceptualizing alternatives to patriarchy, providing a normative foundation for a culture of peace. Human rights learning is, in fact, a dynamic form of the pedagogy of critical engagement. Many—certainly most peace educators and growing numbers of human rights educators—are coming to recognize that the requisite political process is dialogic, as is the pedagogy that prepares us for the politics. It requires us to interact with each other, to exchange ideas, concerns, fears and positive visions. Most of all it requires us to listen, respectively, reflectively and deeply with the genuine respect for the other that informs authentic dialogue. It is a mode of interaction in sharp contrast to the didactic and authority based instruction that has educated for centuries to think within the patriarchal paradigm as it is revealed in the quote from Roy that opened this presentation.

Authentic dialogue is the medium of learning facilitated by the pedagogy of engagement. Learners and citizens engage with each other, and together they engage with the substance of the problems. I tend to think of the dialogic process of the pedagogy of critical engagement as being like sculpting clay. The clay is the substance that is the problem or issue to be transformed. We work with that substance intellectually, while not actually manually, in truly "hands-on" mode, with ideas as our fingers and sculpting tools, the challenges of the problem as the quality of the clay. We plunge our ideas into the substance, shaping it into a representation of the vision of transformation with which we approach the problem in hand. We engage with each other, asking: Do you see the alternative to the problem I am conceptualizing through our inquiry? What do you see as the possibilities? Which of them do you think most possible? How should we shape and mold our shared ideas? How might we exhibit this image of the transformed problem in wider dialogue with the larger society? How might we make our discussions the subject of a generalized public discourse that can achieve political results? In what ways can we mobilize for change? Without such dialogues among and between those at all levels of the patriarchal pyramid of power, it may not be possible to transform the prevailing paradigm into a paradigm of a culture of peace.

In sum, the achievement of a culture of peace requires confronting and transcending patriarchy; it requires social learning pursued through the pedagogy of critical engagement rooted in the values, visions and the concepts, principles and standards of human rights as indicators of progress toward human equality and social justice as the foundation of a robust peace. Achieving universal equality and durable social justice requires establishing a non-violent, disarmed and demilitarized, gender equal political order, secured by the renunciation of war, weaponry and all forms of coercive violence and gender oppression. These are the essential elements of a transformed world order of mutually enhancing human relationships at all levels of human society, from interpersonal to global. It involves liberating a world now trapped in the structures of patriarchy and patriarchal thinking and setting it on the learning path that will lead us to a culture of peace.

~ June 30, 2008
SGI-USA New York Culture of Peace Resource Center

Moving Beyond Tolerance in Race and Human Relations

Lessons From and For a Global Los Angeles

Robin S. Toma

Executive Director, Human Relations Commission, Los Angeles County

Robin Toma was appointed by the Los Angeles County Board of Supervisors in 2000 after working five years with the commission. He was invited to be a member of the U.S. delegation to the 2001 UN World Conference Against Racism, held in South Africa; the Japanese American Leadership Delegation to Japan in 2003; and the Climate of Trust Delegation to Russia in 2005. He is co-author of the manual *Day Laborer Hiring Sites: Constructive Approaches to Community Conflict,* and author of *A Primer on Managing Intergroup Conflict in a Multicultural Workplace.*

Toma was lead attorney in seeking redress for more than 2,200 Japanese Latin Americans who were forcibly brought to the United States and imprisoned by the U.S. government during World War II. He is also part of an ongoing gathering of leaders known as the Executive Session on Criminal Justice and Human Rights, organized by Harvard University's Kennedy School of Government. Previously, he served as staff attorney with the American Civil Liberties Union of Southern California for nearly seven years, promoting human rights and building multiethnic coalitions to bring about institutional change.

Mr. Toma addresses many of the eight action areas in the 1999 United Nations Declaration and Programme of Action on a Culture of Peace, most notably the sixth, advancing understanding, tolerance and solidarity. As he says: "Democracy is very messy. But it is critical to understand that this is a time of relationships. If you can build a relationship with somebody, you're going to get much more value in the long term than if you pursue a short-term gain and exclude a person who doesn't offer anything today but really should be part of the equation. You will run the risk of later not having that relationship to call upon later if necessary."

I am a product of this community. I'm sansei, a third-generation Japanese American, born and raised in the Echo Park and Silver Lake neighborhoods of northeast Los Angeles.

I am the son of U.S.-born parents. My mother is of Japanese ancestry, my father is of Okinawan ancestry, and I feel Okinawan. Both sets of grandparents migrated to the United States in the early 1900s – my father's family to Hawaii, and my mother's to Washington state.

Growing up, I learned about my mother's experience in World War II internment camps. I always wondered why my father never talked about such things. After all, he was raised in Maui, much closer to Pearl Harbor, and one would think that fact especially would cause him to be considered a potential threat to U.S. security. But because the Japanese in Hawaii were the majority, they didn't exist under a cloud of prejudice and therefore were not put into internment camps.

My mother's life, on the other hand, was completely disrupted. She was living in Washington, thousands of miles from Pearl Harbor, working with her family farming strawberries. Yet, they were the ones pushed into the internment process. They found themselves first detained at a local racetrack, where they lived in horse stables, and were eventually moved to Tule Lake in Northern California, and then to Minidoka, Idaho.

So, early on, the idea of national security became very unclear to me.

Because of how the world works, my parents' paths eventually crossed when they both ended up in Salt Lake City. While my mother is from a very strong Buddhist background, and my father is from a very strong Christian background, their time in Salt Lake City resulted in us having Mormons in our family as well.

Within my family, then, there is diversity. That is also something I experienced attending public schools here in the Los Angeles area, and then in college at UC Santa Cruz and at UCLA. An acceptance of diversity, for me, has just been a fact of life.

This is why I ended up in the field of human relations. I lived in Spain for a couple years, and I think of myself as a global citizen. I know ours is a small world and is becoming increasingly so every day.

My understanding of how we all affect one another is continually growing. What we do here locally has a profound impact on what happens to
people in other parts of the world. Our demand for hamburger, for example, contributes to rainforest destruction in Brazil. What happens in the
Middle East has reverberations in terms of hate, discrimination and conflict here in Los Angeles.

This idea of global connection struck me deeply when I was living in
Spain. I'm fluent in Spanish, and I also speak Catalan. My life was good
there, and I thought, *Maybe I should just live here permanently.*

But then I returned to the United States. On that trip back, I had an
extended layover in New York City, so I took a train into the city and visited Central Park.

I looked around and had this feeling of being at home because of
the diversity. All races seemed to be there. I realized, then, that I hadn't
experienced that during the time I'd been in Spain. In fact, I had struggled with being stared at constantly, like a strange alien in the land of
Spaniards who did not know what to make of me because I spoke Catalan, which is unusual for that part of the country. To hear Catalan coming from an Asian face was just inconceivable; once the people there saw
me, they would switch to Castilian Spanish. And they would stare at me
on the subway. I got used to it, but I realized I really am more at home in
a diverse world.

Part of the work that I do is to try to figure things out in order to help
the rest of the world. The tremendous diversity we have experienced
here for generations is now becoming a reality for Europe and the world.
Accordingly, I want to focus on the United Nations Programme of Action
on a Culture of Peace, because advancing understanding, tolerance and
solidarity is critical to create a culture of peace.

We have never needed that more than now. Today, in so many places,
we have a collision and confluence and connections among people of
different backgrounds, of different ethnic and religious faiths, of different
heritages, of different spoken languages and of different perspectives on
how the world works.

I've framed my talk as "beyond tolerance," because tolerance is a very
low target. We want more than that. We want to create a world where
people are accepted for who they are, where they feel that they belong,
that this is their world as much as anyone else's, and that they have a say

in what happens to them and to their families and to their communities.

One thing we are constantly working at is how to build solidarity among communities so that we're not just worried about what happens to our own community, our given ethnic group or however we define our group, but that we also care about what happens to people in other places.

This is not always easy to achieve. People have a lot to deal with in our world, and it's very easy to say, "Let others worry about their stuff, and I'll deal with mine." But the survival of our society, its ability to thrive, depends on us appreciating and supporting others so that they understand that we all care about one another. They, in turn, can reciprocate.

If you feel as though no one else cares about you, it's very hard to care about other people. But our world right now demands that we have people willing to make the change and to say, "Just because our community wasn't victimized doesn't mean we're not going to stand up with you and denounce that mistreatment, too."

Today, I want to tell you a little bit about Los Angeles County.

The county has eighty-eight cities and Los Angeles is just one of them. It's the biggest by far, but there's also Long Beach, Glendale, Pasadena, Santa Monica and so on. It's a big, big county.

In fact, it is the most populous county in the United States, with nearly ten million residents. Only eight entire states (including California) have more people than Los Angeles County, which contains almost a third of California's population.

We have forty-seven police agencies. We have eighty-six school districts. And for all of that, we have five elected officials who oversee county government.

These are my bosses, the L.A. County Board of Supervisors. That government body is in charge of an annual budget of $22 billion—24 percent of which comes from the state government, 21 percent from the federal government and 21 percent from property taxes.

Our budget, unfortunately, is not large enough, because the county's responsibility is to provide a safety net of basic services, such as health services. When people don't have health insurance, they go to a county hospital.

In terms of public health, who's going to ensure that the latest West Nile virus threat is contained, that we can provide education and have teams ready to move? It's L.A. County's Public Heath Department.

Who makes sure that the amount of gas the pump says you're pump-
ing and paying so wildly for is accurate? It's the L.A. County Agricultural
Weights and Measures Department.

Public protection—the L.A. County Sheriff's Department is the largest
in the country. It runs a vast jail system, the largest in the world, sadly to
say, which also has one of the largest mental health facilities in the state.
There's also the whole court system—jury duty, probation, juvenile hall,
all of that is the county.

For the very poor, those who are completely out of luck, who don't
have a job, or any means of income, it's the county that administers programs such as General Relief and Food Stamps.

And, of course, there are elections, which are run by the County Reg-
istrar Recorder.

Admittedly, I learned all this after I started working for L.A. County
government. You probably wouldn't know these things. In fact, it's likely
most of you don't even know who your supervisor is. I was the same way.
Yet, the county has a lot of responsibility.

I'm but one small part of a very large county government. With twenty-
seven staff members, we're considered a micro department. Almost no
county department is as small as ours. But we have a tremendous challenge because we're charged with supporting this exceptionally diverse
county in order to promote the understanding and sensitivity we need to
maintain harmony, to have healthy inter-group interaction, to reduce hate
crime and so forth.

First, as you probably all know, L.A. County is likely the most diverse
place in the world in terms of the number of international communities
here; and these are the largest communities of their respective nationali-
ties. The number of languages spoken, of religions and faiths practiced is
astonishing.

I speak Spanish and not Japanese because I grew up in a neighborhood
that had many Spanish speakers, and that was back in the 1960s and '70s.
Latinos made up 10 percent of the population in 1969. Today, they're 44
percent, and we're in a changing environment.

Also, the Asian population grew tremendously. Until the mid-1960s
when immigration laws changed, my grandfather, despite having been
here since the beginning of the century, could not become a citizen. Now,
people from Africa, Asia and Latin America can become citizens, so there

was a big shift in immigration demographics. For a period, this was a major characteristic of our lives. We have seen a tremendous amount of change in communities, and that has been quite a challenge for our agency to make things work.

When we talk about all these differences—race, ethnicity, national origin, religion, language, sexual orientation, gender identity, disability, immigration status—it's important to recognize that we do not have a level playing field. There are dominant groups and less-dominant groups, the minority groups. And the composition changes depending on what level you're talking about. For the United States as a whole, it's one thing. If you're talking about the city of Los Angeles, it's another. This matters in terms of how institutions react, how institutions perpetuate themselves, how communities are affected.

I marvel at the fact that, talking about change, we're in a moment of history that could result in the first African American to be elected president of this country. As I was saying to a group of young people earlier, I would never have imagined this growing up. (*Editor's note: Barack Obama was elected in November 2008 as the forty-fourth U.S. president, the first African American to hold the office.*)

And there are elements of change we often don't recognize. For example, as the number of interethnic marriages continues to grow, so does the number of multiethnic people. Census data reveal that the percentage of people who mark the multiracial/multiethnic box is increasing. Just from looking at our young people, we can see the large increase of those who have multiple-ethnic heritages. We're going to become harder and harder to pigeonhole.

We're not fitting into those neat boxes anymore, and that's a good thing, because it helps us appreciate what we should always have appreciated: that people are, within themselves, incredibly diverse; that we are not easily categorized; that we defy stereotypes.

At the same time, I'm reminded that there is a clear dominance of certain groups. I'm married to someone who was born in Korea, raised in Brazil, and who then grew up here in California. She speaks four languages: Korean, Portuguese, Spanish and English. I speak English and Spanish.

Our children speak Korean, but that's because my wife's parents mainly speak it, and they spend a lot of time helping us raise them. But we've noticed that our children don't really like speaking in Korean.

I've heard similar stories from other people. As children grow and real-ize where the dominant power is, who the people in control are and what language those people speak, they want to be a part of that. They watch television, it's in English. To my children, Korean is a secondary, subordi-nate language. It's not the language of the ones in charge.

Something similar, I believe, was experienced in the social experi-ments that impacted the famous Brown vs. Board of Education case. When young African American girls were asked to choose the "more beau-tiful" between dolls that were identical except for one being light-skinned and the other being dark-skinned, overwhelmingly, the light-skinned doll was chosen. What does that tell us about self-image and sense of self-worth for minority cultures amid the dominant culture? Such subtle but omni-present and pervasive messages regarding self-identity have been around for a long time.

> *We want to create a world where people are accepted for who they are, where they feel that they belong, that this is their world as much as anyone else's, and that they have a say in what happens to them and to their families and to their communities.*

Incidentally, growing up, I never saw a doll that looked like me. Later, though, I found out that there was actually a G.I. Joe doll in the image of a Japanese-American soldier from the famous 442nd battalion that fought in World War II. But I could only find the doll online.

Events like the Olympics are great, as they provide the chance to see capable people of different backgrounds winning gold medals and com-peting on a more-or-less level playing field.

The first lesson I want to share is that we have the ability to be so much more than we are. One way we can become so is by learning more languages. We live in a world that, unfortunately, has mainly been English-only. There's a joke I used to hear all the time in Europe: What do you call a person who speaks three languages? *Trilingual.* What do you call a person who speaks two languages? *Bilingual.* What do you call a person who speaks only one language? *American.*

Almost everyone in Europe speaks more than one language – usually, it's English in addition to one's native tongue, but there are examples such as Belgium, where they learn Flemish and Dutch along with their native French. In Japan, too, children learn other languages. And it's easy for young kids to do it. My children pick up Korean so much more easily than I ever could. It's effortless for them.

In the United States, however, we generally offer language study in the eighth grade and essentially give children only a few choices. Why are we not taking advantage of the fact that we live in such global communities? Why are we not enabling our children to learn more languages? It can only help them, because we know we're not the only ones here on this planet. Even though English is a dominant language, it isn't the only thing spoken. It is a gateway, certainly, but all languages are gateways to other worlds.

I was blessed to learn Spanish, and I have loved traveling through Latin America. When I travel, I don't just visit buildings and museums; I talk to people. I try to understand their lives and their world perspective. It's a much more fruitful experience than if you're simply sightseeing.

We're losing out on a wonderful opportunity, which, I think, is a critical issue. Here in Los Angeles, when we work with communities, people will tell us things like: "I'm having trouble with my neighbors because they've got a rooster that wakes me up every morning. And I don't know how to talk to them because they don't speak English."

So, part of what's going to bridge cultural gaps is language. Language can be a barrier or provide a great advantage. This is one issue I see as critical to the success of our society, and it's one area in which we're behind other communities. But we certainly can catch up.

I think it is sad that there are children who can't even speak to their grandparents in a common language. In my own case, my grandparents who were still alive when I was growing up spoke very little English, and I spoke very little Japanese. Maybe it was because of my mother's family's internment experience, but my parents did not feel it was important to teach me Japanese.

Regarding their children, perhaps my parents were thinking, *We want our children to succeed in the United States. Why would we want to emphasize our differences?*

But what we are talking about is "English plus," an added value, because no one loses English fluency by learning another language.

Another lesson I think we should all take home is that race is clearly a social invention, a social construction. Race is categorized by whatever a country decides it is.

Visiting South Africa some time ago, I was told that there were seventeen different racial categories there based on how people looked. In fact, some brothers and sisters had to live in different communities, because if you were light-skinned, you were considered "colored" and had to live in one place, and if you were dark-skinned, you were "black" and had to live in the township—you couldn't both live in the same place.

Although arbitrary, that's how categories were defined under the apartheid regime. Using such divide-and-conquer tactics was a great way for that regime to remain in power for many years.

Now, does that mean we can just make such classifications disappear or ignore them as if they never existed? The truth is that we have lived so long with race, with ethnicity, with various differences being the focal point of how we organize ourselves, that we have to acknowledge their impact, that the experiences of communities based on such distinctions are very real. To dismiss or ignore that reality, I think, would be very foolish.

What we see with children growing up in various school communities is that they are generally going to go where they feel most comfortable. On any campus today, what do you see? Mostly segregation at lunchtime. This is not because students don't all speak English; it's simply because they feel more comfortable in their own group.

That's how human beings are. If we move to a new country, we usually gravitate to communities where there are people like us so that we can communicate with others who understand something about where we came from. It's very natural.

The error we make is when we don't create a space where everyone can come together, where it's safe to step out of your group and connect with other groups.

There's that whole thing about the "melting pot," where you put things in a pot and they all become the same. I certainly don't experience that when I get a kosher burrito or Muslim Chinese food or fusion food. We have a diversity of heritages, of cultures, and, thankfully, we're not all the same.

Other people say: "We're really talking about a salad. We've got the lettuce. We've got the tomatoes. We've got the onions. We're all separate but thrown into the same bowl." That's not right, either, because we're more than that.

It's more like a stew, that's my theory. You've got your carrots, your potatoes, your onions. They all retain their own flavor, but they also add to the flavor of the gravy, which, in turn, affects what the carrots and the potatoes taste like.

The potato in a stew is much tastier because it picks up the flavor of the rest of the food. That idea, I feel, represents a vision for our society— that we should all cherish, respect and honor our own histories and our own cultures, but we should also recognize that we're part of something new. This is a good thing, because studies show that with diversity you come out stronger, with a much greater variety of ideas and approaches. It's a real danger when a society becomes so insular that people believe that theirs is the only correct way.

Another lesson is that in order to effectively advance understanding, tolerance, acceptance and solidarity, you have to foster a culture of peace through education. By *education*, I'm specifically referring to schools.

Schools are critical places where we must incorporate the teaching of fundamental skills our citizens will need in the twenty-first century. Unfortunately, the schools fall far short of that. In fact, when we go to campuses that are exploding in racial or other kinds of violence, there are scarcely even opportunities to talk about what's going on.

People then align according to race because they don't have anywhere to discuss issues that lead to violent incidents. Schools should be where we can teach critical skills of character education, of social and emotional intelligence, which we know are even more important than IQ in terms of one being successful in the world. But we have campuses in neighborhoods that are just terribly neglected, where students have to worry every day whether they can get to school and back home without being injured because gangs in the neighborhood might prey on them. Those communities also suffer from joblessness and a lack of places to go after school.

If you don't have sustainable economic and social development, what you have is a community where people are miserable, and they're looking for scapegoats to blame.

In order to for us to have a harmonious society, it is critical that we take away those factors driving the divisions among many communities.

So, out of the $22 billion, 20 percent goes to health services, 27 percent for public protection, and 25 percent for social services. We have been on a track for many years where, not just L.A. County government, but our state government and our nation have been spending a vast amount of money on incarceration. California has built way more prisons than they have universities.

We have been on this track because we have expected law enforcement to solve the problem in communities where the only organized youth activity is the gang. The police come in, they arrest everyone they can get their hands on, send them to the jails and prisons, and guess what happens? Within months you've got new recruits coming in. The reason gangs are successful in perpetuating themselves was not addressed – that there are limited alternatives for young people in those communities.

Investment in social services and in young people has been far too inadequate, and therefore the strategy we've had for dealing with gangs over the past twenty to thirty years has been a complete failure. It's not just me saying this. This is what former Los Angeles Police Chief William Bratton and Los Angeles County Sheriff Lee Baca have also been saying. We cannot arrest ourselves out of this situation; we have to invest in youth, in gang prevention and intervention.

The police will tell you that 90 percent of the gang members are not the ones responsible for gang crime. It's only 10 percent. The other 90 percent are in the gangs for a variety of reasons: protection, self-preservation, they merely like to hang out with the guys "with the juice." But unless we provide motivation to peel those guys away and give them opportunities, then we'll continually have gangs in our communities. It's sad that, in all this time, we have not meaningfully eliminated gang violence in any neighborhood. And we're not going to until we invest in youth programs, after-school programs, etc.

I raise the question, because we know even in personal relationships there is conflict. If even among people from the same background there are conflicts and personality differences, imagine when you add culture and language to that mix—there is a real potential for conflict, and we experience it. That's part of our challenge as an agency and a challenge for the community as well.

At the same time, as I mentioned, what a sad world it would be if we were all the same. How, then, do we harness the power of diversity while minimizing prejudice and discrimination, fear and hatred? The way I see our world is that there is a tremendous opportunity to bring that diversity to bear on our society and make it what we want it to be. So, if we don't want to live in a homogeneous world, how do we make diversity work?

At one time, before severe government cuts occurred in the '70s and '80s, we had more than seventy staff members. Actually, our agency originated way back in the 1940s as a result of the Zoot Suit Riots. If you ever see the play or film *Zoot Suit*, while it's not exactly the same as having been there, you will get a sense that many years ago there was a lot of violence in the streets of Los Angeles. Out of all that was created the Committee for Interracial Progress, later renamed the Los Angeles County Commission on Human Relations.

As to the vision of the commission—we want to inform multicultural and diverse communities; to connect people through interaction, compassion and understanding. We are committed to justice, equity, opportunity, accountability, respect and dignity for all.

I was asked earlier when I met with the youth, "How can you address such big problems with twenty-seven people?" Clearly, we have to prioritize, and what we focus on is public safety. We want to enhance public safety through the prevention of, and in our planned responses to, hate crimes and discrimination.

One of our programs is called the Racialized Gang Violence Prevention Initiative. A lot of gang-involved conflict starts off not as racial but then takes on racial overtones, which has quite an impact on the larger community. A core part of the solution, then, is derived from looking closely at the cause: What are the sparks? What are the triggers for violence in many communities?

Gangs are a big part of it. How do we deal with the issue of gangs? As

I said, law enforcement suppression is critical, but if that's not supported by other things you can forget about its efficacy.

Our key initiative has been in that area. We've had tremendous success in communities where we've merely spent a year, simply bringing different groups together to focus on change. Unfortunately, we don't get enough chances to do that because we don't have the resources. But that's what communities need, to go from "let's arrest everyone" to "let's bring together all the programs we need in order to address the root causes of gang violence.

In reference to what I said about how critical schools are, we have our schools initiative. We selected five high schools around Los Angeles County at which we are creating human-relations school models that can be replicated by entire school districts. These models demonstrate that when you address issues through student leadership development, teacher training, parental involvement and community collaboration, your campus doesn't have to fear racial riots. You'll actually see a variety of improvements: reduction in disciplinary actions, reduction in calls to the police, reduction in on-campus bias-related harassment incidents.

We have worked hard on this for the past two years. We're entering our third year, and we think this critical program can affect the key institution of public schools.

We are responsible for producing an annual report that highlights the level of hate crime in our communities, which always gets big news. Of course, our efforts to show different ethnic groups working together in various school communities rarely gets the kind of coverage our hate-crime report does.

We also have a Hate Crime Victim Assistance & Advocacy Initiative, through which we fund seven community-based organizations in communities hit hardest by hate crime. Those organizations reach out directly to their communities, and they support one another so that when one community is victimized, partners from other communities stand together with them.

Crisis response is another responsibility. We're known for our major urban riots—Zoot Suit, Watts, the civil unrest after the Rodney King trial in 1992. Sadly, even people from abroad know about us for that last one. Again, we have to identify those causes and make sure we don't allow one thing to lead to another and another and have an explosion of violence as occurred in 1992 and 1965.

Also, there's capacity building, which requires culture change, building a culture of peace. It's going to take a long-term process to bring about the long-lasting change our world needs. It entails working with institutions, not just schools but city governments and police departments. We do a lot of police training, working to bring police together with civil rights groups. All of that is critical to our work and, I think, a critical lesson for the world.

People often react to big crises by saying: "OK, let's take a break. Let's have an assembly. Let's all talk about this. Lots of talking." But in the end, unless changes occur in everyday practices in those institutions, then only very incremental changes will occur, such minimal changes that it can be gone in a few years. That's particularly true with schools but certainly with workplaces as well.

It's easy for us in our world to believe that material gain is of the utmost importance. In relationships, for example, we are often trying to figure out, "What can we get out of this?" Sometimes we are so short-term-goal oriented that we just say, "Maybe if I can make a deal with this person, then, when we're both finished with our jobs, we'll be able to benefit ourselves more effectively.

It's always more complicated when there are more people. Democracy is very messy. But it is critical to understand that this is a time of relationships. If you can build a relationship with somebody, you're going to get much more value in the long term than if you pursue a short-term gain and exclude a person who doesn't offer anything today but really should be part of the equation. You will run the risk of later not having that relationship to call upon later if necessary.

Leaders are being trained to not be so short-term oriented but rather to understand that there is something much larger to be gained. Mutual respect means keying on relationship building, on power sharing as opposed to power control. Instead of turning the tables, you're going to share the table and open it up. The trust and positive relationships you can build will be critical to changing the way we view the world.

People ask, "How can you know how things are in Los Angeles?" The truth is, it's not that easy. If you read the media stories, you mostly get crime. You get conflict. You get the movie *Crash*, in the sense that there is a lot of conflict in a short time period. Not to say that that stuff doesn't happen, but it doesn't happen in all of two or three days.

School data is tough to get, and it is often very poorly reported, so it can't necessarily tell you how things are going. And school data is just about our youth population—it is only one indicator. I wouldn't say it tells a whole story.

I spoke earlier about the rate of interethnic marriage and about persons considered multiracial. Those, too, are concrete indicators but again just pieces of the puzzle.

To be clear, a hate crime has to actually be a crime, not merely a dirty look or an epithet thrown. On top of that, it must be shown that the motivation behind it is based on the victim's sexual orientation, ethnicity, race, gender, religion or disability. It can't be just that the person is wearing a Boston Celtics t-shirt, for example.

We've been compiling yearly hate-crime totals longer than almost any other agency in the United States. In 1980, when we started doing this, the numbers were very low. As you might imagine, it doesn't mean we had very few hate crimes, just that the reporting system was underdeveloped, that many people and agencies did not file reports because they didn't know they should.

In the 1990s, we hit a plateau, and then we had our huge spike in 2001. After September 11, the amount of scapegoating and attacks on people who looked Middle Eastern or Muslim was historic. It caused that huge bump up to 1,031, the highest total we've ever had.

I can report that since 2001 we've dropped. But more recent headlines report that the hate-crime figures we released show that it's up 28 percent, to 763, and it's the highest it's been in the past five years. That's bad news because it's going up in 2007 when general crime went down from 2006; it's contrary to the general crime trend.

We don't know all that's going on with that statistic. We get the numbers reported to us, and we look at the communities involved. We know that violence has increased across the board: racial, ethnic, national-origin-based hate crime, the largest category, experienced a significant increase; sexual-orientation hate crime, a significant increase; religion-based hate crime, a significant increase. All those categories. I'm not sure what's driving it, but it's coming from various parts of the county.

Why do we care about hate crime? Because it's extreme behavior. For a county our size, 763 hate crimes is really a small number. On the other hand, we know that it's part of a larger pyramid of hate. People commit hate crimes when they feel like there is an atmosphere in which it could be tolerated or supported. Somebody gives you the idea that it's OK to shout these epithets, to attack or target someone over characteristics.

Those prejudiced attitudes sit at the bottom of it. Moving up the pyramid, we find acts of prejudice that are non-criminal. Then there's discrimination, which can be non-criminal as well. But then you get into violence, and then at the top is genocide. If you allow violence to become the way of dealing with group differences, it can lead to the extreme.

Hate crimes from 2003 to 2007 were pretty much scattered throughout the county. While no community is immune from hate crime, we see clusters develop in different parts of the county that sometimes correspond to targeted populations. For example, we see a lot of sexual-orientation-based hate crime in West Hollywood and Hollywood where there's a strongly established gay community. People will go there specifically to carry out attacks.

In the San Fernando Valley, South Los Angeles, the San Gabriel Valley and the Santa Clarita Valley there are a great variety of types of hate crimes, a targeting of all sorts of groups.

Throughout the county and state, the vast majority of hate crimes, 68 percent, are based on race, ethnicity or national origin.

The next slice of the pie is sexual-orientation-based hate crime, which is about 17–18 percent. And the largest slice after that is religion-based hate crime, which is 15 percent. Then there are disability- and gender-based hate crimes, both very lightly reported. Partly, I think, it is because law enforcement has never come up with a workable definition of gender-based hate crime; there's a great divide when it comes to what is characterized as being gender based. The same goes for hate crimes based on disability. The lack of clarity on those two issues presents ongoing challenges.

For targeted groups in 2006 and 2007, by far the largest segment is anti-African American hate crime. That makes up 39 percent of the targeted hate crime in L.A. County, and yet African Americans are 9 percent of the general county population.

Gay and lesbians are next—102 hate crimes—about 15 percent of the total.

Anti-Jewish hate crime makes up the largest amount of religion-based hate crime, consistently about 80 percent.

Anti-Mexican and anti-Latino come next. If you put those together, they become the second largest group.

Anti-White hate crime follows. Anti-Asian/Pacific Islander, anti-Armenian, anti-Christian, anti-Transgendered, anti-Middle Eastern, anti-Chinese, anti-Catholic … and the numbers get smaller and smaller.

It's highly diverse in that practically every group is targeted for hate crime in our county each year.

But the rates of violence differ. For 2007, the highest rate of violence was against Latinos—anti-Latino hate crime was 85 percent violent. Anti-White was 81 percent violent; anti-African American, 70 percent; anti-Middle Eastern, 60 percent; anti-Armenian, 47 percent; and anti-Asian, 43 percent.

All this data, by the way, is in our hate crime report on our website, which you can download for free.

This is just to highlight the year-to-year trends in terms of gangs. You can see the bottom red line is the number of gang-involved hate crimes. And the one at the top is the total number of hate crimes.

Although the numbers fluctuate year to year, there's been a climb in the past few years in gang-involved hate crime, which is very troubling. And this is anti-immigrant hate crime—crimes that involve anti-immigrant remarks, as well as those targeting people of certain national origins. The purple line on bottom represents anti-Latino hate crime. The total number of racial and ethnic hate crimes is at the top, and the total number of hate crimes involving national origin is in the middle in yellow.

I was surprised that our reports didn't show higher totals after the contentious debates in 2006. But, we know that there's severe underreporting in immigrant communities because people feel insecure about their status. Also, there was a huge, historic demonstration bringing a million people to the streets of Los Angeles over immigration rights. So, in some cases, because of strengthened, organized communities some would-be hate-crime perpetrators were discouraged from seeing the citizens as such easy prey.

I think this data also illustrates that the tenor of our debate—how well we handle it—will be a critical factor in whether there is resultant hate crime.

For instance, the same-sex marriage issue that's coming up is something that can create a spike in sexual-orientation-based hate crime. It depends on how the debate is carried out in both the media and by people on the street day to day. If the issue becomes an opportunity to spew anger and animosity toward gays and lesbians, it can very well trigger increased violence. On the other hand, if we conduct respectful and civil conversation, it doesn't have to bring about violence. This is something upon which we ourselves can have an impact.

Also, Department of Education statistics show that students who are gay or perceived to be gay were five times more likely to report being threatened or injured with a weapon. In terms of people most targeted and most at risk, then, gay, lesbian and transgendered students are tremendously vulnerable to hatred and prejudice.

Public-opinion surveys will tell you that, surprise, a majority of L.A. County residents believe race relations are poor. I do think that's affected by what we see in everyday news coverage, but it doesn't necessarily reflect our daily interactions.

But 53 percent believe racial profiling is widespread in their area of the county. That means government agencies, police department, etc. 54 percent believe race relations will improve in five years. And that's a positive sign. People, as a result of their personal experiences, still seem to have a great deal of hope.

There was a very interesting study done by Harvard University's Robert D. Putnam, one of the most comprehensive national studies examining the way communities develop what he calls "social capital." We can think of social capital as trust in our relationships. What Putnam found was in some cases not so surprising, and in other cases, very surprising—that increased immigration and diversity reduces trust, social solidarity and social capital; that people have a tendency to hunker down within diverse neighborhoods; and that even trust within your own group declines for those who live in diverse neighborhoods.

He also makes a very clear point, that immigrants comprise a disproportionate share of America's Nobel Prize winners and distinguished scholars and artists. He points out that economic productivity is often higher, and crime rates lower, in places with a greater number of immigrants. Ethnic diversity is increasing and inevitable, and in the long run it is a valuable asset for advanced countries.

Putnam concludes that becoming comfortable with diversity is not accomplished easily or quickly, but it will be speeded by a collective effort, and in the end it will be well worth that effort. One great achievement of human civilization is our ability to redraw more inclusive lines of social identity. That's what we are trying to do every day, redraw the lines so that people who are on the outs, who feel excluded, who feel disenfranchised can feel like they matter, that they're part of our communities, that they actually have a say in what goes on.

A somewhat recent multilingual poll, the first of its kind found that nearly every minority group tends to strongly believe negative stereotypes about other groups. To me this was a very clear sign that we have a lot of work to do in providing education and in battling discrimination within our own communities. At the same time, we can also see that a majority within each group wants to work together to better their communities. They believe that people have a lot in common, that change is possible, and they want that change to happen.

How many people here have heard of *implicit bias*, the idea that we're all prejudiced or guilty of promoting stereotypes, etc.? Even so, people frequently say: "I'm not racist. I'm not sexist. I'm not a bigot." Because we human beings are very good at filtering our actions and responses to match what society thinks are the right things to say and do.

Deriving from the latest research coming out of Harvard, there is a project in which people's reactions are measured without giving them time to think. The subjects aren't able to say: "Ooh, I shouldn't say that because it might sound racist"; or, "That doesn't sound right if I say, 'Those people ...'" In this test, pictures are flashed, and they create associations in the brain. The subjects then hit keys to respond as they associate faces and characteristics. Results from the test have shown that, unfortunately, there is a tremendous amount of unconscious bias. Because if you were to ask the same subjects their feelings directly, they'd likely say, "Oh, no, I don't think that members of this or that ethnic group are sneaky and can't be trusted."

But if that's the image you have been fed most of your life and you have not been exposed to relationships that would counter that perception, then this test will likely show that that's what you think because in a quick response that's where you go.

Broadly speaking, this means that when there is a high level of stress, fear, anger and emotion—perhaps during a time of war—you're going to be distrusting those people toward whom you maintain implicit bias. We are finding this to be a major challenge. Surely, most of you would be willing to go through a process to help eliminate prejudice deep in your souls. But the truth is that such prejudice can only change through everyday exposure to other people, through counterbalancing what we see in the media with real interactions with others.

A lesson for Los Angeles is that we have to expect this change to come from within. We also have to work on making it happen around us. We have to recognize that we're facing a very difficult period. The economy is getting worse. And that means tensions are going to rise, unemployment is going to rise, more conflict is potentially upon us, all at this time when we have less resources, less tools like language instruction to help bridge communities.

I want to be clear, there are a lot of reasons for hope. And you being here today is obviously one of them. You care about this issue. There are many other people in this community, in this society working on it, too. The upcoming presidential election is creating a discussion we can't avoid, and I think there's going to be greater leadership coming from Washington.

I believe that will be good because, compared to other nations, we are far behind in terms of having national leadership on this issue. Canada has a Ministry of Multiculturalism. Great Britain has a Commission on Human Rights that systematically addresses these issues. Mexico City has a Human Rights Commission that is 200 times larger than ours. Other nations, too, make this issue part of the daily work.

We've kind of ducked this issue. We've tried to avoid focusing on intergroup relations. But the truth is, change of culture requires everyday attention. We have to make it part of our daily lives, and we all can make a huge difference.

I recently came across the Manifesto 2000 pledge; it is something wonderful, which we can all adopt to help us keep our focus and keep on the path. It reads:

> I pledge — in my daily life, in my family, my work, my community, my country and my region — to:
>
> 1. respect the life and dignity of every person without discrimination or prejudice;
>
> 2. practice active non-violence, rejecting violence in all its forms: physical, sexual, psychological, economical and social, in particular towards the most deprived and vulnerable such as children and adolescents;
>
> 3. share my time and material resources in a spirit of generosity to put an end to exclusion, injustice and political and economic oppression;
>
> 4. defend freedom of expression and cultural diversity, giving preference always to dialogue and listening rather than fanaticism, defamation and the rejection of others;
>
> 5. promote consumer behavior that is responsible and development practices that respect all forms of life and preserve the balance of nature on the planet;
>
> 6. contribute to the development of my community, with the full participation of women and respect for democratic principles, in order to create together new forms of solidarity.

If we all took this pledge to heart, we would have a very different world. It's hard to do, no question about it, but I think that we need to ask, not only of ourselves but of our government and of our private institutions, that we make these ideals part of our mission. It shouldn't be someone else's job; it has to be the work of all of us to change the culture to a culture of peace.

Questions and Answers

AUDIENCE MEMBER 1: We surrender our kids to the education system daily for 12 years, so societal change has to take place in education. But because of the bureaucracy and related factors, the necessary change isn't happening fast enough. As a concerned parent and advocate in the community, I get frustrated sometimes.

TOMA: Bureaucracy certainly presents challenges, and I, of course, work in a very significant county bureaucracy. But when I go to school districts like the Los Angeles Unified, for example, there is a real challenge. You have to have stamina and patience. First, we have to connect with the principal, because a principal is often given a lot of free rein. They're sort of the captains of their ships, their campuses. Often, when we establish relationships with them, they then help us navigate the bureaucracy.

And if they understand what we need to do, then they can help make it happen. For instance, in Pomona we have been successful in establishing one of our model schools by connecting with the principal and having her see what we were doing. As a result, she got promoted because the school was doing well. She then, in turn, spread our example to other schools.

In this circumstance, we created change from the ground up. Other times, we have to hit it from different directions—top-to-bottom, bottom-up. We need to be committed and strategic and focused, and we can help schools do that.

We've talked to the L.A. County Office of Education, had seminars with the various superintendents and asked them: "Do you want to get beyond managing crises? What are you prepared to do so you can actually prevent crises in the first place?"

The superintendents can become absorbed in the challenge of test scores, etc. They become so focused on such matters that you need to help them understand the importance of those larger questions. It's a difficult task, but they tend to get it when they see it in action. At Pomona, they saw test scores improving over those at other high schools with similar demographics, so they realized the Zero Hour program must be working.

AUDIENCE MEMBER 2: I'm sad to see what's become of our great city. But how do we counter it when we have no jobs for adults, let alone for children who can't read or write very well? We do live in a global society, but we're being left out. Jobs are being sent to China, to Mexico, to Taiwan, to India, and we don't even have jobs for the average citizens who know how to read and write. And these kids are making in one night up to $20,000. They're driving around in $100,000 cars.

TOMA: They also risk being shot at, being arrested and being sent to prison.

You're right; we can't compete purely on the economic level. But you combine all those circumstances and, you know, they've all lost homies. Almost everyone in a gang or who has been in a gang has lost friends, so they understand that there's a real risk. They can live high and short or they can have a longer horizon. There are ways to address that.

You're right; joblessness is a huge factor. We've actually tapped into a new county program with the idea that we've got to get jobs into these communities. That's the way you start to peel off the high-risk youth who are attracted to gangs.

It's multifaceted and complicated, but jobs are a central part of it. We have to provide real opportunities to help young people go on to higher education, to have hopeful horizons, to have a chance at creating a family, to have a sustaining job, perhaps even a union job or other means of making a living wage. Probably the most important policy issue facing this community is whether we can turn around the gang issue, which will have ripple effects and improve quality of life in so many different ways.

Even if you live in a community where there aren't gangs, you're being affected indirectly, because police are responding to the problem areas and therefore maybe not responding as well to lower-level crime in your area. Also, how the gang culture affects other young people growing up is something we all have to make a huge priority to address in the coming period.

~ August 30, 2008
SGI-USA Santa Monica Culture of Peace Resource Center

Forging Coalitions Among People of Faith

Efforts at the United Nations Toward a Better World

Hiro Sakurai

Hiro Sakurai is the Soka Gakkai International representative to the United Nations in New York and has managed the SGI's United Nations Liaison Office since 1997.

Soka Gakkai International is the global support organization for practitioners of Nichiren Buddhism and has had consultative status with the UN Economic and Social Council since 1983.

Since 1997, Mr. Sakurai has participated in various activities and taken on a wide range of responsibilities, including: President, Committee of Religious NGOs at the United Nations (2004–07); Member, Civil Society Task Force, General Assembly High-level Dialogue on Interreligious and Intercultural Cooperation and Understanding for Peace (2007); Troika member, Tripartite Forum on Interfaith Cooperation for Peace (2006–07); Member, Council of Trustees, Temple of Understanding, a global interfaith organization in consultative status with ECOSOC (2004–present); Member, Board of Directors, NGO Committee on Disarmament, Peace and Security, a substantive committee of the Conference of NGOs in Consultative Relationship with the UN (CONGO) (2002–present); Member, International Steering Committee, Global Action to Prevent War (2006–present); Advisor, Toda Institute for Peace and Policy Research, a research NGO associated with the Department of Public Information.

Mr. Sakurai has been actively involved in the work of religious NGOs, their relations to the United Nations and Member States since 1999. Since 2005, he has worked closely with representatives of the United Nations and Member States to co-organize conferences with religious NGOs at the United Nations. These experiences have given him unique perspectives on issues related to interfaith cooperation at the United Nations and UN-civil society relations. He has also worked on developing interfaith cooperation in such critical fields as nuclear disarmament, education for sustainable development, and building a culture of peace and nonviolence.

Hiro Sakurai addresses many of the eight action areas in the
1999 United Nations Declaration and Programme of Action on
a Culture of Peace, most notably the fifth, fostering democratic
participation. As he says: "Building a culture of peace requires
efforts on many issues, from human rights to the environment,
as are laid out in the eight action areas. To tackle all those issues
and challenges, we need the participation of all actors, not just
governments and international bodies like the United Nations.
We need the so-called ordinary people, like us—people from all
walks of life."

Today, I would like to share with you some of the things I have learned
and experiences I have gained through my UN activities that I think
are relevant to the discussion of a culture of peace.

First, I would like to briefly go back to the origin or the early history of
the concept of a culture of peace. We know that the UN General Assembly proclaimed the year 2000 as the International Year for the Culture of
Peace and 2001–2010 as the International Decade for a Culture of Peace
and Non-violence for the Children of the World.

But how was the concept of a culture of peace born?

Some say the idea of a culture of peace was foreshadowed in the mandate of UNESCO when it was founded in 1945. The preamble to the
UNESCO Constitution reads in part:

> That a peace based exclusively upon the political and economic
> arrangements of governments would not be a peace which could
> secure the unanimous, lasting and sincere support of the peoples
> of the world, and that the peace must therefore be founded, if it is
> not to fail, upon the intellectual and moral solidarity of mankind.
> (*Basic Texts*, Paris: UNESCO, 2012, p. 5)

And of course the famous phrase: "since wars begin in the minds
of men, it is in the minds of men that the defences of peace must be

constructed" (ibid.). Today, we would say "the solidarity of humankind" and "the minds of men and women" or "the minds of people"....

But the actual phrase "culture of peace" was first coined by Peruvian Jesuit scholar Reverend Father Felipe MacGregor. MacGregor headed the publication of a peace education book titled *Cultura de paz* (Culture of Peace) in 1986. In the same year, a group of scientists met in Seville, Spain, and issued a statement in which they laid out a foundation for the culture of peace. Then, in 1989, the International Congress on Peace in the Minds of Men was held in Yamoussoukro, Côte d'Ivoire, where the culture of peace became the central theme for the first time.

What was inspiring to me was that in 1991, around the time of the first Gulf War, a university professor who was concerned about the United Nations being pushed to be militarized decided to take a sabbatical and work at UNESCO. He wanted to help redirect the United Nations away from the use of military force and toward the use of peaceful means to promote peace. His name is David Adams. Later he designed UNESCO's Culture of Peace program and worked as director of the International Year for the Culture of Peace.

What inspires me most is that David Adams designed the Culture of Peace program because he saw culture of peace as a means to change the United Nations.

The key UN document for a culture of peace – the Declaration and Programme of Action on a Culture of Peace – lists eight action areas identified as essential components for building a culture of peace. Shortly before I left New York to come to Chicago for this lecture, I spoke with Ambassador Anwarul Chowdhury, who came here last February to speak about a culture of peace. He is a great leader and advocate for a culture of peace. As Bangladesh's ambassador to the United Nations, he steered the negotiations among governments to realize the adoption of key documents for a culture of peace, such as the Declaration and Programme of Action that I just mentioned.

In addition to the eight action areas, there are also six key points that were identified in 2000, the International Year for the Culture of Peace, when UNESCO launched a signature campaign called Manifesto 2000. The idea was to make this new concept of the culture of peace widely known to the world's people, so organizers made an effort to "translate" these UN documents into language we non-diplomats use.

The six key points were prepared as a pledge to sign, and 75 million signatures were gathered from around the world.

The Manifesto 2000 does not appeal to a higher authority; instead it is a pledge of individual commitment and responsibility. It was drafted by a group of Nobel Peace Prize laureates, translating the resolutions of the United Nations into everyday language and making them relevant to people everywhere.

Manifesto 2000 for a Culture of Peace and Non-violence

The year 2000 must be a new beginning for us all. Together we can transform the culture of war and violence into a culture of peace and non-violence. This demands the participation of everyone. It gives young people and future generations values that can inspire them to shape a world of dignity and harmony, a world of justice, solidarity, liberty and prosperity. The culture of peace makes possible sustainable development, protection of the environment and the personal fulfillment of each human being.

Recognizing my share of responsibility for the future of humanity, especially for today's children and those of future generations, I pledge—in my daily life, in my family, my work, my community, my country and my region—to:

1. respect the life and dignity of every person without discrimination or prejudice;

2. practice active non-violence, rejecting violence in all its forms: physical, sexual, psychological, economical and social, in particular towards the most deprived and vulnerable such as children and adolescents;

3. share my time and material resources in a spirit of generosity to put an end to exclusion, injustice and political and economic oppression;

4. defend freedom of expression and cultural diversity, giving preference always to dialogue and listening rather than fanaticism, defamation and the rejection of others;

5. promote consumer behavior that is responsible and development practices that respect all forms of life and preserve the balance of nature on the planet;

6. contribute to the development of my community, with the full participation of women and respect for democratic principles, in order to create together new forms of solidarity.

The International Decade for a Culture of Peace and Non-violence for the Children of the World was launched in 2001 and will come to a close in two years (2010). We don't have much time left. What have we accomplished in these seven and a half years?

I would like to share with you two examples from my work at the United Nations that give me hope and confidence that we are making real progress in building a global culture of peace. One is interfaith dialogue and cooperation, and the other is nuclear disarmament.

As a representative of the SGI, a Buddhist NGO, I have been involved in interfaith work at the United Nations since 1999.

From 2004 to 2007, for example, I chaired the Committee of Religious NGOs at the United Nations. This is the oldest NGO committee for religious organizations in New York. The executive bureau consisted of Catholic, Jewish, Muslim, Presbyterian, Methodist, Baha'i, Buddhist and interfaith representatives.

I was very fortunate that, during my tenure as president of the committee, we saw what I hope will prove to be the start of a long-term change. And that is the sudden increase of interest in interfaith issues among governments.

This began in 2005. A group of governments, including the Philippines, Indonesia, Pakistan, Germany (and Spain at the very beginning), approached our committee with a proposal to organize an interfaith conference at the United Nations. I must say that my colleagues and I at first felt quite cautious, since we had never been extended such an invitation by a group of governments before. Typically, it is we NGOs who approach governments with ideas rather than the other way around. Our basic sense was that many governments have reservations about dealing with religion at the United Nations or working with religious NGOs. In fact, some governments tend to think of religious organizations as a different category from other NGOs.

After the careful review, we decided to take part in this process. The conference was held in June 2005 and was a great success. It was co-sponsored by a total of sixteen governments, three UN-system organizations (including UNESCO and the World Bank), and our group, the Committee of Religious NGOs. In total, it brought together more than four hundred representatives from governments, the United Nations and civil society. That led to the formation of the Tripartite Forum on Interfaith Cooperation for Peace, which was launched in 2006 with fifty governments, fifteen UN-system organizations, and the members of our committee.

This tripartite partnership is certainly a new phenomenon in interfaith activities at the United Nations. This partnership was most effectively utilized during the High-level Dialogue on Interreligious and Intercultural Cooperation in October 2007, convened by the General Assembly. This was the first time in the history of the United Nations that the General Assembly, the largest and most representative UN body, convened a high-level event focusing on interfaith cooperation.

The original resolution co-sponsored by the Philippines and Pakistan did not include the participation of civil society in the high-level dialogue. After we urged the two governments to include this, they put forward a follow-up draft resolution that provided for the convening of the civil society hearing as part of the high-level dialogue. It was this resolution that was finally adopted by the General Assembly.

Of course, things have not always been rosy or perfect. When dealing with different governments, we sometimes need to be careful not to be co-opted by their agendas. For example, as religious NGOs, we must carefully consider how to deal with governments that have bad domestic records in such areas as human rights, environmental protection and so forth? How do we encourage governments to grasp the true meaning of Tripartite? These are some of the issues we need to consider.

Nevertheless, different actors are now coming together and collaborating, which is still unique at the United Nations. What was truly rare was something that happened toward the closing of the first conference in June 2005, as we were finalizing the conference summary for adoption. There were government officials, UN staff and NGO representatives all gathered around a single laptop computer working to finalize the language of our joint statement, all working in a spirit of openness and equality. Normally, governments make such decisions in closed sessions. I can't tell you what a moving sight this was.

Immediately following the conference, the committee hosted a reception at the Church Center across the street from the United Nations. Shortly after the reception began, a rainbow appeared over the UN Headquarters. Many of us—again, not only NGOs but also ambassadors and UN officials as well—went out to the Center's balcony to see it. It appeared to be bridging the General Assembly Building and the UN Secretariat. It really seemed to be a metaphor for the mission of interfaith initiatives: to close the gap between the religious community, the UN and member governments.

The other example that I would like to share with you is about nuclear disarmament. Last year, the SGI marked the fiftieth anniversary of the declaration, calling for the abolition of nuclear weapons, made by the Soka Gakkai's second president, Josei Toda, in 1957 in front of a gathering of 50,000 youth members. In 2006, as part of his proposal for UN reform, the SGI's current president, Daisaku Ikeda, issued a proposal for a "decade of action by the world's people for nuclear abolition."

Declaration for the Abolition of Nuclear Weapons

Josei Toda, second president of the Soka Gakkai, made a declaration on September 8, 1957, that reads in part:

Although a movement calling for a ban on the testing of nuclear weapons has arisen around the world, it is my wish to go further, to attack the problem at its root. I want to expose and rip out the claws that lie hidden in the very depths of such weapons. I wish to declare that anyone who ventures to use nuclear weapons, irrespective of their nationality or whether their country is victorious or defeated, should be sentenced to death without exception. Why do I say this? Because we, the citizens of the world, have an inviolable right to live. Anyone who jeopardizes that right is a devil incarnate, a fiend, a monster.... Even if a country should conquer

> ✒ *The United Nations defines the culture of peace as a set of values, attitudes, modes of behavior and ways of life that reject violence and prevent conflicts by tackling their root causes, solving problems through dialogue and negotiation among individuals, groups and nations. This means that it has to start with each of us.*

the world through the use of nuclear weapons, the conquerors must be viewed as devils, as evil incarnate. I believe that it is the mission of every member of the [Soka Gakkai] youth division in Japan to disseminate this idea throughout the globe.

So, to commemorate the fiftieth anniversary and to launch the people's decade, we created a new exhibition on nuclear abolition. We have displayed it in Hawaii, New Zealand, Malaysia, New York and many other places, but most recently at the UN headquarters in Geneva, Switzerland, during a round of negotiations related to the Nuclear Non-proliferation Treaty.

What is significant about this exhibition is that it makes the connection between human security and nuclear disarmament explicit. To date, nuclear disarmament has been discussed almost solely in the context of traditional national security frameworks. The negative impact of the very existence of nuclear weapons—even if they are never used—is rarely discussed. Nor are the benefits to the world—the enhancement of the quality of people's lives and security through the reduction and elimination of nuclear weapons—given much attention. To many of us, this may seem like common sense: of course nuclear weapons are threats to the security of people's lives. But, unfortunately, that is not how many governments think. They continue to see nuclear weapons as a symbol of power and prestige.

I think, however, that this is starting to change, and the positive reaction our exhibition has received is a sign of this change.

Frankly, the kind of support that we have received for this exhibition has been far beyond our expectations. In fact, when we brought it to Geneva, it wasn't our idea. It was the UN officials for disarmament affairs who strongly encouraged us to do so. In Geneva, we received positive reaction from a wide range of participants to the NPT session, including government officials and NGO experts. People appreciated the SGI's effort to bring the concept of human security into nuclear disarmament.

One UN official with whom I spoke said that many exhibitions tend to present issues and problems and how serious those are, but not solutions or ways to respond or make a difference, so people end up feeling helpless. But the SGI's exhibitions always present ways forward—what each of us can do. That's why people feel empowered by them. I was truly encouraged by this response, and we are determined to continue our efforts to empower people to make a difference toward the goal of a world without nuclear weapons.

Last, I would like to share with you two aspects of a culture of peace that I am inspired by most:

One is its inclusiveness.

A culture of peace is not a simple, one-track idea. For example, we cannot build a culture of peace just by accomplishing nuclear disarmament. Building a culture of peace requires efforts on many issues, from human rights to the environment, as are laid out in the eight action areas. To tackle all those issues and challenges, we need the participation of all actors, not just governments and international bodies like the United Nations. We need the so-called ordinary people, like us—people from all walks of life. Because there are many, many problems that are impacting the lives of people, every effort is important and can contribute to the building of a culture of peace.

The other aspect is personal change.

The United Nations defines the culture of peace as a set of values, attitudes, modes of behavior and ways of life that reject violence and prevent conflicts by tackling their root causes, solving problems through dialogue and negotiation among individuals, groups and nations. This means that it has to start with each of us.

Our efforts don't have to be on a grand scale. We can start things within our reach, close to home in our daily lives. Or it can be just putting a little additional effort into something we are already doing. Any conscious effort for peace is a great start. If each of us takes just one extra step forward, the positive impact will be enormous.

Buddhism teaches that everything we think, say and do creates either a negative or positive cause. I personally find this way of thinking very strict and also very empowering. It means that *everything* matters.

And I think this is what is so wonderful about the culture of peace. It is a grand, global transformation of human history—after thousands of years, humankind finally quitting our terrible habits of violence and exploitation and finding a way of living together in peace, mutual respect and dignity. It is something that starts right here, right now, in our daily lives.

~ September 13, 2008
SGI-USA Chicago Culture of Peace Resource Center

Peace and Love

Shigeko Sasamori

Hiroshima Atomic Bomb Survivor; Hiroshima and Nagasaki Peace Projects, L.L.C., Chief Executive Officer

Shigeko Sasamori is one of twenty-five women known as the "Hiroshima Maidens" who survived the atomic bombing of Hiroshima on August 6, 1945, and were brought to the United States for reconstructive surgery in 1955. Norman Cousins, editor of the Saturday Review, rallied support from his readership to sponsor the reconstructive surgeries. In the same way, he arranged medical care and education for four hundred Japanese children orphaned by the explosions. Cousins became Shigeko Sasamori's adoptive father. Her story of survival revolves around her transformation from a thirteen-year-old in delirium after the atomic bombing to an international peace activist in the tradition of her adoptive father. The mission of the Hiroshima and Nagasaki Peace Projects, L.L.C, is to stimulate an active, worldwide dialogue to protect humanity from nuclear harm. Its activities advance the work of Norman Cousins, who demonstrated the power of international dialogue in promoting mutual understanding, good will and peace.

> Ms. Sasamori speaks compelling on many of the eight action areas in the 1999 United Nations Declaration and Programme of Action on a Culture of Peace, most notably the eighth area: promoting international peace and security. As she points out, "Once war starts, everybody is a victim."

I am a survivor of the atomic bomb that was dropped on Hiroshima. I was thirteen years old at the time, but [today] it seems as though it just happened. My story extends over many months and years, so I can't tell you every detail.

A Beautiful Day

The houses in Hiroshima were built very close to one another. Although the big cities had been firebombed many times, Hiroshima had not. However, expecting that a firebomb would be dropped at some point, the city wanted to clear a fire escape route. To do this, houses were demolished. Young students had the job of helping to clean up the streets.

It was my first day of work on this clean-up project. The sky was a beautiful blue that morning, the weather nice and warm. Just before work started, I heard an airplane and looked up at the sky. The plane was a beautiful, shining silver color and it trailed a tail like a white cloud. I said to my classmate standing next to me, "Look up! The airplane is so beautiful!"

In that same moment, I saw white things coming down and immediately felt a very strong force that knocked me out. I don't know how long I was unconscious, but when I finally sat up, everything was pitch black. I couldn't see anything, just black. And I didn't feel anything; didn't hear anything. The city seemed to be dead.

Little by little, like a fog fading away, the blackness disappeared and I could see around me. Everything looked completely different. The people didn't look like people. It's very hard to explain how they looked. Their face and hair hung from their bodies by skin. Most had no clothing, just skin hanging and swelling and bleeding. Their hair was burned, and they were covered in ash.

There was no sound. I couldn't hear anything. People were walking very slowly. I have never been in hell, but if there is one, it is probably like that. I followed people to a nearby river. When I got there, there were already so many people in the water.

I must have been in shock. I didn't feel or hear anything. Then, I heard a baby scream. I looked down. A baby with burnt skin was crying and screaming terribly. The baby's mother was also hurt. She didn't look like a normal person, but she tried to nurse her baby.

My ears cleared. Somebody was saying, "Go across the bridge; cross to the other side of the river." So I just followed the people. I arrived at a schoolyard and sat down under a big tree. That much I remember, but after that, I don't recall anything clearly. I know I was lying on the floor. I could hear people talking, moaning, screaming and crying—so much noise.

I realized that a firebomb must have dropped near me and that my parents must be looking for me. I repeated my name and address out loud and also: "Please give me water. I'm sick." I said it over and over, again and again, but nothing happened. I stayed there for five days and four nights, without food, water or treatment. I didn't really know that time was passing by in that way. I only know because my mother told me later.

I didn't know the difference between day and night. I just kept saying to myself: "One more time. I'll ask someone to give me water one more time, one more time." I kept pushing myself, "One more time, one more time." I still remember saying that.

A Miraculous Rescue

So, miraculously, five days after the bomb dropped, a man saw me. He went to my parents' home on the other side of the city. My parents didn't know it was me he had found because he only told them where I was. My parents didn't really know whose child the man had found. But my father said, "It could be anybody's child. Let's go get her. Maybe someone is looking for her."

My mother had been looking for me every day after the bomb dropped. She looked at everyone, even dead bodies, even people who didn't look like me. She looked all over, calling my name. When she came back home at the end of that day, she was so tired. She was about to sit down when she heard that my father was going to pick up the child the man had found. She wanted to go with him. My father tried to stop her, but she said: "I want to go. Maybe it's Shigeko. Maybe."

It was a good thing that she came when she did. At the time they arrived, I felt I was in a dream. It was a beautiful day and I saw yellow pumpkin flowers on the ground. A water well was nearby. My body felt so heavy. I wanted to go to the water. As I crawled toward the well, it changed into a stream. As I continued to crawl, the stream turned into a river, the river into an ocean. Still my body was craving water. Suddenly, the ocean turned into the sky.

My body was light and it shot up so fast into a beautiful place. It was so beautiful all around me. Imagine that someone melted pure gold and poured it into your own gold, how you would feel. There was nothing there—just shiny, beautiful, pure gold. My body was as light as a feather as I continued to crawl. But at the same time, my throat was very dry; I was so thirsty.

> *I feel that the people's power is much stronger than the government's power. I believe in that —especially when I see young people. Their energy is so strong.*

Although I was dying for water, I can't explain what a good taste I had in my mouth. To say "a good taste," is not enough. I can't explain it. My ears also heard wonderful music. Yet there wasn't any music, just a very good sound. I felt happiness in this place, happiness I couldn't explain.

Then, from far away, I heard, "Shigeko!" I said to myself, "Here I am!" And then the gold went away along with those things I was seeing and feeling. I was in a dark sort of place. I saw a little light down below. At the same time, I had a pain in my chest and I heard a voice say, "She has a strong heart; that's why she's alive." That was the first night since the bomb had dropped that somebody took care of me.

On the way home, I felt movement [of being carried] and heard comments such as, "It's still burning there." "Oh, there, too."

Then I heard someone say: "Maybe under the house, the dead bodies are still burning." When we drew near my home, I heard people all talking at once:

"You found Shigeko!"

"Oh, how nice!"

"Wonderful! You found Shigeko!"

That's when I felt, "Oh! I am home!"

The next thing I remember is being under a mosquito net. In Japan in the summertime, each room had a big mosquito net. People slept under there. Fortunately my father had two houses. One house had burned down. Nothing remained. The other house, the one we called the summer house, hadn't burned. It was slightly damaged, but it had survived and some clothes and futons were there.

I feel that if my parents had not survived, I would not have survived. And also, if the house had not survived, I might have died. Every day I heard people coming to see my parents and me. Those people were saying: "Is she still alive? Is she still alive?" People thought I would die any minute because one-fourth of the front of my body was severely burned.

Not only that, can you imagine being in that condition for five days with no food and no medical care in the hot, hot summer of Japan? My mother stayed under the mosquito net with me all the time, except when she went to the bathroom. There was no medication available, so they rubbed cooking oil all over me. That was how I healed. Miraculously, I survived.

Help from the "Enemy"

Eight years after the bomb dropped, the minister of my church, Reverend Hiroshi Tanimoto, took nine girls, including me, to Tokyo University for reconstructive surgery. Before the operation, we went to Tokyo to see the people who donated money to cover the cost of surgery. I had already had nine operations by that time.

Shortly after the surgery, we met Norman Cousins in Japan. When he went back to America, he asked people to donate money to bring the twenty-five "Hiroshima Maidens" to the United States for plastic surgery. It took him two years to organize everything.

Before I left, people asked me: "Why are you going to America? The Americans dropped the bomb." Or, "Aren't you scared to go to America?" But I wasn't scared of coming to America. After the war, many American soldiers came to Hiroshima with their families, including their wives and children. They were very nice people.

During the war, we heard that American people were monsters and that if the soldiers saw you, they would kill you. We were brainwashed. Fortunately, when we came to America, we were put into the care of a group of good people. Most of our hosts and hostesses were Quakers. They treated us like their own daughters. How could I be afraid of American people or have anger toward them? The people all smiled and were nice to me. I was very happy and comfortable. We felt lucky to stay in the United States.

Once the project was finished, just before going back to Hiroshima, Mr. Cousins asked everybody, "What are you going to do when you go back to Japan?"

I said to him: "I would like to become a nurse, because when I was in the hospital, a nice doctor and kind nurses were very helpful to me. They were so good to me that I would like to do something to help other people."

Mr. Cousins said, "Come back to the United States." I was so naive. I didn't speak English and here I am, thinking of coming to the United States to study nursing. When I went back to Japan, I asked my parents for their opinion. My father said: "As long as you live and I am here, of course you can always stay with me. But we can never tell what may happen in the future. So, you make your own decision about what you want to do."

Life in a New Country

I liked American people and also doing and learning new things. I must have been very naive, but I came to the United States. Ever since I came to this country, it has been so wonderful. People have been very good to me.

When I first came to the United States, once or twice a year around August 6, the anniversary of the bombing of Hiroshima, people from the media would ask for an interview. Over the years, the world situation has gotten worse. What is happening in the world now is horrible. Now, more and more often, every year, people ask me about what happened in Hiroshima and my thoughts about it.

I met many people in peace movements who wanted to learn. Gradually, I got a very strong urge to do something. So many people died from severe burns and had such a horrible experience, but I survived. This is a miracle. God gave me a mission to do something. He gave me a new life.

Once war starts, everybody is a victim. Many Americans have said to me, "I'm sorry for what you had to go through when we dropped a bomb on your country." But I don't feel that way.

I have said to people: "No, don't be sorry. You didn't do it. It was the war. If you feel bad about what happened to Hiroshima and Nagasaki, please put that feeling into the entire world. Think about all the nuclear weapons in the world now. Please don't say, 'I'm sorry.'"

I really feel that way. Yes, I'm upset and angry at the war, but not the American people. The people who have sympathy about what happened to us in Hiroshima have a good nature, a good heart.

Today I am so happy to meet all of you, because you care about peace. That's why you came here to listen to me.

Although people have felt sorry for me because of the hard life I have had because of my burns, the ones who had a harder time are my parents and my sisters and brothers. When I became a mother myself, I understood how my parents felt seeing my injuries.

I almost died, but even though I survived, I wasn't normal. My hand was crippled, and my face didn't look normal. My parents must have suffered much more than me. Since I understand how I feel about my children, when I think about other people's children, I hope nothing will happen to them as they grow up. Stopping war is the most important thing — stopping nuclear weapons and nuclear war.

Today's Danger

Currently we have a very dangerous situation. America has more than twenty-six hundred nuclear warheads. Each of these bombs is one hundred times more powerful than the Hiroshima bomb. And many other countries have started to make bombs. They are very, very dangerous things. Many people don't realize this.

Just one month ago, I went to a study group in Los Alamos, New Mexico. They told me that the United States not only is holding nuclear weapons, but is still making them. Also, they are going to make a new building, because the existing one is getting old. It was built more than sixty years ago. It's a huge amount of American tax money that they're using. Many people don't know that. They are making poison. It's a bad thing that they are doing.

Two days ago, I got back from a weeklong stay in Missoula, Montana. I talked to university students and local people. Over the years, many people have become more interested in what is going on in the world and what they can do to stop war. I was surprised to meet so many people. There was one group of more than three hundred people and another one of more than two hundred. This makes me feel very hopeful.

I feel that the people's power is much stronger than the government's power. I believe in that—especially when I see young people. Their energy is so strong. That good energy can be used for peace work. When I arrived at an elementary school in Missoula, Montana,third, fourth and fifth graders were sitting on the hard floor, more than 260 in all, sitting close to one another. They didn't move. Not only were they not moving but also, when I talked, their eyes were like strong beams coming toward me, really strong. They had What's-she-going-to-talk-about? eyes.

I said to them, "Hello, everybody!" and they said, "Hello!"

"I'm going to talk about something that might make you scared. You might not like it. It's a horrible story. Is it OK to tell you?"

They said, "OK!"

Everybody responded! I talked for almost an hour.

I said, "Don't you think that war is horrible?"

They responded, "Yeah!" Just like that! They reacted so positively.

I said, "When you go home, tell my story to your mama and papa and no more war, OK?"

They said, "Yeah!"

Every time I said something, they nodded their heads. They were so wonderful! I said to myself, "My God, what kind of world is ruining these beautiful, beautiful children? We must do something, urgently, very urgently."

I hope people will get together to oppose nuclear war. Just think about it. Even though we may not see them, people hear that there are so many children dying in Iran or Vietnam, that there are so many war victims in the world. It hurts inside. I am sure that if everyone has this feeling, it can give us the energy to get together and do something to oppose war. I believe this.

Some people in the audience in Montana asked me, "Do you believe war can end and we can get rid of nuclear bombs?"

I say: "Yes! It has to end! There can be no more nuclear weapons." That's the only answer: "Yes, I believe it." It's the only way people will survive.

One peacemaker told me that right now there is a new United Nations treaty on this subject. It says, "Let the countries make atomic bombs, nuclear weapons, or don't make any more." There are only two choices, they say. What will happen if the United States decides to make more weapons? We could lose our whole world. We can't do that.

That's why I say, "Yes, I believe that we will work together and one day there will be no more nuclear weapons." I believe that very strongly. It's the only way to do that.

Questions and Answers

AUDIENCE MEMBER 1: Are there any DVD resources available that tell your story?

SHIGEKO SASAMORI: Yes, just last year there was a documentary released called *White Light/Black Rain*. It shows fourteen survivors talking about what happened to them that day. I was in the film a little bit. The [American] pilot was also in it and four other people, American pilots and technicians. It's a very wonderful movie. It's not just the survivors talking. It also shows what happened in Japan and America during the war. It's a very good movie to suggest.

AUDIENCE MEMBER 2: How were you able to overcome feelings of hatred and bring yourself to forgive?

SASAMORI: This is why I feel that people's love and caring are important. I survived not only physically. My emotional mind also survived. [I didn't have] any hatred, anger, suicidal thoughts or anything like that. I think I never felt that way because people loved and cared for me. If people care for each other, they can have hope. Then, no more war.

Norman Cousins has a very famous theory that laughing is a medicine that can cure illness. Laughing is very important. Fortunately, my parents, two sisters and younger brother weren't hurt. I was the only one in the family who was hurt. It helped that my family cared about me and that I was in fairly happy surroundings.

I thought to myself, why should I get angry if people are smiling at me? If a stranger smiled at me, I couldn't make a bad face at them. Instead, I smiled, right? That's why it is very important to care and love.

AUDIENCE MEMBER 3: Have the other Hiroshima Maidens forgiven the United States for the bombing of Hiroshima and Nagasaki?

SASAMORI: When we first came to America, the media surrounded the twenty-five of us. They asked so many questions. Some of the other girls said that, in the beginning, they wanted to die. Well, I couldn't die because my mother wouldn't let me. Or, they said that they didn't want to go outside because they were afraid people would stare at them. Of course, they were talking about the difficult time they had. When I heard them say these things, I felt odd, I had a feeling of not belonging with them.

I could have said the same kind of thing, but I didn't feel that way. I couldn't be dishonest. I felt a little uncomfortable, but as we stayed through to the end of the project and then went home, the other girls became much more relaxed and happy and they liked their American host families. I think maybe by then they understood me.

AUDIENCE MEMBER 4: How many people were in the city when it was bombed? How did it affect their health?

SASAMORI: That's a very good question, but to be honest, I don't know. I know many, many people died. Many died from being severely burned while others died from radiation illness. Some didn't look bad, but they had been exposed to radiation and later on developed what we call "atomic bomb illness," which was mostly cancer. The cancer didn't appear right away. Today there are still many people suffering in Hiroshima.

Five years ago I had cancer in my intestines. About twenty inches of my intestine was removed in surgery. I also got thyroid cancer and still have it. Over the years I was very healthy but then we found cancer. So, I am sorry, I don't know how many, but many people died.

AUDIENCE MEMBER 5: Prior to the dropping of the bomb, was the population in Hiroshima informed that the attack was coming?

SASAMORI: At the time, many people thought that there had been a warning but we didn't hear about it. This is not true. An American study group later told me that there had been rumors that fliers warning about the attack had been dropped from the air, but this turned out to be a rumor.

AUDIENCE MEMBER 6: What action can we take to abolish nuclear weapons?

SASAMORI: I think that we are all different individuals. What is most important is learning. Educate yourself. Learn from experts about what is happening in the world and find out what you can do. No matter what you decide to do, I think you can find a peace group to work with. There are many ways to participate. The important thing is that you want to do it. It's the first step and you've already done it.

AUDIENCE MEMBER 7: What advice do you have for youth who want to take action?

SASAMORI: That's a very good question. Young people are waiting for a big future world, but they have to learn what kind of future is waiting for them. That's number one. The next thing is education. Young people's energy is very powerful and very important. I love them. Yes, young people are so wonderful.

AUDIENCE MEMBER 8: How long did it take you to overcome your injuries? How were you able to overcome your suffering?

SASAMORI: I don't know exactly, but it probably took over a half year [to heal]. As for the second question, I was able to overcome my sufferings from the time I was able to go outside. When I saw how the city had burned how many people had died and I heard many stories, I said, "Thank God I lived." I was also thankful that everyone in my family was OK. I think I overcame my suffering at that moment. (Ms. Sasamori calls her family to the stage, including children and grandchildren.)

You can tell what a happy person I am with this family. Think about the future of these children. How can people abuse young innocent children? They are so important. We have to do something. We have to stop people from fighting and killing one another.

~ September 20, 2008
SGI-USA Santa Monica Culture of Peace Resource Center

Gandhi and a Culture of Peace

Joseph Prabhu

Professor, Philosophy
California State University, Los Angeles

Dr. Prabhu was educated first in economics at Delhi University, studying with Amartya Sen, future Nobel Prize winner, among others. He then went to Europe to study philosophy and religion, spending time at Heidelberg University and the University of Munich in Germany and Cambridge University in England, where he received his master's in philosophy. At Boston University, he secured his doctorate with a thesis on "Hegel's Philosophy of Religion."

Dr. Prabhu has taught at California State University, Los Angeles since 1978, but has also been visiting professor at University of California, Berkeley; Harvard University and the University of Chicago. His teaching interests are in metaphysics, ethics, philosophy of religion, social and political philosophy, and comparative religion. In addition, he has presented more than 100 guest lectures at universities in Germany, Spain, Turkey, Japan, Australia and India.

The National Endowment for the Humanities has granted Dr. Prabhu nine fellowships, and he has also garnered fellowships at the Center for the Study of World Religions at Harvard and the Martin Marty Center at the University of Chicago.

Dr. Prabhu has edited *The Intercultural Challenge of Raimon Panikkar* (Orbis Books, 1996) and *Indian Ethics: Ancient Traditions and Contemporary Challenges* (Ashgate Press, 2005). His own book, *Liberating Gandhi: Community, Empire and a Culture of Peace*, is being reviewed by Rowman and Littlefield. In addition, he was a co-editor of ReVision, a journal of philosophy, spirituality and psychology, for a six-year period. He serves on the Executive Committee of the Society for Asian and Comparative Philosophy; is a member of the Board of Trustees of the Chicago-based Council for a Parliament of the World Religions; and a member of The Toda Institute, an independent, nonpartisan, nonprofit organization committed to the pursuit of peace through peaceful means and a complete abolition of war.

Dr. Prabhu addresses many of the eight action areas in the 1999
United Nations Declaration and Programme of Action on a
Culture of Peace, most notably the first area: fostering a culture
of peace through education. He says: "When it comes to peace
education, we need to go quite deep in terms of establishing
for ourselves and those we teach and learn from the principles
that can have wide resonance and can effectively neutralize the
forces of darkness and destruction. One thing I will emphasize
is the fearlessness of Gandhi. Imbued with his sense of truth, he
was fearless facing any opponent. Again, to seek the roots of this
fearlessness, this confidence, is valuable for us today when so
much fear and anxiety has gripped the human spirit."

The teachings of Gandhi and the teaching of the Buddha, especially
as mediated through Nichiren, can be seen as quite similar to each
other. In fact, the great Indian poet Rabindranath Tagore, who received
the Nobel Prize in Literature in 1913, compared Gandhi to the Buddha,
and said it had been a while in India since a message of illumination,
applied now to the social and political realm, had come from India. So,
we can find a lot of similarity.

The point of recognizing this similarity between Buddha and Gandhi
is to say that both of them are living traditions. I cite Gandhi as a person
who didn't so much give us doctrines as principles, attitudes that we can
live in our own lives and creatively apply. I would argue that the same is
true of the Buddha.

Some of you are familiar with that rather harsh Zen Buddhism saying, "If you see the Buddha on the road today, kill him." The point of that
remark is that Buddha's last words to his disciples were, "Do not cling to
me, work out your salvation for yourselves with diligence."

This is, by the way, the same as the sayings of Christ after his resurrection, when he says to Mary Magdalene, "*Noli me tangere* (do not cling to me)." What's implied in Christ's message is: "I have to rise and so do you."

There are two or three contexts I'd like to cite, referring to this sort of common space between Nichiren Buddhism and Gandhi. One is the wonderful book *For the Sake of Peace, Seven Pathways to Global Harmony*, by Daisaku Ikeda (president of the Nichiren Buddhist lay organization Soka Gakkai International), in which he graphically tells the experience of his family in Japan during World War II. Three of his brothers had gone to war. Ikeda recounts an instance where his mother had made some rice cakes to take to soldiers going to the front, which led to a heartwarming scene at a railway station as the soldiers were going off to battle, many of whom did not return, including Ikeda's older brother Kichi. From such visceral experiences, Ikeda developed a sense of horror at the idea of war. He's 80 this year, and, I feel, some of his tireless peacemaking activities around the world are exemplary.

Another context I want to mention is that of the Parliament of the World's Religions, which started in 1893 in conjunction with the Chicago World Fair and represented America's first meeting of the world religions. As you may know from your religious history, America in 1893 was a strongly Protestant country, and any sort of contact with religions beyond Christianity was hardly known.

It took the daring of monks from the Rama Krishna mission to suggest to the conveners of the World's Fair that it might be a good occasion, given that trade and commerce and the arts were coming together at this fair, to have a meeting of religions. It was a very dramatic event, likely the historical marker of the kind of pluralism we today take for granted. You walk out here on the streets and you're going to see Hare Krishnas, people from some Buddhist organization, Christians, Jews—and that sort of multi-religiosity was without question sparked by the Parliament of the World's Religions in 1893.

For reasons unknown, it took another hundred years before people could get up the courage to organize another parliament. The modern parliament started in 1993, exactly 100 years later, again in Chicago, out of which emerged a very important document that I would urge you to look at. It is called the "Declaration Toward a Global Ethic," which has now made it all the way to the United Nations, and it serves as the basis for deliberations toward a document called "Religion and Human Rights."

The 1948 UN "Universal Declaration of Human Rights" is a strongly secular document. People felt that bringing in religion might lead to more strife and contention than was worth it. But I think people today, some 60 years later, recognizing the importance of religion in people's lives, feel that there should be a more balanced document. In any case, "Declaration Toward a Global Ethic" was one of the most important documents coming out of the 1993 Parliament.

The next Parliament, which I'm going to talk about later, is to be held in Melbourne, Australia, which was chosen largely because of its indigenous peoples. As you know, at the Australian Parliament, Australian Prime Minister Kevin Rudd made an historic apology for the treatment of indigenous people. Those of you familiar with American history know the disgraceful treatment meted out to Japanese-Americans during World War II. You can imagine, then, what indigenous peoples around the world have been going through. In any case, that's only one aspect. There's much more going on about the Parliament, but I thought I'd mention that because one thing I'm going to talk about today with reference to Gandhi is the importance of interfaith and interreligious dialogue.

As an introduction to my talk about Gandhi, let's take a peek at our global situation today. I contend that Gandhi's actual message is timely as a counter view to the notion that his techniques of non-violent resistance might have worked against the British because the British were an essentially civilized people given to traditions of law and dialogue. To that, the Indian defense minister had the appropriate response when he said, "The sun never sets on the British empire because God doesn't trust the British in the dark."

The idea that somehow British imperialism was a very kindly and humane form of domination is historically inaccurate. In fact, at every step of the way after returning from South Africa, Gandhi had to fight inordinately against not only the British but also his fellow Indians, who were keen on taking up violent forms of resistance. This double struggle testifies that the principles are by no means local or confined to a particular instance.

Nonetheless, we live in dark times, however one wants to characterize them, whether with the latest financial crisis or the fact that wars are going on around the world—not only the war in Iraq but the genocide in Darfur, the instability in the Middle East, the trouble between India and Pakistan over Kashmir, and so on.

When we talk about religion—and some of these wars, unfortunately, have had religious causes—it's overstating the case to say that religion has been the prime motivator. Yet, while there have certainly been other factors, political and economic, there's no question, if we're honest with ourselves, that religion has contributed a great deal to these wars, especially the perversions of religion that have given rise to religion-based terrorism. Accordingly, we have to be honest and critical about our own religious traditions and practices, and, if anything, these times call for the transformation of religions themselves, the kind of inner purification stressed so much in Buddhist theory and practice.

Two things about the global situation: on the one hand, there is this ongoing so-called war against terrorism, which has indeed spawned various attitudes non-conducive to peace; on the other hand, there are the Gandhis, the Martin Luther Kings, the Desmond Tutus, and the Vaclav Havels of the world who are fighting to bring about a more peaceful world. These are two forces in a kind of spiritual war with each other.

Also, when we talk about religion, we have to acknowledge this duality that has been recognized by thinkers as diverse as Sigmund Freud and Thomas Hobbes. On the one hand, human nature is prone to a kind of self-destructive dark side, balanced by, in Freud's language, the force of Eros, the force of love, the force of constructive desire. That is also a thread that runs through the tension at the founding of the American nation, where John Locke, on the one hand, represented the side of human nature that is peaceful and good, while other thinkers invoked Thomas Hobbes and said that the primordial condition of human beings was destructive and warlike.

Gandhi unequivocally supports seeing human beings' peace-loving side as primordial and our warring side as an aberration, rather than the other way around. When we talk about a culture of peace, it's important to recognize that the word *culture* is a biological, agricultural metaphor. It comes from the medieval French and means "to grow," and it is from there that we get the word *agriculture*.

When it comes to peace education, we need to go quite deep in terms of establishing for ourselves and those we teach and learn from the principles that can have wide resonance and can effectively neutralize the forces of darkness and destruction. One thing I will emphasize is the fearlessness of Gandhi. Imbued with his sense of truth, he was fearless facing any opponent. Again, to seek the roots of this fearlessness, this confidence, is valuable for us today when so much fear and anxiety has gripped the human spirit.

This is not an easy thing to apply; Gandhi's fearlessness was hard won. By the way, how many of you saw the 1984 film by Richard Attenborough, called *Gandhi*? It is without question the best simple introduction to Gandhi. But one thing not covered in that particular film is that after Gandhi trained as a lawyer and went to court for his very first case, he was petrified and tongue-tied. He had to leave the court in disgrace because he was commissioned to defend somebody but just could not get the words out. For someone like him to end up where he did described a long trajectory of rigorous, relentless practice in non-violence.

> *Whatever victories are achieved through violence, then, are really short-lived victories, as the history of war will amply demonstrate.*

I'm going to share with you the text of a recently published lecture I gave, titled "Gandhi, Empire and a Culture of Peace." I'll just read from a short section, and then go on to apply some of these ideas to the inter-religious scene. This particular section of the lecture is called "Gandhi's Moral Universe."

Gandhi is a moralist through and through, and yet it is difficult to talk philosophically about his ethics. This is because Gandhi is fundamentally concerned with practice rather than theory or abstract thought, and such philosophy as he used was meant to reveal its "truth" in the crucible of experience. Hence the subtitle of his famous autobiography, 'The story of my experiments in truth." The experiments refer to the fact that the truth of concepts, values and ideas is fulfilled only in practice. Prior to that practical fulfillment, they remain spectral and abstract. Furthermore, Gandhi's ethics are inextricably tied up with his religion, which itself is unconventional. Though an avowed Hindu, he was a Hindu in a philosophical rather than sectarian sense, and there was much Hindu ritual and practice that he subjected to critique.

In fact, he lost his life as a result of this critique because the person who killed him was a Hindu who felt that Gandhi had betrayed Hinduism.

In accordance with this religio-philosophical ideal, his religion could be described as the life of the self attempting to realize itself as Self, with a capital S, and thus achieving *moksha*, or spiritual liberation. But *karma yogi* that he was, his self-realization had to be achieved through work in the world and the details of daily life, rather than through renunciation of the world.

This was a longstanding tradition in India where people seeking liberation or renunciation felt that they had to leave the world. Gandhi was one very strong proponent of saying that it was not renunciation of action but renunciation *in* action that was the goal.

Gandhi's own ethics have a decidedly spiritual caste, but because he takes pains to express them in a neutral philosophical manner, he intends them to have general validity. Thus, when he switches from affirming that "God is truth" to saying that "truth is God," his rationale is that "truth is God" is a more general statement that has resonance even for unbelievers.

This is a quote from Gandhi: "God is Truth. But God is many other things also. That is why I prefer to say that Truth is God ... you may simply worship what you find to be the truth for Truth is known relatively. Only remember that Truth is one of the many qualities that we name. It is the living embodiment of God, it is the only Life, and I identify Truth with the fullest life and that is how it becomes a concrete thing for God is His whole creation, the whole Existence, and service of all that exists" (M.K. Gandhi, *Collected Works*, vol. 68 (New Delhi: Publication Division, Ministry of Information and Broadcasting, 1958–1994), 81).

That statement is a testament to Gandhi's inner sense of tolerance and inclusiveness in that he believes that his ideals of truth and non-violence are accessible even to those who do not share his particular religion.

Truth for Gandhi is not merely, or even primarily, the property of statements, though Gandhi does not deny the importance of factual truth or the correspondence between propositions and states of affairs in the world that either confirm or refute them. Rather, his multifaceted notion of truth emphasizes ontological, moral and existential aspects. Ontologically—that is, in terms of how we see reality—*satya* is derived from *Sat*, the self-existent essence, both the "is" and the "ought" of reality. It was this derivation that led Gandhi often to say, "Nothing exists in reality except Truth, everything else is illusion." Beyond the illusory temporal flux of phenomena lies the eternal Truth, what Gandhi also called "Absolute Truth." We humans with our finite capacities, however, can have access only to relative truths, an assertion Gandhi uses to justify his humility and tolerance. All our perceptions of truth are inevitably partial, and therefore claims of cognitive absoluteness are both unwarranted and dangerous.

While the ontological aspect of truth points to a more objective notion, the moral and existential aspects move toward a more subjective, almost Kierkegaardian notion of truth as subjectivity—the deeply personal intuition of truth that can be experienced only through action. Raghavan Iyer brings out the duality between the subjective and objective aspects of truth, stating: "Gandhi could not regard truth either as solely the object of reason or as simply the product of human decision. For him ... truth is nothing less than the splendor of reality and cannot be gained without an understanding of the Eternal Law of Nature, but when it is perceived and seized it must be acted upon. In this sense truth must be both discovered and created, found and enacted ... In this activist view of truth ... it is not enough for thought to be based upon truth; the life of the thinker must express it, must represent it visibly in his actions" (Raghavan Iyer, *The Moral and Political Thought of Mahatma Gandhi* [Oxford: Oxford University Press, 1973], 154).

As already intimated, the idea of truth for Gandhi found its fullest expression in the field of politics, which, in accordance with his moral outlook he regarded as the arena for doing good on the largest possible scale. The idea that Gandhi used to encapsulate this moral conception of politics was *satyagraha*. This was conceived as a practical experiment to introduce truth and non-violence into the political field. Gandhi adopted this idea early in his political career when he chose *satyagraha* as the name for his resistance movement against the repressive South African government. Explaining his decision, Gandhi wrote, "Truth [*satya*] implies love and firmness [*agraha*] and therefore serves as a synonym for force. I thus began to call the Indian movement *satyagraha*, that is to say, the force which is born of truth and love of nonviolence" (M. Gandhi, *Satyagraha in South Africa* [Madras: S. Ganesa, 1938], 172).

The forceful and activist character of *satyagraha* should correct a common misperception, namely that it denotes a passivity of resistance, a mere turning of the other cheek. On the contrary, Gandhi insisted that violence be met with love and understanding. The non-violent means chosen should not obscure the powerful end — that of establishing justice and truth. In fact, he is on record as saying that if the choice were between passive acceptance of injustice and violent resistance to it, he would choose violent resistance. He was convinced, however, that there was a third alternative superior to both, namely non-violent resistance.

Satyagraha begins with reasoning with one's opponent or adversary in an attempt to arrive at a just solution, recognizing that no party has a monopoly on the truth or is wholly in the right. The purpose therefore is to work out a rational compromise agreeable to both sides. It is only when such processes of reasoning, persuasion and compromise have been tried and have proved unsuccessful that one adopts the direct action techniques of *satyagraha*.

Satyagraha involves performing actions such as noncooperation (strikes, boycotts, fasts, lockouts, etc.); civil disobedience (nonpayment of taxes, disregard of specific law or injunction); publicizing one's cause through marches, rallies, picketing and other forms of peaceful protest; and finally, and actually very importantly, constructive programs (low cost housing, education facilities, cooperative banks for the poor).

It's important when we talk about the culture of peace in connection with Gandhi to keep in mind that, even though he's known as a political leader in the conventional sense, four-fifths of his life was really spent in the countryside forming these ideal communities. His real energy goes as a person who wants to build the culture of peace through these model communities. He formed two such communities in South Africa and then two such in India, and, as I've said, that's where he spent most of his time. A big part of such non-violent resistance is *tapas*, the willingness to suffer for one's cause.

As Thomas Pantham puts it, "It is the assumption of *satyagraha* that when reasoning fails to move the head, the argument of suffering by the *satyagrahis* helps move the heart of the oppressor or opponent. Self-suffering, moreover, is a truth-serving alterative to the truth-denying method of inflicting violence on others" (Thomas Pantham, "Habermas's Practical Discourse and Gandhi's *Satyagraha*," in *Political Discourse: Exploration in Indian and Western Thought*, ed. Bhikhu Parekh and Thomas Pantham [New Delhi: Sage Publications, 1987], 292–310).

Contained in the idea of *satyagraha* is the question of means and ends, which for Gandhi are two sides of the same coin. Gandhi strongly disagrees with the conventional political idea that the ends justify the means. To the contrary, he held that immoral means taint and distort potentially good ends, and to that extent he placed as much, if not more, emphasis on the means, which he described as ends in action. "The means may be likened to a seed, the end to a tree; and there is just the same inviolable connection between the means and the end as there is between the seed and the tree" (Gandhi, *Collected Works*, 10:431).

The forceful and activist character of *satyagraha* leads naturally to the idea of non-violence. Gandhi is obviously invoking the Jain precept of *ahimsa*, or not causing deliberate injury or harm to any being. But Gandhi takes the precept far beyond its merely negative formulation to mean by *ahimsa* "the largest love, the greatest charity." To quote Gandhi: "If I am a follower of *ahimsa*, I must love my enemy or a stranger as I would my wrongdoing father or son. This *ahimsa* necessarily includes truth and fearlessness" (Letter in *Modern Review*, October 1916, quoted in Iyer, op. cit., 180).

Ahimsa, then, is the deployment of moral force to persuade one's opponent or adversary. It differs from violence in that it respects the autonomy and dignity of the other, whereas violence does not. It differs from violence in the perpetual willingness to dialogue and negotiate with, and to listen to the other, and, as far as is consistent with rightness, to come to a compromise. Given that one's grasp of the truth is at best partial, it is imperative to see and appreciate the truth in the position of the other person and to try and achieve a higher reconciliation of conflicting ends. This negotiated compromise has the opposite effect of violence, which involves vanquishing and putting down one's opponent that merely sets up another cycle of resentment, ill will and further violence.

Whatever victories are achieved through violence, then, are really short-lived victories, as the history of war will amply demonstrate.

Of course, Gandhi was not so naive as to think that such moral persuasion would come about easily. He was all too aware that people who exercise power over others are not likely to give it up without some pressure being exerted. All the means of *satyagraha* mentioned above should be adopted as a way of morally coercing one's opponent to negotiate. It is true that coercion is being exercised, but it is a coercion that still respects the moral agency and dignity of the other, not least by the willingness to undergo self-suffering.

The strategy presupposes that the opponent does have a minimal openness to such moral appeal, a trait Gandhi was willing to grant to most people. We can argue with this assumption. He also recognized, however, that there are madmen and tyrants, rapists and aggressors who would not fall within that category of people open to moral appeal. But it's not a blanket policy. Non-violence is really a question of the heart, and not a rigid principle. In those extreme cases, Gandhi was willing to use physical force for the purpose of self-defense, as when he sanctioned the use of military force to drive back the Pakistani army in what he considered to be the invasion of Kashmir in 1948.

We don't have to agree with everything Gandhi says. I personally find less than satisfactory his response to the Jewish philosopher Martin Buber, when the latter skeptically asked Gandhi whether he thought the Jews should use *satyagraha* against Hitler, and Gandhi said, "Yes," which sparked a long correspondence between Buber and Gandhi.

The three concepts I have discussed, *satya*, *satyagraha*, and *ahimsa*, give us some idea of the texture of Gandhi's ethical thought. As mentioned earlier, the ideas of truth and non-violence are certainly to be found in the Jain, Buddhist and Hindu traditions, but there's a big difference between Gandhi's conceptualization of these ideas and traditional ones. The high standards of moral and spiritual discipline that Gandhi invokes were traditionally a part of the spiritual practice of monks and saints but decidedly not of people in political life.

Even in the case of King, there are people who, when they compare his life with Gandhi, begin to see that this importance of a moral and spiritual discipline was emphasized more by Gandhi than by King. Though, to grant King his own growth – he died, after all, at age thirty-nine – I think toward the end of his life he was beginning to see that this aspect of Gandhi's teaching was equally important.

Gandhi considerably softens the traditional dualism between religion and politics. Instead, he attempts to forge a nondual relationship between them, but of course with sharply different definitions of the two. Religion is now seen as reverence for and service to all of life. True service must necessarily lead to politics, the arena for the greatest potential for public service. Politics, in turn, is to be saved from powermongering and the conflict of factional interests by the moral purification involved in religion at its best.

It is very important to distinguish between Gandhi's highly moral notions of religion and politics from the ideological conceptions of them all too common in our time. Certainly the rise of religious fundamentalism and right-wing religious groups would make any peace-loving person nervous about some of the marriages effected between religion and politics. It should be clear, however, from what I have discussed, that the moral checks and balances Gandhi exercised over religion and politics purified both domains and offered the world a far different and nobler conception of them to which we have yet to measure up.

I'm going to say a little bit about the importance of interreligious dialogue and the Parliament with reference to Gandhi. First, as far as the culture of peace is concerned, the notion of peace is rich and comprehensive. It's far richer than thinking of peace merely as the absence of conflict or war. In fact, it's because people begin from the assumption that war is inevitable that peace is by contrast seen as a default position. I would argue that it's the other way around, and Gandhi does, too.

This is portrayed even by an examination of some of the words for peace in the respective religions. I'll look at just three, which the Parliament uses quite often in speeches and prayers. *Shanti* is the word for peace in Sanskrit and Pali, *salaam* is the word for peace in Islam, and *shalom* is the word for peace in Hebrew. All three words have a comprehensive and deep meaning in all three traditions, and in other traditions we would likely find something similar.

There are at least three dimensions to peace seen in this rich and comprehensive way. One is to be at peace within ourselves. It would be highly ironic if people teaching techniques of non-violence went about it in a violent and angry way. It happens, unfortunately, some of the time. The second dimension is peace with our fellow humans, and with all living beings, is a principle that comes from both the Jain and Buddhist traditions. The third dimension of peace is peace with nature and the cosmos, which now the ecological movement is trying to draw upon.

If I had time, I would try to show that Gandhi's culture of peace in the communities that I spoke about was as comprehensive as this. It certainly embraced the first dimension—trying to be peaceful within ourselves—through prayer, through penance, through working and sharing the products of our work. And it certainly had to do with trying to solve social conflicts within communities. Again, those of you who saw the film might remember the tussle between Gandhi and his wife, Kasturba, over the cleaning of latrines.

In Indian caste society the cleaning of toilets and latrines was not a job for someone in the caste to which both Gandhi and his wife belonged. But Gandhi insisted that such work would be shared equally in all of the communities, and that he and his wife were going to clean not only their own toilets but the toilets of others as well. His wife, naturally, was furious and said she hadn't married him in order to become a toilet cleaner. But Gandhi, stubborn as he was, insisted that he was going to do it. And he won her over by his example—he would clean the toilets that she was assigned to clean, and she finally relented.

~ October 11, 2008
SGI-USA Santa Monica Culture of Peace Resource Center

Philosophical Challenges in Building the Culture of Peace

Lou Marinoff

Professor and Chair
Department of Philosophy
The City College of New York

Lou Marinoff – a Commonwealth Scholar originally from Canada – is professor and chair of philosophy at The City College of New York, and founding president of the American Philosophical Practitioners Association. Marinoff collaborates with numerous global organizations that contribute to building cultures of peace, prosperity and harmony including Biovision (Lyon), Festival of Thinkers (Abu Dhabi), Horasis (Zurich), Soka Gakkai (Tokyo), Strategic Foresight Group (Mumbai), and the World Economic Forum (Davos). Marinoff is author of *Plato, Not Prozac!* (1999), which has been translated into twenty-seven languages. His other books include *Therapy for the Sane* (2003), *The Middle Way* (2007), and *The Inner Philosopher* – a dialogue with Daisaku Ikeda (2012).

Dr. Marinoff addresses many of the eight action areas in the 1999 United Nations Declaration and Programme of Action on a Culture of Peace, specifically focusing on five:

1. Fostering a culture of peace through education;
2. Promoting sustainable economic and social development;
3. Promoting respect for all human rights;
4. Ensuring equality between women and men;
8. Promoting international peace and security.

Dr. Marinoff says "We can always find despair in the world if we look for it. But if your hopefulness is more abundant, then hopefulness will prevail. Make your ideals compatible with justice, and you will realize them. Make your actions selfless, and they will engender enduring peace."

I t's a privilege to have this opportunity to interact with you tonight and
to present a lecture in the Culture of Peace series.

I know that all of you are on a path of action. You're activists for peace,
for prosperity, for betterment, for creating value. And I want to give you
some philosophical challenges. There are many deep questions posed by
the United Nations program, the eight action planks. I want to cover just
five of them.

Before I do so, I want to express my profound appreciation to SGI President Daisaku Ikeda for his tremendous encouragement. He has shown
me an enormous amount of generosity, has given me his time, has shared
with me deep insights concerning philosophy, which he understands perfectly well, has helped me to do a better job at what I do, and has encouraged me in every conceivable way.

As much as he gives of his energy to encourage us all, I'm going to try
to encourage you as well.

The eight action areas comprise an incredible program, very idealistic,
very thought provoking. There are deep philosophical challenges embed-
ded in these areas. It's impossible to address one of them without implicat-
ing the others. They're all connected in vital ways. I hope to make some
of these interconnections plain.

I will tackle action items 1, 2, 3, 4 and at the end, 8. That's my ambi-
tious program for you.

(1) Fostering a culture of peace through education is the first point.

The purpose of education is to awaken and manifest inner greatness.
Everyone has inner greatness. We also have inner terribleness. But we
maximize our potential, fulfill ourselves and help others, by focusing
always on greatness. The middle way of education is to awaken and manifest inner greatness. Its focus must be on the individual student. Those are
Daisaku Ikeda's words, and I ask you to bear them in mind.

The content of education must be, as Matthew Arnold said, "the best
which has been thought and said in the world," and its outcome is the celebration and renewal of human greatness.

How important is education? Diogenes Laertius references Aristotle:

"Being asked how the educated differ from the uneducated, 'As much,' he said, 'as the living from the dead'" (*The Lives of Eminent Philosophers*, trans. R. D. Hicks [London: William Heinemann Ltd., 1925–38], 5.19).

President Ikeda has said, "Education is a process of becoming fully human" (*To the Youthful Pioneers of Soka: Lectures, Essays and Poems on Value-Creating Education* [Hachioji, Japan: Soka University Student Union, 2006], p. 156). So nothing could be more important than education, surely.

As an educator, I've devoted my life to this. To date, I've spent more than three decades in higher education as a student, graduate student, teacher and professor. I have a lot vested in this. I think it's first and foremost the important thing.

The middle way of education is hampered by two extremes—I'm speaking globally: the global lag, which is a conspicuous and tragic lack of education in the developing world. And the deconstruction of higher education and now lower education in the United States of America. In my view, these are the two extremes that need to be rectified and remedied in order for humanity to progress in the middle way.

If we look at the global lag, it's appalling. The disparity and the extent of illiteracy in the developed world are truly shocking. In many developing countries, that the male-to-female literacy ratio is inexcusably high. In other words, not enough women are literate: There is as much as two to four times more literacy among men than among women.

When Americans took that first step on the moon in 1969, the leading edge of the written tradition had taken us there. At the same time, about 80 percent of African women were illiterate in that year. Now it's improved to 50 percent, a 30 percent increase in about fifty years. But we still need to accomplish more. We need to aim for 100% literacy among women.

Illiteracy has corollary effects. If women do not read, then they do not take as good care of their children. And the support structures are weaker in a culture that lacks literacy. This is reflected, for example, in infant mortality rates.

There are many other factors, such as war, epidemic, disease and all of that. But as literacy rises, so will the standard of living rise and so will infant mortality fall, among other things. The importance of literacy cannot be overemphasized.

Another unspeakably tragic issue involves child soldiers. This is what we see in cultures that have not understood the importance of education. Books and ideas are incomparably more constructive and empowering than guns, and far less expensive, and far longer-lived. Children belong in school. Not only are their childhoods being stolen from them, but also they will possibly be scarred for life.

Adults who participate in combat are often traumatized by their experiences. What about children? This is an unconscionable horror. We must do something to stop it.

I am also absolutely appalled by the global sex trade. I have a Japanese friend who was rescuing girls as young as five in Thailand.

We have to speak about these things in order to remedy them. Child soldiers around the world, and young girls being used around the world like this. This is a global disgrace. We have to find a way to do something about it.

Mahatma Gandhi said, "You can judge the morality of a nation by the way the society treats its animals." If that's true of animals, how much truer is it of children? The moral character of a global village can be judged by how it treats and mistreats its children. We're not doing as well as we need to do in many places.

Martin Luther King Jr., in one of his most memorable utterances, said something about the world in which he wanted his young children to grow up, a world in which they would be judged by "the content of their character" (*I Have a Dream: Martin Luther King Jr. and the Future of Multicultural America*, ed. James Echols [Minneapolis: Fortress Press, 2004], p. 7).

The politicization of higher education in the United States represents the other extreme. Allan Bloom wrote a bestselling book in the 1980s called *The Closing of the American Mind*. Everybody read it, but for some reason, nothing was accomplished. It just kept happening, like an epidemic. *Tenured Radicals* by Roger Kimball describes how power was consolidated in the '80s. I will quote from *Professing Feminism*—Daphne Patai and her colleague Norreta Koertge, two women who wanted to teach humanities but were forced to teach political indoctrination instead. Their careers were sabotaged when they refused. *The Shadow University* is the most shocking of all. It's a more current book by a courageous professor of history, Alan Kors.

Read *The Revolt of the Primitive* if you want to go into the psychological roots of political correctness. Howard Schwartz has done a remarkable job. And last, *The Middle Way* summarizes all these works and gives you a bibliography of them all.

Daphne Patai, who wrote *Professing Feminism*, teaches romance literature, Spanish and Portuguese. She says that she wanted to speak as a human. She wrote, "Over the years, this has become ever more difficult to achieve." She was pushed into activism and radical feminist studies. And then she went back to romance languages. "When I speak as a heterosexual woman," she says, "lesbian women could trump me. But if they're white, they could in turn be trumped by non-white women, lesbians or not. But it is my conviction that this is no way to run an academic life for teaching, and that identity politics has a pernicious effect on education." She concludes, "Evidently I'll have to wait for another life to be able to speak as a human."

I asked Daisaku Ikeda what was his philosophy of education, and this, in a nutshell, was it: Students must always be kept center stage in any educational effort. Anything that ignores their individuality, force feeds them knowledge, or pushes them into uniform mold must be rejected.

Of course I agree with this. That's been my lifelong philosophy, too. But it just so happens that mainstream American higher education has succumbed to ideologies that oppose what Mr. Ikeda and I both uphold. In the US, identity politics ignores individuality; political correctness force-feeds indoctrination; authoritarian administrations impose cookie-cutter molds on campus culture. This is utterly dehumanizing.

Those are the two extremes we need to work on: Insufficient literacy and inadequate education in much of the developing world, and politicization of the curriculum and conspicuous neglect of the content of character in the US and the developed world.

Raphael's "School of Athens" hangs in the Vatican, on public display. It was originally called "Knowledge of Causes." Raphael followed this dictum: Assemble the best that has been thought and said. In his imagination, he brought together Ptolemy and Euclid and Pythagoras and all of the great minds that he was aware of, and he put them in this wonderful academy. It's a beautiful painting. This is what education should be like, and must be like. It leads to blue skies and open archways. It's not a cloister. People go out from the university and disseminate their learning throughout the world. That's the open system, the good system.

This is brilliant and reflects, of course, Daisaku Ikeda's philosophy of education. It also reflects the New England Transcendentalist philosophy of education. This painting, a replica, hangs in Emerson's home in Concord, Massachusetts. I've seen it. It hangs over his dining table. He saw it every day and was inspired by it. It's also what we chose for the APPA logo, long before I met President Ikeda or encountered the SGI.

(2) Promoting sustainable economic and social development, is a huge area of responsibility. It's the second plank of the action program. Buddhism emphasizes the transitory nature of all phenomena. Consider the doctrine of dependent origination. Nothing is permanent. We finally found something that's permanent. The catch is, it's nothing.

What does this mean? "Sustainable development" has become a buzzword. I've been around this buzzword for more than twenty years, in the academy, in the applied ethics industry, and as a consultant to corporations. It means one of two things. There's the sincere meaning: people really trying to work to make things that last and minimize corollary damage from development. And then there are the very cynical ones to whom *sustainable development* means "let's make a pile of cash and get out before the whole thing collapses." This is, unfortunately, the un-salutary connotation that sustainable development has acquired.

Let's put it in context. Let's not be afraid to step back and take a cosmic view of sustainability. Let's ask ourselves—this is a philosophical question—"So what exactly is sustainable, and for how long?" The universe? A few trillion years. For us, that's an immeasurably long time. Now consider the sun, which will last only a few billion years. It's just a flickering ember in the cosmic hearth.

Life on earth will not last longer than the sun. When the sun reaches a supernova stage the earth will be incinerated. About 95 percent of all terrestrial life forms that ever existed are now extinct anyway, some of them no thanks to us. There were three great extinctions in biological history: at the end of the Permian period (about 245 million years ago), the late Cretaceous period (about 65 million years ago), and now we're in the midst of the third one. Not good. But most of evolutionary life doesn't survive. It's just simply not viable.

Here's something that survives quite well: Lingula, the lampshell. It's an inarticulate brachiopod, and it has survived for 400 million years. It's very sustainable, right? This thing is not too smart, but somehow it's figured out how to survive a long time. It's also asocial. Perhaps there's a moral in this somewhere. Now consider another interesting bunch of creatures, the hymenopterans or social insects: Ants, wasps, bees and also saw-flies. Remarkably, they've survived for around 140 million years. We know this because some of them have been preserved in amber, and we can date them. Economically they're really sustainable, except for honeybees whose populations are currently collapsing. Scientists call it "Hive Collapse Disorder," as though that explains why the hives are collapsing.

Well, we're probably doing something to the bees. Bees are socially rigid, in case you didn't know. Their social strata are rigidly caste-based; they're social and political lives are proto-totalitarian. If you're hatched in a beehive, your life is predetermined according to the caste that you're born into. You have no choice. Bees identify only with the collective. By definition they belong to a certain hive or formicary. They're ruled by a queen. And 95 percent of them are females, two-thirds genetically related. This explains altruism under kinship theory, a very important biological development. The 5 percent who are males are kept for breeding purposes. Social insects have no rights, but their societies are nonetheless sustainable.

Now here's an interesting correlation, which I discovered by accident in the British Library. I was looking at the life spans of primates. Humans are apparently the latest branch. If you graph the brain size of hominids starting with the Dryopithecine divergence about 15 million years ago — which produced the prototypical ancestor of ape and human — it becomes clear that the bigger our brains, the shorter our life expectancies as a species. In other words, the smarter we became, the quicker we became extinct. I guess that's the epitome of being "too smart for one's own good." Australopithecines were much smarter than apes, but they only lasted a quarter as long. The Proto-hominids were brilliant compared to the Australopithecines, but they only lasted a million years; Cro-Magnon, maybe half a million years or so. We have to find some better ways to exist on this planet if we're going to defeat this curve. This is our challenge.

For a long time we humans were an endangered species. Our natural population density is closest to wolves, if you look at the data. We were living in hunting and gathering bands of about 30 humans, more or less, ranging over about a thousand square miles — 0.03 people per square mile

was our optimum density. That meant if you had come to the five bor-
oughs of New York fifty thousand years ago you would have encountered
about ten people. Now our population density in New York and other
mega-cities is typically 25,000 to 40,000 people per square mile—1,000,000
times greater than 0.03. We have figured out how to sustain ourselves in
unbelievably dense agglomerations. But this produces all kinds of strange
behaviors.

> *Violence itself never prevents violence. Force*
> *can prevent violence—especially moral force.*
> *On the other hand, peace at all costs can*
> *lead to war at unimaginable cost. That's my*
> *cautionary tale to you.*

For a while, such increases in population density were very sustainable. But as we evolved more technology, especially since the Industrial
Revolution, this curve is shooting straight up. Some people say it's going
to level off, but we can't extrapolate. We only know it's not sustainable at
the present levels—unless certain parameters change drastically. (*Soylent
Green* being one among many possible futures.)

When you're "under the radar" (not significantly affecting natural
resources), the planet doesn't even know you're there. For most of our existence, the planet never knew or cared.

When population gets very, very dense, we end up depleting natural
resources. How do we correct that? We introduce synthetic resources. And
then we become dependent on the synthetic resources, because there are
no more natural resources. But there's a lag in the delivery system of the
synthetic stuff.

If you're living with nature, there are cycles, not lags. You're foraging,
you're hunting, you're fishing, you're gardening. But if you're inhabiting a
big city, you're dependent on complex supply chains, and there are bound

to be technological glitches and temporal lags. There are many ways in which people can be affected by lags. Certain kinds of goods may be in short supply; parts may be on order; supply chains may be disrupted at any time. In the developing world, the so-called "digital divide" is an example of a persistent technological lag, which still shuts millions of people out of cyberspace.

What is stability? It's sustainability. Human hunting and gathering tribes lasted as long as a hundred thousand years. They were economically sustainable but socially static. Nothing really changed. World religions have been with us for only a few thousand years. Relatively speaking, that's just like yesterday, at least from a philosopher's viewpoint. Just "yesterday," we started debating moral issues. Religions have been economically sustainable, too, but they require periodic social reform, don't they? All religions have evolved either by allowing reform, or by being reformed.

Most democratic nation-states are only a few centuries or decades old in their current form. This is a very short time. Democracy is a political experiment. Democracies have been economically sustainable, but with setbacks. They experience depressions, recessions and bubbles. But they're socially progressive. The golden age of capitalism lasted only about thirty years. It was economically unsustainable, but socially revolutionary.

The Summer of Love 1968 lasted only two to three months. I was there. It was great. But it was not sustainable. Those of us who were there will always remember the Summer of Love, sustainable or not. The memory is very sustainable.

The moral is that there's a tension between economic sustainability and social progress. If you want long-term economic sustainability, you might end up with a harsh political system, and a rigid social structure.

If we want to accentuate human qualities and introduce progress, which presumably we do, then we have to risk the sustainability factor. So please consider this when you're trying to build sustainable things. Ask whether they're progressive, and what kind of tradeoff is worthwhile for you.

Voyager I was launched in 1977, and it's carrying a gold record. They didn't have digital recording in 1977. They put the music on a record coated with gold. At this writing, Voyager I is just about to leave our solar system.

The record includes Glenn Gould performing music from Bach. This is like a message in the bottle. The record includes music from fifty cultures. Now this is sustainable. Because maybe eons from now, some intelligent advanced alien civilization is going to recover this thing and they're going to listen to this record, obviously. And they're going to say, "Wow, who was this guy?"

If you want to sustain something for a long time, send it into space. I'm serious. It's not just for our sake. It has to be for everybody out there, whoever they are. Let's put our best foot forward into space. Notice when people collected material for Voyager I, they did not send, for example, *The Rise and Fall of the Third Reich* into space. They didn't send Gibbon's *Decline and Fall of the Roman Empire* into space. They sent our most valuable gifts: music, not histories of empires (no matter how well-written). They sent up things that epitomize human culture at its best: creativity and artistry. Now that's sustainable.

(3) Promoting respect for all human rights. Of course, this is a vital plank.

Pop quiz. I am a professor, so I have a right to pop quiz you. What's a right? Anyone? A right is an entitlement, whose exercise entails an obligation.

Where do rights originate? Do rights exist in nature? I think not. There are no rights in nature, where only "might is right." You have perhaps the instinct to preserve yourselves, but that's it. On this planet, rights emerge only in human cultures.

Are rights automatically conferred on people? That's an easy question. Unfortunately, not. Rights usually need to be won, safeguarded, defended, and preserved. Rights are precious; they don't come easily, nor are they effortlessly self-perpetuating. They have to be sustained. We have to work at it.

Can rights be exercised in a social or political vacuum? No, they can't. Why? Because the exercise of a right entails an obligation. This is a very serious proposition; ethicists call it the correlativity thesis.

The exercise of a positive right entails an obligation to provide something. For example, to exercise our right to vote, we need candidates and ballots. The state has an obligation to provide these things. If it fails to do so, our right to vote cannot be exercised, even if it exists on paper. This goes for all positive rights.

A negative right is not necessarily bad. "Negative" has a negative reputation. Negatives can be very good. Defendants want verdicts of "not guilty." We all want medical tests to come back "negative." In terms of rights, the exercise of a negative right entails an obligation not to interfere. For example, if you have the right to freedom of expression, then I have an obligation not to interfere with your expression. If you have a right to peaceable assembly, then I have an obligation not to interfere with that assembly.

Rights and obligations go hand in glove. Wherever obligations are not met, rights, even if mandated, cannot be exercised. This poses problems. We have many menus of rights that we say must be applied to all people everywhere. But the structures and the infrastructures that do not buy into the obligatory part of the thesis are not allowing these rights to be exercised.

The problem is not so much the consciousness and definition and articulation of rights. The problem is getting people and governments to live up to their obligations. Especially in the case of governments, this can be a challenging mission. Governments are generally fearful of social unrest, so sometimes they can be persuaded that granting people rights and living up to governmental obligations may make society less prone to upheaval.

But what rights should we have? This is a normative philosophical question, and extraordinarily challenging.

I'm going to tell you something that strikes me as inevitable—that we're guaranteed cultural conflicts over certain questions. If we want to introduce rights, we have to ask what rights we're going to introduce and universalize. And if we do this, we are going to have disagreements. Why? Just look at the menus with which we're already saddled—human rights, for example. What about animal rights? Peter Singer has a chair at Princeton University for saying that animals have rights, too. In fact, he thinks that animals have more rights than humans. I wouldn't go that far. Meanwhile, I have never heard of an animal rightist who applied his ethics by feeding himself to the sharks, whereas many Buddhists have self-immolated to protest wrongdoing against their fellow humans.

As Buddhists, we respect sentient life in all forms, do we not? We have to respect sentience that is not restricted to human beings. Therefore it follows that animals deserve to be treated well insofar as they're sentient. But sometimes that will bring us into conflict with our own rights -- such as when we decide to eat other sentient beings (be they reptiles, fishes, birds, or mammals) – to exercise our fundamental right to self-preservation. This represents a potential ethical conflict for non-vegetarian Buddhists.

Individual versus group rights – individuals have rights; groups don't. There are many, many people in the United States and the developed world, however, who think that group rights take precedence over individual rights. This signals a mutation of the philosophy of rights and the theory of rights since their inception. And I think a very dangerous one, because it ends up denying individual rights. If group A has rights that some other group B doesn't have, then everyone in group B is denied their individual rights. Whereas if everyone has equal rights, membership in one group or another can never be used to deny anyone his or her rights. And nota bene, those who have strayed too far to the other extreme: Racism is unjust, and so is reverse-racism. Sexism is unjust, and so is reverse sexism. Rights can be justly granted on one basis only: the basis of one's humanity. Membership in any other sub-group is irrelevant to one's entitlements, because equal rights are granted to all individual humans. Group rights fostered by identity politics have eroded equal rights for all, just as bigotry erodes them at the other extreme. Group rights dis-empower people; individual rights empower everybody.

Heterosexual versus LGBT. We have numerous conflicts going on now in our country, including legislative battles, judicial challenges, and social disputes over the nature and norms of human sexuality. Heterosexuality is a long-standing norm, but numerous other kinds of sexual expression have accompanied human evolution and civilization in every generation, and many for that matter are observable among the apes. We currently see many human beings with different orientations, and they're saying they're entitled to rights, too. And I think they are. I am close to 100% libertarian on this topic. I believe that consenting adults have a fundamental right to do pretty much whatever they please behind closed doors, provided they aren't harming sentient beings or disturbing their neighbors. That's close to John Stuart Mill's position in *On Liberty*, which according to Isaiah Berlin is the greatest defense ever written of individual liberty.

I think human beings merit human rights no matter what their sexual orientation, subject to them being adults and not harming anyone. But this opens a door onto dispute: to begin with, at what age will they be considered "adult"? There is no universal agreement on this.

But I also believe that we can't debate these issues rationally until the media circus is tamed. Pierre Elliott Trudeau, the former prime minister of Canada, said – this was back in 1967 – "There's no place for the state in the bedrooms of the nation" (see http://www.cbc.ca/archives/categories/politics/rights-freedoms/trudeaus-omnibus-bill-challenging-canadian-taboos/theres-no-place-for-the-state-in-the-bedrooms-of-the-nation.html). I guess Trudeau had read *On Liberty*, too.

If gays and lesbians are demanding the same rights, for example the right to marry, there are a lot of people who say the sacrament of marriage is only between men and women because its purpose is to bring forth children. It's very complicated.

Then there's abortion: If you think you have a right to an abortion and someone else thinks that the right to life mandates the protection of the fetus, there's a conflict.

Perhaps you think you have a right to euthanasia, which means "good death." I've counseled clients who are dying, and their worry is not that they're dying, but that they just want a good death. Doctors, however, won't allow them to stockpile medication. There's a lot of fear among people who receive terminal prognoses because they're afraid they're going to die in pain, for example. Physician-assisted suicide is still not really available, and I don't think Dr. Kevorkian is the answer.

Perhaps you believe you have a duty to preserve life at all costs because you value life, but someone else may say, "I'm dying, and I should be able to choose my death." This is a conflict.

There are many such conflicts: Higher education, right or privilege? I think it should be a privilege, earned by good performance on a level playing field. Primary and secondary education, kindergarten through high school, is obligatory in any civilized country. But those who are able to earn the privilege of higher education should be able to do so.

Health care, right or privilege? You're individuals who all have opinions on this, and they're all important. But is it a right or a privilege? In socialized democracies, it's a right. In this country, it's a privilege. We have too many people who have no access to healthcare because it's a privilege. But even where it's a right, it doesn't always work. For example, in Britain, the national healthcare system is considerably under-funded. In theory, people have a right to a hip transplant, for example, if they need one.

The catch is that the waiting list is six years long. The system is actually killing people. There were 1,500 deaths annually in London alone last time I tracked this—elderly people dying of hypothermia or pneumonia, because they're not moving around enough. A lot of them are not going to live long enough to actually exercise the right. The just obligation would be to deliver what you have a right to in a timely way. No matter what you do with health care, this is a very difficult question.

So if we're going to assert that we need to respect all human rights everywhere, then we're basically making an incoherent statement. We have to say what those rights are, and we have to give good reasons for asserting the value of some rights, and perhaps diminishing our commitment to others. A very difficult question. Who will determine the menu of universal human rights? You will, over time, so please choose wisely. At least make informed choices. That's my purpose here, to get you thinking about these things.

(5) Equality, meaning equality and not something else—let's talk about this a little bit. Think about this: One plus four is five, right? Two plus three is also five. These sums are equal, but they're not the same. "One plus four" is not the same as "two plus three." They are equal but they're not the same. Equality is not sameness, in this case.

I'm saying to you that matriarchy equals patriarchy. This is radical equality. Matriarchy equals patriarchy. Equal how? In their importance to humanity. But they're also different in their complementarities. The rules that matriarchs play by and the rules that patriarchs play by are complementary rules, and they're different rules at times.

Think of the game show *Let's Make a Deal*, where contestants are offered a choice of three doors. In our case, it's really three planets. There are three kinds of inequality in the male chauvinist planet. The male has more of everything than the female. Right? And the male has also a disproportionately large influence in the female's life. She has a disproportionately small influence on his life. Right? Those are the three kinds of inequality.

What's the second planet? We have the same thing in reverse, with exactly the same disproportions, but in favor of women. If you're a militant feminist, this is your idea of utopia, definitely. And then you have the third planet. This is the egalitarian, humanist planet where we share equally. We have a division of power. We have the same amount of control and the same amount of influence over each other's lives. We honor and cherish and respect our differences. We also know that we're complementary parts of a greater whole, namely humanity. And we come in two flavors, male and female. That's the planet I think we have to live on. I don't see any other choice. We have to live on the egalitarian humanist planet.

Humans are the sum of nature plus culture. There are two things going on with us, what we're born with and what we acquire. They're both important. Ignoring the power of culture, which is what the chauvinists do, leads to sexual segregation based on exaggeration of differences. That's the chauvinist answer. Others base everything on exaggerating differences between men and women. That's the caveman model. That was adaptive a hundred thousand years ago. It got us here. It's not adaptive anymore.

But, on the other hand, ignoring the power of nature leads to social engineering based on denial of differences. For example, a militant feminist extreme. It's a Marxist model. Equality of opportunity between men and women does not guarantee sameness of outcome. Equality is not sameness. We don't have to be the same to be equal. We can be different. It's OK to be different.

The danger of revolutions is that the extremists take over. This is the unfortunate chronicle of human history. When we make revolutions even for a good cause, all too often the extremists get control of the reins. So what starts off as a well-intentioned, progressive exercise turns into another kind of manifestation of extremism. It has happened the world over.

Many revolutions have gone wrong because the extremists got hold of the process. For example, can we liberate women without destroying men? Yes, I think we can. Are we doing it that way? No, we're not. Those of you who are working for the equality of women see inequalities that you want to remedy, and I think it's very important that you do. On the other hand, you don't have to demonize or destroy men to do this. Matriarchy does not have to destroy patriarchy. Matriarchy, to be equal to patriarchy, has to respect it, just as it wants respect in return.

This is what some call the gender wars. Christina Hoff Sommers does a good job of explaining who were the radicals who hijacked the revolution and the feminist takeover, patriarchy and matriarchy in two decades. There's a lot of hatred of men, a lot of disrespect for men. I feel it very strongly. I feel it in the public media and elsewhere. Hatred is wrong no matter where it occurs, in all minds. It's a poison and it spreads like one. Hatred of anything is wrong.

That's why I'm here, to remind you that one extreme is not better than another extreme. We need the Middle Way. All of you are brilliant activists. You're all young, vibrant, intelligent, and you have the right heart and the right mind. But understand the problems on the ground and then you can do something meaningful to address them. There is a war against boys in this country, and it's going to destroy this culture if it gets out of hand. The war against men is also ongoing. And the war against the family. All those things.

Liberating women is necessary and has been necessary for a long time. But it's not necessary to destroy patriarchy in order to do so. We have to have an egalitarian humanist planet. That's what we have to inhabit. It's not dominance of one over the other; it's sharing of our humanity.

I want to introduce you to Elaine Newman, a mentor of mine. She's a great Canadian scientist, an exemplary professor, and a humanist. She's a wonderful person. I think she represents a model for the feminist revolution. She went to Harvard and earned a doctorate in microbiology back in the late 1950s. She was the only woman in her class, and she had to put up with a lot. Being the first is always difficult, no matter what mountain you're climbing. She was a pioneer.

What did she do? Did she avenge herself on men? No. She developed a great career in Canada, became an important professor, raising millions in research funds for her laboratories, and training young PhDs, men and women alike, from around the world. Being even more visionary, she created Science College. She wanted to encourage more women to get involved in science, so that women would not meet with the same challenges she met with. But she didn't say we have to hate men, or need quota systems.

She recruited some men, too, because she was interested in minds at the end of the day, and minds have no gender. She was my mentor, and under her mentorship I became a Commonwealth Scholar, and went to graduate school in London. Professor Newman gave me a very solid foundation through Science College. She was a great woman.

Then she was offered the directorship of the Simone De Beauvoir Institute at the same university. Simone De Beauvoir was a fine philosopher, but this Institute was a thin cover for a militant patriarchy-smashing agenda. That's why Elaine refused it. She said she didn't become a professor to teach hatred or contempt. She stayed with Science College, and she encourages women and men alike. That, for me, is exemplary humanism.

(8) The last point I want to make today is about promoting international peace and security. Let's try to understand some of the philosophical challenges we face. This is most important, because if the world is at war, everything else is going to be in a holding pattern. So how do we promote international peace and security? Thomas Hobbes showed us why it's such a daunting challenge, seemingly in every generation.

Hobbes (1588–1679) was an Early Modern philosopher, a contemporary of Descartes and Spinoza. He founded two fields—political science and empirical psychology. A remarkable philosopher, Hobbes lived to ninety-one; but his life was often in danger owing to his then-heterodox political and religious views, especially after publishing *Leviathan*, his magnum opus, in 1651. In it, Hobbes gave us an enduring blueprint for separating church from state, for removing political power from religious authorities and placing it in the hands of secular government. Anyone who studies modern political science begins with *The Leviathan*.

Hobbes explored the rapacious dimension of human nature. To understand the nature of war and conflict and its resolution, he had to probe the darker recesses of the human psyche. In fact, he anticipated Freud. In the sections on human nature in *The Leviathan*, you will find at least three major ideas that Freud later went on to make great hay with.

Hobbes is an important figure for many reasons. For one, he gave us a dilemma. A Hobbes scholar described this dilemma as a "bone." Hobbes didn't create the problem, he only identified it, but it is a bone lodged in the throat of international peace.

It goes something like this: Hobbes wanted to resolve the problem of civil war, but he realized that the resolution of the problem of civil war itself would potentially lead to international conflict. That was the dilemma. If you want civil peace, you run the risk of international conflict. This was Hobbes's problem. Why? Because civil conflicts are resolved by establishing a secular, sovereign government, he said, and enforcing a binding social contract.

Modern social contract theory originated with Hobbes. He stimulated Jean-Jacques Rousseau, John Locke, and many others to think about this problem. Even if it's a fair and just contract, Hobbes said, it would still need to be enforced, because some people will always try to cheat one another, and the system. Hence, we need law enforcement. Use of force is mandated, which can change into violence if we're not careful. If you need to arrest somebody, usually you have the power of arrest, which sometimes entails force.

Enforcement versus violence is an important distinction. Law enforcement exists for this reason. It's not crime prevention, it's law enforcement. Every single nation has this power of a sovereign with control over the justice system, as well as control over defense. That's common to all autonomous nation states. There was no general conception of what we today call a *nation state* until after the Napoleonic Wars. Hobbes, however, was a prescient philosopher. He saw this coming, 150 years before Napoleon.

The problem is that sovereigns themselves are subject to no overarching authority. There's no automatically or easily enforceable international contract that anyone can impose upon sovereigns. Wars are often fought over whose law is going to prevail.

We can't force a sovereign to join a social contract without violating our own principles. If force turns into violence, then we're doing the very thing we tried to prevent. At the same time, if we don't stand up to tyrants, then we're allowing them to inflict violence on their own people, and possibly their neighbors.

This is a cautionary tale: After World War I, the allies were so terrified of war that they allowed Hitler to get away with everything and anything in order to keep peace. He had taken the Rhineland. He had annexed Austria. Hitler kept saying, "This is my last demand." And everyone wanted peace.

Then Hitler said, "Now I need Czechoslovakia, because we have some German-speaking people there, and they should be part of the Reich." Everybody said "OK" (except the Czech government!). In 1938, Neville Chamberlain, the British prime minister, gave Hitler Czechoslovakia. It was tragic. The Czechoslovakian government was kept outside in a waiting room while the Germans, the English and the French carved up their map. Then Chamberlain and Hitler came out and said, "Your country doesn't exist anymore, but it's for the sake of peace." It wasn't. In fact, it made the war much worse. When war came, it was the most devastating war yet fought.

The point is that it could have been stopped. In those days Winston Churchill was a voice in the wilderness. He was politically ostracized when he said about the Munich deal, "We have sustained a total and unmitigated defeat." Later the British elected him leader, and he saved England but at huge cost. We're still paying the price. The Cold War came out of that war.

The whole thing could have been stopped if they had stood up to Hitler. That is to say, made a show of force, not of violence. Force is not violence.

What I want to say to you is that the price of delusion can be high, and sometimes force is needed to prevent violence. Violence itself never prevents violence. Force can prevent violence — especially moral force. On the other hand, peace at all costs can lead to war at unimaginable cost. That's my cautionary tale to you.

Please be careful about tyrants. The twentieth century was the worst century ever for war, but there's great hope here at the end. I want to share hope with you.

This sovereign terror (of Hitler, Tojo, Stalin, and World War II) was exactly a Hobbesian problem. No one could arrest these sovereigns, because they had mobilized the entire resources of nations in order to resist arrest, and in the process tens of millions of people were murdered. Unbelievable. The only one to repent was Hideki Tojo, prime minister of Japan. He was hanged as a war criminal, but he at least apologized before he died.

Tsunesaburo Makiguchi (founding president of the Soka Gakkai and mentor to Josei Toda, who followed him as Soka Gakkai president and, in turn, became mentor to Daisaku Ikeda) died in prison, where he had been confined by the Japanese militarist government. Mr. Toda was also imprisoned, and later released. Anybody who stood up to the government would have been imprisoned or killed. That's the problem. They had no respect for the moral dignity of the human being.

How do we apply moral force? This is the beautiful part. Terror does not have sovereignty. It is not sustainable. Moral force has sovereignty and is sustainable. Non-violent resistance to oppression works in certain conditions. It has to be undertaken by fearless activists. Throughout human history, we have a long record of fearless activism and non-violent resistance to oppression by the wielding of moral force.

Mahatma Gandhi was assassinated by a fanatic, but not before he led India to home rule via moral force. Gandhi had no army. Gandhi had no official position. Gandhi had no business card. Yet he single-handedly persuaded the British to give up the jewel in the crown of their empire. How did he do that? By applying moral force, *satyagraha*, a firm and unflinching adherence to truth. Moral force proved stronger than the Imperial power of Britain.

Martin Luther King was also assassinated. It's hard to believe that he accomplished so much in such a short life—civil rights for African Americans via moral force. He and Gandhi were both inspired by Thoreau and civil disobedience. Like Gandhi, King never took up arms.

What do they have in common? They were willing to die for their principles but not to kill for them. That's the quintessence of moral force. You have to be courageous enough to be willing to lay down your life but not to take other life in defense of your principles. Thank goodness that we have had such courageous people in every generation. This is the courage that you must exercise, too — your moral force. You will not kill for your principles, but you will die for them if need be. That's the hardest price to pay, but it is what makes moral force sovereign over terror.

How do we internationalize moral force? Socrates was born in Athens, and he exercised it there. Nichiren exercised it in Japan; Gandhi in India; Dr. King, here in the United States.

Now the question is, how do we transplant moral force internationally? We have to be able to export that moral force and bring it into the regimes of other tyrants so that it can flower there. That's what the culture of peace has to do, and that's your mission, to transplant the culture of peace into other countries.

The *noosphere*—have you heard this word? It's made up of Greek components, and it means "the thinking envelope of earth." It was coined by a French scientist named Pierre Teilhard de Chardin. He was Jesuit, a paleontologist, and a mystic. He conducted research into the natural history of our species. He discovered Peking Man. He said the real evolution that has to take place next—he was speaking around mid-twentieth century—is the evolution of human consciousness.

Now this is the beautiful part. The evolution of consciousness, he said, has to be manifested in this thinking envelope of earth. There's a zone of thought that encircles the globe and influences human behavior and human identity. That's the noosphere. This is where we will live and work.

You know that there are necessary partnerships between public sector, private sector and civil sector organizations. Governments and businesses and NGOs have to partner in order to manage planetary affairs. No one can do it alone. These conceptual partnerships envelope the earth in a plan for sustainable progress, peace, rights, education. This is all happening in the noosphere.

Cyberspace is also part of the noosphere. How do we get connected with people all over the earth instantaneously? Via the thinking envelope of earth. The understanding that we all inhabit one place, namely the global village, permeates the noosphere. Wherever you happen to be locally, you're still a part of a global network. Every locality is a region of globality. Everything is global now.

So this is where we have to build a culture of peace: in the thinking envelope of earth. We must help to evolve a new consciousness for humanity. Surely this is what the real revolution is about. It unfolds in the noosphere, in the thinking envelope of earth, and so it embraces us all.

My encouragement to you is to carry on in this great spirit that you've shown. First, make your foundations as deep as your aspirations are lofty, and your edifice will stand tall. Then make your hopefulness more abundant than the world's despair. We can always find despair in the world if we look for it. But if your hopefulness is more abundant, then hopefulness will prevail. Make your ideals compatible with justice, and you will realize them. Make your actions selfless, and they will engender enduring peace. It's not for you or for me. We don't act for ourselves. We act for the greater good, for the cosmic consciousness of humankind.

Questions and Answers

AUDIENCE MEMBER 1: Could you give a definition of world peace in maybe one or two sentences?

MARINOFF: One sentence is that it has to be the absence of war. There has to be an absence of overt conflict in order for peace to take root. But there has to be more than this. This is an old story, but this is the other side of peace and the dimension that's often neglected.

Signing a treaty doesn't end conflict. We have to have peace in each human being's heart and mind, and then we'll have global peace. It starts with you.

AUDIENCE MEMBER 2: I read your bio and some of the discussions you had with President Ikeda in 2003. I am curious to know, are there any topics that stayed on your mind since then, and that you studied further more deeply since those discussions.

MARINOFF: Much more has transpired since. I've been twice to Tokyo and met with President Ikeda on both occasions. For our first dialogue, we were scheduled to have two hours. Instead, we had three. We stayed overtime because it was a tremendously inspiring experience. He said to me afterward that he had asked only 15 to 20 percent of the questions that he had prepared.

Consequently, we continued our interchange. As a result, we met again in 2007. At that meeting, we resolved that we would commit to a written dialogue. All of the issues have been revisited in deeper and more elaborate ways. And there are also new things on the table.

AUDIENCE MEMBER 3: I read the dialogue as well and it mentioned poetry and freedom, also how they link to art and its influence on philosophy, as well as philosophy and its influence on art and artists.

MARINOFF: Poetry is almost an indescribable art. We can teach music. We can teach dance. I've been a student of music almost all my life, and a teacher of music at certain points. But poetry is much more difficult. It seems to be very compact, almost like chanting. Both are compact, and powerful. I think that poets have to be inspired in some way, but they don't need to know exactly what they're doing when they're writing poetry. People at this high level of composition/creativity often say they're just vehicles for what's coming out of them. It's a process that's unfolding through them. I think poetry is like that.

How does it relate to philosophy? Well, maybe poetry is the most compact expression of philosophy. There's so much that one can read into a good poem. But philosophy and art are deeply connected.

Those of you who read The Middle Way, you know that I devote some time to expressing the same thing, that philosophy and music and mathematics are very closely related. These are extremely interesting matters.

AUDIENCE MEMBER 4: I was also reading the dialogues and I was fascinated by the definition of philosophy and how it uses doubt as an instrument to reveal the truth. The only time I feel like my mind and my heart really come together is when I'm chanting. At other times, I go back to the debate between my mind and my heart. How does one find balance between the heart and the mind, or is it even possible?

MARINOFF: I wish I could tell you that. That's a great question. Many schools of Buddhism teach this, about the discursive mind. We have an ongoing dialogue with ourselves a lot of the time, anyway, if we're not disciplining our minds, or if we're not focusing and being attentive to other things that are going on, we will end up in this cycle of a discursive mind, a grasping mind. There's no end to that. I think when philosophers are wrestling with a problem we're trying not to do that. We don't want to have a fruitless discourse. We would like to be very focused on a particular problem. We need to have mental acuity to do this.

Insofar as we're using words to challenge ideas, I think doubt is useful. Doubt is not a way of life in and of itself. I believe that all of us have the capacity for faith and all of us have the capacity for doubt, and these things are balanced in us. When we need to make inquiry, if we resort only to faith, the danger is that it can become blind, and blind faith allows people to be swayed by dogma. President Ikeda, for example, is a relentless inquirer. Why? Because he's always wanting to reveal more truth and get to the bottom of things. He is a philosopher in this, using dialogue as an instrument of inquiry. If you're asking questions, they can't be leading questions like a lawyer asks.

This kind of inquiry, which is doubt based, opens the mind, and so that seed of doubt can be very useful.

On the other hand, people who have too much doubt and don't manifest enough faith can become bitter and skeptical and cynical.

We need faith in our lives, and we need doubt in our lives. How do you attain the balance? I think by practice. That's the only way.

AUDIENCE MEMBER 5: Do you think there is a universal beauty?

MARINOFF: Yes, because I'm a Platonist. It seems clear that Plato, who learned a lot from Pythagoras, who learned a lot from India, may have been connected to some Indian, including Buddhist, teachings. Plato certainly came after Shakyamuni, so it's possible that he learned something from the Buddha.

He had, for example, the doctrine of reincarnation. The Greeks had a doctrine they called *metempsychosis*, "transmigration of souls," which sounds a lot like the Indian doctrine of reincarnation. It seems that Indian philosophy had already made some inroads into the Western world at the time of Polemic civilization.

I find this fascinating. Is there beauty? Yes, of course. Plato said that everything has a form, and that these forms are outside space and time and not susceptible to causal forces. So, there's permanence in form. Music has a form. Chanting has a form. These forms may be copies of pure forms, which the mind can apprehend. As humans, we are uniquely gifted with minds that can apprehend what Plato called "the pure forms." Indian philosophy and subsequently Buddhism have refined to a much more sophisticated model, if you like, of mind.

AUDIENCE MEMBER 5: I asked because I realized that, for example, with modern arts and modern music, they seem more dissonant. I feel that things that are somewhat chaotic or asymmetric are more and more appreciated.

MARINOFF: Yes, insofar as art represents what we experience in life, it may reflect what people relate to. Certainly, postmodern life is chaotic. Think of Chaos Theory. Out of chaos comes order. When things get chaotic enough, very deep order becomes apparent.

AUDIENCE MEMBER 6: History has shown that major movements have often been driven by youth, and that philosophy behind the youth has been very poor. What is your assessment of how healthy we are philosophically? Also, would you share with us your thoughts about where the youth are in terms of philosophy? What do you think we can do to change it?

MARINOFF: This is also something that affects me very deeply because I inherit a lot of these kids when they get to the university. They're not youth anymore at that point. One can see from the way they react in the classroom, the way they think, the way they speak and the way they write. One can infer a lot about their upbringing.

Aside from that, I'm on the record as a crusader against the "big pharma" drug culture, the prescriptive diagnostic culture we have in the United States, and the extent to which the pharmaceutical industry has colonized the medical profession so that every human complaint attracts a diagnosis now. Where there's a diagnosis, there's a drug. These things never touch at all the heart of what I think is really afflicting most people. I'm not against medicine, far from it. Thanks to modern medicine, our life expectancies have almost doubled. Vaccination and antibiotics and all the "miracles" of modern medicine are wonderful. But allopathic medicine at its extreme doesn't treat the person. It treats the ailments. You become an inconvenience. And you become an inconvenience if you have a question. Doctors don't have enough time to interact with their patients.

The educational system has failed. It comes hand in glove with not engaging young children's minds in cognitively salutary pathways. Kids are watching four-and-a-half hours of television a day from the time they're born. They're cognitively impaired by the time they get to school. They're playing way too many video games.

Vision is our preeminent sense. This is how we're different from the other animals. We evolved to use vision in important ways. But the best way to learn is not through television. The best way to learn is through the written tradition, mediated by personal contact with a teacher or mentor. But the written tradition is being replaced by visual and digital traditions. And this has caused what I'm calling "cognitive impairment" in a whole generation of people.

Add to this the sociological factors, including latchkey children and skyrocketing divorce rates. A couple of years ago, America crossed a Rubicon in that more than 50 percent of its families have less than two parents in the house. This is another kind of catastrophe. I firmly believe—I'm very traditional and I really believe—that children need to have both parents in order to experience the maternal and the paternal sides of humanity. Regardless of the gender of the child, children need both parents in their lives. Developmentally it's much better. They also need a peer group. When the peer group has to play the role of the parents, then you have gangs.

One could highlight sociological and pharmacological and familial and other factors. The schools are afraid to educate now. There are so many other things that are going on that are not healthy. Yet youth will always respond to something positive. Youth is so full of hope and enthusiasm and optimism. It is malleable. Unfortunately, it can adjust to appalling conditions and doesn't know the difference. Kids aren't full of judgment, which is their blessing. But if they're getting substandard cultures, if their enculturation is not as effective as it should be, they'll respond to that in ineffective ways and become dysfunctional.

What can we do about this? Many things. In a certain way, this should encourage you. We want people to reach their potentials. But if the culture is not doing it, then obviously it's the culture itself that needs to be reworked. The Soka Gakkai International as a movement has a tremendous amount to offer if it can find a way to bring its message into a broader education.

In Japan I met with many of the children and educators in the Soka school system, as well as the university. We need somehow to make that kind of system more accessible to more people, and then they will gravitate to it. There's no question. Children are not fools. When they see something good, they will respond to it. We need to offer them a better quality of life and a better culture than they're getting now.

AUDIENCE MEMBER 7: You talk about "nobody rules truth." That concept and things like political and religious dogmas can cloud issues. How would you characterize what's going on politically now? Is anything useful?

MARINOFF: I am not a party political animal in this country. I don't like extremism on the left, and I don't like extremism on the right. I would like to see the middle way better-represented in politics. We have this two-party system, and the pendulum swings from one party to the other. One party is in for eight years, and half the population is totally disgusted with it. Then the next party comes in for eight years, and the other half is totally disgusted with it. When things go well economically, politicians take credit. When things go badly, they blame the opposition. It's just posturing.

I think that there's a real opportunity for change. This was one of the planks of [then president-elect] Barack Obama's platform – change. We certainly need some things to change. I remember the Clinton administration promising to change healthcare, but that didn't really happen. And education was something that Bush wanted to change, but he only made it worse.

The president of this country is not a dictator, thank goodness. But that means that each president has to make compromises. That's the democratic way. Consequently, things get watered down because you have to get enough people on your side.

There's been a lot of optimism in Europe already. This I know from my European colleagues, who are expressing expectation that the new administration is going to make some positive changes.

AUDIENCE MEMBER 8: In one of Obama's speeches he talked about the young generation, "Generation Z," as having the ability to reject the myth that we're an apathetic generation, that we don't care and all we do is play video games.

MARINOFF: You're still a youth, and the twenties is a great time. But on the other hand, you're a young adult. That means you need to be a role model. What youth need are people to be there. Youth do not need people on TV. They don't need talking heads. They need people in the room, in their lives. They need people to be there. You may need other people to be in the room with you. Maybe I and others of my generation can serve that purpose for you.

We need real human contact. This is one of the things that's been eroded by technology.

The extended family was a wonderful institution. It had drawbacks, but it allowed at least three generations to cohabitate. Young people could learn from the stories of their grandparents and parents.

Looking that far back would give us windows onto the future, whereas many kids today inhabit a timeless and placeless shopping mall. There's no sense of continuity. They've lost that grounding in the extended family. That's why presence is really important, being present for them. They need this. We all do.

AUDIENCE MEMBER 9: You also talked about encountering people who have no sense of purpose in life. How can you encourage that kind of person?

MARINOFF: That's a very difficult question. If people want a dialogue, if people want to come to the table, then we can do many things. This works also in political realms. We can solve a lot of problems when we dialogue with people. A lot of violence can be curtailed or even prevented if we can talk.

But sometimes people don't want to talk, and then we have a dilemma. How do we get them to the table without compromising our own principles? That's a big challenge.

What I've seen is that technologies really do a disservice to us. This problem is widespread in Japan now. I was working with Soka counselors who were describing this problem, and we were brainstorming about how to resolve it. You know, technology tends to dissociate people from reality and from one another. Everyone is wired to his or her own universe. Again, it's about human contact.

If you wanted to have music in your home a hundred years ago, you had to play an instrument. Everyone was playing an instrument and making music as a family. They were producing culture, and that act of creation and production brought them close together and strengthened human bonds. Now people are wired to their own mp3 player, and they're not even talking. They've become consumers only.

With people who are totally withdrawn or totally apathetic, we must try to bring them into the circle. Don't pressure them or make them feel they have to contribute, but let them be with others who are in dialogue. Just invite them to sit there and say, "Just be with us." And then see if that doesn't awaken in them the desire to join a human circle and to contribute. Maybe that will work in some cases.

AUDIENCE MEMBER 10: Thank you for what you've said about connecting. You put it down on the youth today. That's really true.

What do you feel is the global philosophy, the global way of thinking, that gets us into these constant conflicts and wars? How can we really change that and create a new world, a new history where that doesn't constantly happen?

MARINOFF: I like your enthusiasm. You're already making a difference. We have a very positive thing that's going on with technology, because it connects people who are very far away and brings them very close, which shrinks time and space. But I'm not saying spend all your life online.

I'm saying that cyberspace makes us aware of what Buddhism taught along time ago, namely the interconnectedness of all beings. Cyberspace is a way in which we experience being connected to anybody. This is a good thing. This will help to break down xenophobic barriers.

But as far as the conflicts are concerned, it's a biological evolutionary story. The positive side of it is that the human being is capable of what I would call a "psychic evolution." It's the psychic evolution that we need to work on. Biological evolution happens over long time scales, and so we don't see it in our lifetimes. But we have this capacity to evolve cultures. Cultures are not determined; our DNA is determined. You didn't choose your genes, but you do choose your culture, and that's the key.

We're not condemned, as *Homo sapiens*, to be at perpetual war.

If we're in a civil society, if people break the law—assuming we have just laws—people can be brought to justice within a given nation state under its body of law.

But in the international system, there's no equivalent body of law. There are only embryonic forms of government like the United Nations.

When an outlaw resists arrest, we may have to use force to arrest him. Force is OK. Violence is not.

When people can harness the entire resources of nations and resist arrest by the international community, then we're in trouble. If we leave them alone, they will go on a rampage and commit horrible atrocities on the people in their sphere of influence. If we try to stop them, we then have to resort to violence, because force is not enough if they're advanced in their warfare. It's a terrible dilemma.

What do you do with a culture of peace? You go into these countries that do not have a culture of peace, and you help people evolve more enlightened forms of government. That's one way. You hope they will not elect despots or allow themselves to be controlled by despots.

It requires a lot of courage to do this, but we must have, from the grass-roots level in every country, a culture of peace that can spring up and show people a better way to live.

This is such a deep and important question.

I firmly believe that all wars can be averted if the right people intervene in the right way at the right time. But this means having organizations on the ground that will also be present to help to grow alternatives to warfare. It's not about imposing peace on anybody. That's not desirable. What is desirable is people imposing peace upon themselves.

AUDIENCE MEMBER 11: When I look at the problems that are going on in the world—war, terrorism, conflicts and so on —I'm filled with a sense of urgency. We have to do something now to work for a culture of peace and change these trends. In your book you also talk about your faith in music. In that section you stated that you feel like there's a more powerful tool in music to heal wounds. You said music can really bring out a sense in people of shared humanity.

I was wondering if you would elaborate on this.

MARINOFF: Music will charm most people. Only those who are hardened by a life of brutality or the need to exercise naked power over and oppress others, may be more difficult to reach. Most people want to spend time singing and dancing and playing. That's why every culture has music, even going back to prehistoric times.

What I am saying is that, when a despot takes over—and this we can see from every culture—the first people they get rid of are the artists and the intelligentsia. That's because they are afraid of ideas. They're afraid of the beauty of art, which can awaken people. This is why they feel the need to suppress it. Even Plato wanted to suppress poetry in his political utopia, The Republic. He was worried about the effect of poets, because they stimulated strong emotions. He was concerned about citizens feeling too strongly about things.

I think that music and other arts can't be controlled by despotism. During the Cold War, I remember very clearly that Soviet kids wanted rock music and blue jeans, and they found ways to get them. The Beatles got behind the Iron Curtain. One way, or another, records were smuggled in.

These days, it's easy. We have cyberspace. Even China, to take one example, cannot seal itself off from cyberspace. This is a good side of technology, that we can find ways to get music to people. So let's do it.

Only by questioning can we open minds and hearts. If we can get people to ask questions then they will reform themselves and stop persecuting artists, who are doing the most beautiful things that culture can offer.

AUDIENCE MEMBER 12: I work with young kids in a different population from myself, and I struggle to understand four-year-olds taking medication. Then I think about the Soka Gakkai, which was founded almost eighty years ago in a war-torn country.

What you say about philosophical counseling resonates with me. We need an alternative to going straight to the medication, which involves dialogue and opening your mind or freeing yourself. It's a beautiful concept. What kind of philosophy can really impact those who are suffering? I think that's the purpose of any religion or philosophy. How can I influence those who are suffering?

MARINOFF: President Ikeda and I are exploring this in greater depth in our current dialogue (published in English under the title *The Inner Philosopher*, 2012). I think what the Soka Gakkai International and the American Philosophical Practitioners Association have in common —and President Ikeda has fingered this as one of the key issues and I agree with him—is that we are, each in our own way, helping people to connect with their inner resources. We're so fortunate to have these great inner resources to draw on, but they need to be cultivated. No musician would ever be great without practice. You need to practice, and you need to dedicate yourself to it. No matter what gifts we have, they have to be exercised.

When people become too dependent on externals, such as Prozac, it robs them of their own power, and fails to mobilize the greatness of their inner human resources.

What children need is a more dramatic kind of recovery. Maybe one week a year, one month a year, they need a place where they can go to experience being human in a fuller sense than they are in their current lives. If we could set up even one month a year, like a summer camp with these kids, we could wean them off a lot of medication. But they need a total immersion in a new life experience. You can't just give them ideas. It's not going to help them. They need the experience and the context in which to connect to their inner resources. That's vital.

We have some philosophers in our movement who have gone into prisons, for example, and worked with incarcerated juveniles. How do we work with them? They're not in a good environment. They weren't in a good environment to begin with. That's how they got into prison.

We discovered that a lot of them did not exhibit causal reasoning. They didn't understand why they were there. If you asked them why they were in prison, they'd say, "I don't know." Something in their acculturation was failing them. Most children understand causal connections—"If I do 'A,' 'B' will happen."

But these kids were not thinking at all about the consequences of their actions. They needed what we call *critical thinking*. They needed to understand that what we think, what we say, what we do, have consequences. To us, it's obvious; to them, it's not. They needed someone in their lives to explain it to them. What's the virtue of that? It empowers them.

We're not saying, "We're going to give you opportunities." We're saying, "You're going to give yourself opportunities." This is also what children need to know to alleviate desperation. They still need a mentor to work with them in a personal way. You can't just send them a video and say "watch this." It's got to be human to human.

~ November 13, 2008
SGI-USA New York Culture of Peace Resource Center

Foundations of a Peaceful Society
Equality, Diversity, Identity and Inclusion

Stephen Glassman

Chairperson, Pennsylvania Human Relations Commission

Stephen A. Glassman was the first openly gay political appointee in Baltimore, Maryland, where he served for five years as civic design commissioner. He has served on a wide variety of national, state and local boards, including the ACLU, the Human Rights Campaign, the LGBT (Lesbian, Gay, Bisexual, Transgender) Community Center of Baltimore, the Names Project, and the Yale University LGBT Study Center. He is past president of the Common Roads (Bisexual, Gay, Lesbian, Transgender Youth) support group in Harrisburg, Pennsylvania, and the former co-chair and founder of the Pennsylvania Rights Coalition, the largest group in the state working to achieve equal rights legislation on the basis of sexual orientation and gender identity.

In May 2002, Stephen Glassman was appointed to the Pennsylvania Human Relations Commission. Mr. Glassman is the first openly gay individual to receive a statewide gubernatorial appointment subject to Senate confirmation to a Pennsylvania board or commission. In June 2003, Mr. Glassman was appointed chairperson of the Pennsylvania Human Relations Commission, the first openly gay individual in the country to chair a state gubernatorial commission (he served until 2011). In December 2006, Mr. Glassman was appointed vice chairman of the Governor's Cabinet on the Rights of People With Disabilities.

Mr. Glassman has appeared as a media spokesperson on television, radio and in the press on behalf of gay/lesbian/bisexual/transgender civil rights causes, architecture and design, and AIDS issues. He has lectured extensively at conferences, museums and universities across the country and has served as a director on numerous boards of arts and civil rights organizations.

Mr. Glassman touches on many of the eight action areas in the 1999 United Nations Declaration and Programme of Action on a Culture of Peace, especially the sixth: advancing understanding, tolerance and solidarity. As Mr. Glassman says: "If you understand that you can bring things into your life that will alter your perception of the world, your place in it and the difference you can make in this world, that's the kind of purposeful life that builds this society and can ultimately achieve a culture of peace based upon equality, diversity, identity and the inclusion of everyone in the society."

I'd like to illuminate some of the long-standing issues we've struggled with in this country and talk about how we can achieve a culture of peace through an understanding and appreciation of equality, diversity, identity and inclusion.

I think it says something about the SGI that they have included someone of my background in this lecture series. It points to the kind of future we can hope to enjoy, with organizations like this that appreciate aspects of what I'd like to discuss tonight.

Beyond Social Tolerance

One of the most important things I want to talk about is the need to advance beyond the concept of social tolerance, something that has been discussed for years in America but has had the effect of undervaluing our appreciation of one another.

Mere tolerance is not where we need to be in 2008. We need to go far beyond just tolerating or putting up with others. Rather, we need to celebrate, acknowledge and respect one another for our contributions and the diversity and value we bring from our life experiences. We each have a unique perspective on the world that stems from the way in which we have lived and learned from one another. Without an understanding of the value of these varied life experiences, as opposed to merely tolerating these differences, we lose the ability to achieve the kind of change needed to make this world a place that delivers equality and social justice to everyone.

Without this appreciation, we lose the opportunity to enjoy the benefits of the contributions each of us can make. Often we are prevented from making our contributions because, as is particularly true for minorities and women, we have, early in life, been disadvantaged in the way we engage with society.

Equal Opportunity and Early Development

If equal opportunity is not presented to a person at an early age—whether through education, religion or community involvement—then that person is two steps behind from the outset. People base their understanding of their identity on the interactions they have had with others, whether they enter society professionally, through the educational system or through community work. If others devalue a person's very presence and existence, that devaluation is internalized, whether it's internalized racism, homophobia or sexism.

This learned disadvantage is an obstacle to fully appreciating one's own value, worth and empowerment and to making the greatest contribution one can. This disadvantage follows us throughout our entire lives. It takes a degree of personal strength and courage to get beyond the mythologizing and stereotyping about the group to which one belongs or the way in which one interacts with others who are different. It takes a real degree of internal commitment to advance beyond given limitations.

We underestimate one another when we are categorized and classified at the earliest stages of our educational process. Putting people into tracks or groups determines in advance what our expectations are. People's ability to achieve is limited when told that they are only expected to attain a certain level of academic success. It is limited when told they are not worthy or capable or that what is expected of them is different than what is expected of someone from a more advantaged environment.

The damage is internalized early and easily and affects the rest of one's life: the career choices made, the way one engages with others, and the self-esteem that allows a person to fully appreciate his or her own ability to advance and change the world.

It's important to understand that each person has, not just an individual right, but also a responsibility to offer his or her contribution to the world. Change happens through interaction. Change is more effective when we appreciate our ability to work together. It happens incrementally and in varying ways depending upon culture, background, ideology and how those interactions create an opportunity for the world to view itself in different ways.

Eradicating Discrimination and Bias

The work that I do on a daily basis as a member of the Pennsylvania Human Rights Commission addresses this need to eradicate discrimination and bias and allow people to fully actualize and appreciate one another's contributions through education, public accommodation service, housing and the overall environment of the democratic process in our daily lives. We are the largest human relations and human rights agency in the United States and are called on to provide a model for other human rights agencies throughout the country.

As we do this work on a statewide basis, we keep in mind that we are representing the needs of people coming from varying backgrounds and geographic areas: rural, urban and areas that are culturally monolithic or extraordinarily diverse.

According to the last United States census (2000), Pennsylvania is the most rural state in the nation. There are many things about Pennsylvania that surprise people. It tends to vote "blue"[1] presidentially, but internally, Pennsylvania reflects the needs of other states around the nation.

Take New York State as another example. In addition to its big cities, New York State has a very large rural population. What we learn from working with people who come from very different environments,

---

1. The electorate in Pennsylvania has voted "blue," or for the Democratic candidate, in the past five presidential elections (1992, 1996, 2000, 2004, 2008).

especially people who come from limited monolithic perspectives, is that
when exposed to individuals who are different from them, they have an
opportunity to change significantly.

Evaluating Change through a Critical-Edge Issue

Lesbian, gay, bisexual and transgender issues are a telling way of evalu-
ating change. These issues seem to be the critical edge on which many
social justice experiments are discussed in national conversations. The
issue of same-sex marriage points to this understanding of difference in a
way that no other issue seems to.

The fact that people in this country are so exorcised about the idea of
same-sex couples in love being able to make a commitment and having
the same protections and responsibilities to one another as heterosexual
couples is quite surprising when the history of the institution of marriage
is analyzed.

The Evolution of Marriage

Marriage has changed enormously over the last 200 years. There have been
twelve major legal changes to marriage in the United States in the past 200
years, particularly with regard to the rights of women and the acknowledge-
ment of them as full human beings as opposed to chattel or property.

That has been a large shift, but more recently, the case *Loving v. Virginia*[2] abolished the right of states to ban people of different races marry-
ing one another. The struggle that emerged from that issue taking place
from the 1940s through the 1960s, carried on the tradition of discrimination and bias that this country was built upon.

The founding documents of the United States, those we hold most
sacred—the Declaration of Independence and the Constitution—fully
indoctrinate in our understanding of ourselves and our history the kind
of discrimination that we are working to oppose and eradicate today. The
rights of an entire gender were excluded from full recognition under our

2. The Supreme Court of Appeals of Virginia decided the case *Loving v. Virginia* on
June 12, 1967.

Constitution; African-Americans were not even considered full people; people who didn't own property weren't allowed to vote.

Observing the radical change in our appreciation of who we are as a nation over a bit more than 200 years, I believe it is not too much to expect that in a very few years we will ultimately see full equality in this country for lesbian/gay/bisexual/transgender people.

In fact, we are so close that the difference in the ballot initiative in California under Proposition 8[3] compared to the vote that was taken only eight years earlier in 2000, showed a change from 61 percent of the population opposing same-sex marriage or marriage equality in 2000 to 52 percent this time.[4] I believe that's significant progress. I am not discouraged. I believe that this fight is not only winnable but that within a very few years we will achieve the ultimate goal for equality in this country: marriage equality.

Marriage brings with it more than 1,142 federal rights and in most states about six hundred individual rights that have more to do with financial protection than anything else. It's really about money. That's what marriage originally was as an institution: a protection of financial interests, primarily for men over women. We have moved toward a much more equal distribution of wealth in this country. When marriage is taken out of the context of religious rights, it is understood that this civil contract is merely another way of protecting people's financial interests and their responsibilities to one another.

As we look at equality and inclusion in this country, inclusion means not only the rights of people who are obvious but also those who are not so obvious. Today's society is much more subtle and nuanced than it has ever been. People come in many shapes, sizes, gender identities, races, cultures and so on. When we evaluate those differences and attempt to explain how we evaluate one another, we realize we have more commonalities than we do differences. That's not a new concept.

---

3. On November 4, 2008, in a statewide election, California voters approved Proposition 8, adding a new section to the state Constitution that states: "Only marriage between a man and a woman is valid or recognized in California."
4. According to a study commissioned by the Evelyn & Walter Haas, Jr. Fund in San Francisco, released under the auspices of the National Gay and Lesbian Task Force Policy Institute, the total percent of voters supporting Proposition 8 in 2000 was 61%, compared to 52% in 2008. (source: www.thetaskforce.org)

A Majority/Minority Nation

What is a bit new is that our differences are not just to be respected. We now understand that individual differences make us more valuable to one another. It's not only a question of finding common ground. Learning from one another rather than simply doing things as we've been taught enriches us. Globally we are falling significantly behind, because we have been unable or unwilling to recognize that before 2035, we're going to be a majority-minority[5] nation and will look much more like the rest of the world than we have for the last two centuries.

That's an important paradigm shift in this country. Clearly those who are in power are not yet ready to make the adjustment. They've been pushed and dragged and will probably be kicking and screaming until they finally accept it, but this demographic change is overtaking us more rapidly than projected studies indicated just ten years ago.

At that time, it was projected that by 2050[6] we would be a majority-minority nation. Studies that came out last year predict that by 2042, we will be a majority-minority nation. I predict that after the 2010 census, we'll find this date moving even closer. This means we have a limited amount of time to prepare and plan for this change, which will affect, not only the way we interact with one another but the way in which resources are allocated, whether from the federal government, the professions, Wall Street or educational institutions. Those resources will need to match the society being served.

Discovering Needs

In government, our responsibility is not to maintain the status quo. It is to discover the needs of the population being served. Responding to the needs of society is an honorable position and must be approached in a specific way.

One of the most important things I learned in leadership training at the Harvard School of Government was that there are two distinct ways to lead: one is to lead by following; the other is to lead by leading. There's a

---

5. A population where the racial composition is less than 50% white.
6. According to the US Census Bureau [source: www.census.gov].

significant difference between the two. Most elected and appointed officials lead by following. That is, they take polls or look at what will get them
reelected or reappointed and follow those trends, leading by giving people
what the polls tell them people want.

I believe that the way to lead effectively is to listen to your constituency and discover what their needs are, understanding that those needs are
not usually met in today's society. Understanding that those needs reflect
a change in society, we need to redistribute money, services, energy and
time to where the need is greatest.

Redistributing Funds

For example, the way we distribute funding in education is really backwards. We have more money than we need for distribution to those who
are academically superior. People at the top of the academic ladder don't
have difficulty getting money to go to school. This is true whether you're
talking about Harvard or one of the state universities.

In order to advance society and make it more competitive with the rest
of the world, funds must be made available to those who have been disadvantaged from birth. People of ability who have not had an equal educational opportunity are the ones who truly need focused funding and
scholarships so that they can catch up to those who have been advantaged from birth.

So if we reevaluate how we distribute money in this society through
all social programs—such as health, education, business development—
to those who are in greater need, we will become more competitive with
countries around the world that are already doing so. With proper training and development, those in need can advance at the same rate as those
who are advantaged.

Why the United States Is Falling Behind

If you look at the way funding is distributed in India, Bangladesh or even
in China, we see that the methodology is changing. People in the lower
classes or those who have been discriminated against are precisely the ones
who are getting jobs in industries that have fled the United States. This

elevates a country's entire economic society. We are not following a model that is advantageous to the United States.

Richard Florida's most recent book, *The Flight of The Creative Class*,[7] is a wonderful explanation of how we are falling behind other advancing countries and how we can achieve greater success and parity. Florida says we can do this by passing laws that protect the rights of people so they can be fully engaged and find equal opportunity and also by reallocating resources so that we're supporting people from the bottom up rather than from the top down. This approach has worked in the cities in this country that have had the foresight to do so.

Legal Equity and Growth

Let's compare economic growth across the country. The twenty states that have passed equal rights legislation for lesbian, gay and bisexual people and the thirteen states that have also included protection for transgender people[8] are at a higher level economically and are advancing more rapidly in both business and population growth compared to states not supporting legal equity.

For example, Pennsylvania is now the third slowest-growing state in the United States. We are, unfortunately, one of the thirty states that do not have the kind of protections won here in New York. It took, I might add, thirty-three long years of fighting, but ultimately those protections were won in New York. Transgender protections still need to be added here in New York State. I assure you that, when accomplished, it will send a signal, an important message to other people that this is a welcoming environment; this is a place in which you can be celebrated for who you are. People will move here in greater numbers. They will come here for education in greater numbers. They will come here to raise their families if they feel that their children and spouses will be protected. That advances the whole society.

Pennsylvania—the sixth largest state in the country—is not only the third slowest-growing state but, from 2000 to 2004, it grew by only 65,000

---

7. Richard Florida, *The Flight of the Creative Class*, (New York: Harper Business, 2004).
8. According to the Human Rights Campaign (www.hrc.org).

people. Of those 65,000 people, 60 percent were Hispanic. So the change coming here in this country is coming from those who don't look like the people in the majority population today. They infuse our state with a rich culture, vibrancy, sense of commitment and purpose not necessarily evident in the existing community—one that has a sense of entitlement and won't necessarily be giving back to society.

America's Promise

The challenge isn't there for those who have already achieved success. It is there for those who have not yet achieved the success that America promises. Now, whether America delivers on that promise or not is entirely up to us. We must make this decision individually and collectively. We can't look at others saying: "It's your decision. I don't have any power. I can't make change happen." Everybody can make that change happen.

In my own life, the wonderful and rarified opportunity I've been afforded as a Cabinet member has allowed me to make a contribution that otherwise I could not have. Before there was an openly gay Cabinet member sitting at the table, these voices simply were not included in the conversation.

Unfortunately, in every Cabinet meeting, I'm still the voice speaking up about lesbian/gay/bisexual/transgender issues. But more and more, as I speak up about issues of race, gender, ethnicity, national origin, ability and age, people from other groups remember to include LGBT people in the conversation. One of the lessons to be learned is that you can't expect others to be there for you if you're not there for them.

Modeling Change

In my six-and-a-half years in this position that I have loved, I've learned so much from the people that I've met by going to every single luncheon or dinner for the eighteen state chapters of the National Association for the Advancement of Colored People; going to every single luncheon, dinner and event in the state Hispanic American Society; meeting with university presidents in the fourteen state universities and thirty-two major colleges in the state to talk about how to expand minority enrollment; meeting with the chiefs of the 1,217 police forces in the Commonwealth of Pennsylvania to discuss why, based on a study that we initiated, there is not *any* minority representation in three-quarters of the forces. The police officers are all white and all male. There are no women, no Hispanics, no Asians, no African-Americans, zero representation in 60 percent of the police forces.

The response I often get from these police chiefs is, "We don't have any of those people in our jurisdiction."

My response is, "Of course you don't." If everybody looks the same as everybody's always looked in a jurisdiction, there will never be any change. Change must be modeled. That is part of the leadership role. We can't expect that a non-white is going to feel welcome or safe living in an all-white, rural Pennsylvania environment. People are going to be afraid to drive through that environment, let alone live there.

Taking Risks

So, we have to make change happen as individuals, we have to be committed to social change, and we have to take risks. One important thing I hope I have done successfully is to be willing to take risks throughout my career. Risk is critically important. We shouldn't be afraid of risk: if we fail, it's an opportunity to learn what didn't work so we can make it work better the next time. Engaging in risk—and obviously I'm talking about calculated, safe, thoughtful, risk-taking behavior—opens us up to enormous possibilities both personally and for those around you.

When we challenge the status quo, everyone must take a step back to reevaluate what works and what doesn't in order to make a society where things work better. We learn from one another by bringing to the table people who are very different in their life experiences and backgrounds. We won't learn nearly as much by talking to the same people in the same way that we always have. By listening to the voices of those with a different perspective and life experience, we can broaden our own understanding of what works in the world, how things can happen very differently and effectively in ways we've not yet explored.

The greatest gift that this opportunity has given me is learning from many wonderful people from different places and backgrounds, knowing that their life experience is valid, credible and important, offering something that is, as I said at the beginning of this talk, far beyond the level of toleration.

Tolerance gets us in trouble every time because it makes us believe we've done enough. Tolerance makes us believe that our work is finished and that we can stop, thinking that somebody else will carry on the fight. And that's absolutely unacceptable. None of us should be so smug and self-serving that we step back and say we've done enough. None of us have done enough. If we're not engaged in the struggle for changing hearts and minds every day of our lives, then we still haven't done enough.

Making a Commitment

We recognize that few people are going to be able to do this every day of their lives. If you can make a commitment toward change, the world inevitably will change at a faster pace and in a way that's more inclusive of all of us and our needs than if you constantly say to yourself, "It's too much effort, it's too much trouble, I don't have the time, my life is busy, things are complex, the economy is in crisis."

You can always come up with a reason for not engaging in behavior that initiates social change. There are a million perfectly valid and reasonable excuses out there. Why not challenge yourself, saying, "My life will be so much more valuable, so much more interesting, with a greater sense of engagement in the world. I'll be able to make a lasting contribution, even if I touch the life of just one other person." I think you will find a path for yourself that will lead you to the culture of peace we're all talking about.

Teamwork

A culture of peace is not possible if we aren't committed to each step along the way. We can't just talk about an idea in "big picture" terms, expecting it to happen just because we've set it as a goal. We have to work in incremental ways to reach the goal, in partnership with others. One person working alone cannot achieve the goal.

As important as it is to remember the value and importance of every individual in this struggle, it's equally important to remember that social change will be accomplished faster, with greater success and permanence if we do it together: supporting one another, listening to one another, learning from one another and not always certain that our way is the right way. I understand that I make mistakes all the time, every day. But I hope I learn enough from each mistake that I don't make the same ones over and over. All of us have so much to learn from one another.

Identity and Inclusion

The issues of identity and inclusion are particularly critical. Our identities will be limited to our own life experiences if there is no understanding of how we are infused with others' life experiences and of their appreciation for what we have given them. Identity continues to change throughout one's life. For lesbian/gay/bisexual/transgender people, the very act of coming out changes identity – an obvious and extreme example. Identity is an ongoing, changing characteristic that evolves as we allow others' experiences into our own lives.

I started life as a little Jewish boy in Baltimore. I didn't know many people outside of other Jews. Growing up, I had a very limited and restricted life. In college, as I met people from all faiths and backgrounds, I realized how enormous and exciting the world was.

As I got into the work of social change and social justice, I met people from different backgrounds who didn't look anything like me and hadn't had the economic advantages. They challenged me to discover the world in new ways and to learn from their experiences. My world is infinitely more exciting now because of all the wonderful people I've met than it was growing up in a protected and exclusive environment. And I mean exclusive in all the meanings of exclusive. Exclusive meaning that only those identified by one's parents as worthy or valued – and I had wonderful parents – were allowed into one's life.

Retaining Idealism

If we retain our youthful spirit, idealism and sense of commitment to greater goals and aspirations as we grow to adulthood, we have the opportunity to make our own choices. If we just make choices that mirror the ones we've made our entire lives, the world is not going to offer us a great deal of change. If we don't decide to take risks, meet other people, travel, and engage in professions we never considered before, our world will be restricted and limited.

I honestly didn't believe, during my twenty-five years as an architect, that I'd end up as the first openly gay Cabinet secretary in the country. That was not on my radar screen, but my life is so much more gratifying, exciting and learned now than it was with all the academic study that I had. I've learned infinitely more from the last six and a half years than in my entire life. People have given me the ability to see the world through their eyes, through a different lens, both historical and cultural, and have expanded my world. The life experiences of people who have lived very different lives from mine help me understand more about how the challenges we have in this society were created.

When the governor's term is up in two years, I'll be looking for other opportunities, but I don't think they will be in architecture. I hope to work in some capacity to help people who have not yet achieved the American Dream. How can I work to make the world a better place for those who have less than others? That sense of commitment is a change that would not have happened had I not been given the opportunity and honor to serve over these last six and a half years. I'm grateful to be in this position with the opportunity to work with people in the Commonwealth of Pennsylvania and around the country.

Dialogue as Means of Change

Let me give you some examples of the kind of dialogue we've conducted in Pennsylvania that could be replicated here in New York and elsewhere in the country.

When I first came on board, it was very shortly after September 11, 2001. The country was in shock. We were debilitated psychologically from an attack that nobody had anticipated. Our economy was in a very difficult place—maybe not quite as difficult as we're in right now—but by contrast to what we had enjoyed earlier, we were in a state of shock. It seemed to me that we needed to step back and, instead of responding to extreme voices here in the United States, identify voices that were really listening to one another, bring not only moderation to the dialogue but a sense of thoughtful, engaged, intelligent conversation.

I contacted Judea Pearl, a distinguished scholar and the father of Daniel Pearl, the journalist, and Akbar Ahmed, the world's leading authority on Islam and former ambassador to Great Britain from Pakistan who now teaches and has his own chair at American University in Washington, D.C. I brought them together in Pittsburgh, a very blue-collar city, to have a dialogue on television for several hours and then conduct a question-and-answer session with the audience.

It was an unbelievable experience where two people with nothing in common became friends, engaging in a dialogue that affected the thousand people in the audience. We took the dialogue to Philadelphia, and it was even more powerful. Then we filmed it as a two-hour special that was shown on National Public Television several times and seen around the world.[9]

I got a call from the Archbishop of Canterbury in London who invited us to conduct the dialogue in the House of Lords in London. We created an eight-day experience with twenty-four different meetings with ambassadors and community groups from Pakistan, India, Bangladesh, the United States and Britain. You can imagine the impact the dialogue had just among the people who were able to hear it, whether on television or in person. It's an example of how just one person with a creative and thoughtful idea can have a huge effect on many people. I've also been able to do

---

9. In 2003, Professor Judea Pearl, president of the Daniel Pearl Foundation and co-editor of *I am Jewish* (2004), and Professor Akbar S. Ahmed, Ibn Khaldun Chair of Islamic Studies at American University and author of *Journey into Islam: The Crisis of Globalization* (2007) and *Islam Under Siege* (2003), lead a public dialogue in Pittsburgh, Penn., on the divisions between Muslims and the western world and between Muslims and Jews. The event was covered widely in the United States, Arab and Pakistani press. Due to its success, this personal yet public dialogue continued in cities across the United States and abroad. The conversations, which were never the same, covered issues from theology, history and ideology to politics and current news, and encourage audience participation. Two principles guide the conversation; first, no issue is taboo and, second, respect at all times. Professors Ahmed and Pearl believe that these open and honest dialogues are essential for the future of humanity. In 2006, Professors Ahmed and Pearl were among the recipients of the first annual Purpose Prize "in recognition of [their] simple, yet innovative approach to solving one of society's most pressing problems."

things in a more modest way in Pennsylvania that are affecting communities that have not been well addressed.

For example, I started the first Disability Stakeholders Task Force to bring together hundreds of people representing various mental and physical disability rights organizations from across the country. The purpose was to learn from one another and educate those not living with or caring for people with mental or physical disabilities. It has been an eye-opening experience.

As a result of this gathering, the governor of Pennsylvania established the first Cabinet on the Rights of People with Disabilities, of which I am vice chair. We are now engaging people all across the nation in a greater appreciation for and understanding of people who have different kinds of abilities.

Protecting Others Means Protecting Ourselves

We must remember that when we ignore or render invisible a population, whether it's LGBT people, African-Americans or people with different abilities, we have an increasingly harsh economic effect on that community. People with disabilities have a 70 percent unemployment rate in this country. Most people don't know that. And most people are afraid of those with disabilities. They feel uncomfortable and don't want to be near them.

All of us will be part of that community at some point in our lives. It may be from an accident or it may be because we age long enough to become a person with a disability. Ultimately we're all going to get there. We had better learn how to respond to these needs while we're able-bodied and young so that we can have a society that values and appreciates us when we become a person with a disability. That's a great example of how all of us need to get engaged to protect our own futures and the welfare of society.

If we don't engage, if we choose to step back and just live, we can get through life. It may be a life with a lot of money or material things, but it will also be a life that's more isolated and less full. When we look back at the end of our years, we will ask the all-important questions: "What did I do to change the world? What did I leave behind? Why did I spend seventy, eighty or a hundred years on this earth? Was there any reason for me to be here?"

These deep, philosophical questions are the ones that can actually make a great difference in the way we live each day. They are more than just big-picture concepts to study in school or to read about in the newspaper. They are down-to-earth concepts that affect each person differently but can alter our ability to live this life in a full and a self-actualized way.

If you understand that you can bring things into your life that will alter your perception of the world, your place in it and the difference you can make in this world, that's the kind of purposeful life that builds this society and can ultimately achieve a culture of peace based upon equality, diversity, identity and the inclusion of everyone in the society.

Questions and Answers

AUDIENCE MEMBER 1: Is it possible that tolerance is a crucial way station between bias and acceptance, or is it possible to go from bias directly to acceptance without stopping at tolerance?

GLASSMAN: That's a very interesting question, and my response is that tolerance is a way station if you move through it with alacrity and deliberate speed. If it gets you to your goal, then it is a perfectly acceptable place. It's like getting off at a subway stop, getting back on and continuing toward your destination until you get to the end. It's fine if it's a building block that creates greater understanding and acceptance and an ability to listen and learn, but most people get stuck at tolerance.

The real problem with tolerance is that when it becomes a larger goal in society—the end product—then it is being used disadvantageously and actually hurts us. If you lull people into believing that they have achieved their goal by getting to an intermediary place that is not nearly far enough in the struggle, most people will only aim for tolerance. You need to keep the goals really high.

As an example, one organization—and it's a wonderful organization—the Southern Poverty Law Center—well, tolerance is their goal. They now recognize that they've trapped themselves. They're a very thoughtful group and I work with them very closely, but they realize that by their own phraseology they have trapped themselves and are not able to progress as much as they'd like.

People think that the goal they established thirty years ago is the end point. Goal setting is critically important. Stepping back and constantly reevaluating your goals is the path by which you're going to achieve them. That is why tolerance needs to be understood in a very careful and thoughtful way. You recognize that you're allowing people to grow at the rate that they need to grow but that it's part of the growth process, not the place you ultimately want to be.

AUDIENCE MEMBER 2: Can you talk about how your study of architecture and your practice as an architect inform what you are currently doing? Is there a correlation?

GLASSMAN: I could rationalize this for you and say that architects are generalists. They have to study many things and engage with people in many different ways. As an architect, I was not only a designer. I was a sociologist and a psychologist. As an architect, I did lots of couple counseling, straight and gay.

But architecture did not have a great deal to do with how I arrived here. It was more that I had a very rich and full volunteer life for thirty years—from the time I was in high school. I recognized at some point in my career that the thrill, excitement and personal value I was getting from my volunteer work in the civil rights movement was greater than the joy I got from architecture, a field that I love.

I did well, but it affected only a very rarefied audience, a small number of people with lots of money. It wasn't really changing the world in any way. And I wasn't here to just build monuments to myself.

It seemed to me that the important thing is to get beyond academic training and professional experience. I wanted to use my life experience with a sense of purposefulness, commitment and dedication to a cause. I wanted to allow everyone to get to a place of equality and justice so that they could have the same opportunities of education and life that I had.

That seemed to me the life lesson learned. It wasn't about me; it was about others who ought to have the same opportunities but who clearly were not being given them freely. We were going to have to fight to get them those same opportunities.

AUDIENCE MEMBER 3: Although you speak of it as one community, there

is discrimination within the lesbian/gay/bisexual/transgender community. How can we relate to the racism and the discrimination that exists
within the LGBT community?

GLASSMAN: Thank you for making that point. It's not only an excellent
point, but I assume – and I should not assume – that it's clear that,
unfortunately, a society dominated by a culture of racism and sexism is
also one that is being more revealed to be dominated by homophobia
as well. You're absolutely correct that racism exists in all areas of society. And homophobia exists within the LGBT community

For example, there's an enormous need for education about gender identity or expression within the LGB community. The greatest
discrimination against transgender people, believe it or not, is among
other gay and lesbian people as opposed to heterosexual people. Heterosexual people often don't even realize that someone is a different
gender than the one they were born into.

Racism is so structural in this society. Society is limited in its ability
to get us beyond the place where we have been. Our concept of racism
in this society is unilateral, based as it is upon what we've been taught
or what we've seen on television documentaries. If you don't engage
with people who are African-American or people of different colors and
backgrounds and listen to them talk about the authenticity of their life
experiences, then your understanding of racism comes from what you
read in the New York Times or whatever your source of information is.

I think we have done a poor job in the LGBT community of
addressing the issue of racism because we've been focused on our own
oppression. It's been almost a competition of oppressions: who is more
oppressed than the other and who deserves more attention. That has
been a real problem in the LGBT community.

AUDIENCE MEMBER 4: It has to do with the leadership also, because the
leadership is mostly white. If there was more balance…

GLASSMAN: I agree with you. But I also think you have to look beyond
leadership. You have to look at what your commitment as an organization is, not just who's at the top of the organization. People who are
African-American can be less committed to dealing with issues of racism than people who are white. People who are straight can be more

committed to dealing with LGBT issues than an LGBT person might be. It really has to do with the individual.

We need to get beyond categorizing people based upon what they look like. People must prove their worth, value and commitment by the work that they do. We shouldn't just give an automatic pass. "Oh, you're a person of color? Yeah, you get a pass on being fully engaged in the work dealing with oppression and racism." No, we all have to make that commitment, but you're right that the leadership has not caught up with the grass roots.

In the same way that boards of directors are almost always behind the progressive thinking of the staff of an organization, legislators – whom I deal all the time – are way behind the constituency. We do polling all the time that shows that elected officials are terribly afraid of dealing with what they consider to be controversial issues when the polls are actually supportive of doing the work that terrifies them. The reason is that they're worried about winning their reelections – not in the general elections – they're worried about winning primaries. That's what this is about. They're worried about right-wingers running against them in rural-area primaries even when polls say that 88 percent of Pennsylvanians support non-discrimination employment legislation for LGBT people.

AUDIENCE MEMBER 5: My question is about a burgeoning minority population and culture as comprised by the LGBT community, blacks and Hispanics and the importance of established American populations moving past tolerance and into acceptance of these groups. I was wondering in your time moving among the minority groups, if you noticed whether this notion of moving past intolerance to acceptance was something that these groups should be reminded about as well. When you mentioned the census and the idea that the minority population is going to be growing, I wonder if these three groups are going to either unite or fray?

GLASSMAN: Well, first of all, I think you should be giving the talk. You basically answered your own question. I think you fully appreciate the challenges. The difficulty often is that within groups there is tremendous diversity. So, there will be competition for resources as I mentioned earlier within each individual group. There are those who are

better or less well educated with regard to the issues I've been talking about—not academic issues. People will either hold back or help
advance a movement of unity, coalition building and collaborative
work. That's a struggle that's going to be going on for a very long time.

It's been going on for many decades in this country, even within
the civil rights movement. You know from your own study of history
that Martin Luther King had a very low rating in the African-American church community through all of his struggles. He was not able to
preach at many churches in the south because they didn't like his style
or his belief system. There was a great deal of jealousy about the kind
of attention that he was getting nationally. Who was this young upstart?

There's a wonderful book called *Parting the Waters* by Taylor
Branch.[10] It's a brilliant and fascinating biography of Martin Luther
King and the civil rights movement. It talks about exactly the issues
you're addressing, the fractionalization in the African-American community and the need for people to get beyond themselves and their
own particular issues. That still goes on today.

Look at the political arm of the African-American movement today
and think about the campaign we just went through. Think about the
comments that Jesse Jackson—who has made enormous contributions
to this country and is a brilliant orator himself—made about Barack
Obama during the campaign.[11] That answers your question.

We're a long way away from the clear unity of purpose and coalition
of efforts that we need to be. But I believe it hurts us to have expectations that are higher than what we can achieve. We need aspirations
and goals. We need to be able to guide ourselves along a path to our
destination. But we will suffer if we set goals so high in the intermedi-
ate path that we can never achieve them, getting so discouraged that
we stop our movement along the path.

Let's set incremental and achievable goals, as a group or as

---

10. Taylor Branch, *Parting the Waters* (Simon & Schuster, 1989).

11. On July 9, 2008, the Reverend Jesse Jackson finished an interview on Fox News
and made an unguarded statement, unaware that the microphone was still on, that
presidential candidate Barack Obama was "talking down to black people." He apologized and continued his support of Obama's campaign (see http://www.youtube.com/
watch?v=TQl_6buUggM).

individuals. Some success will spur you on and inspire you to achieve more and more until you get to your ultimate goal. If your goal is to have all parts of each group working together in unity in this struggle for fairness and equal opportunity and you set that as your only goal, most people will drop out along the way. It's too difficult, too challenging and too painful.

You need to allow yourself a series of small steps so that, rung by rung, you can get to the top of the ladder. If you're on the ground looking up at the top of the ladder and there are no rungs to get to the top, you may walk away. Very few people are going to leap up to the top.

AUDIENCE MEMBER 6: It was the African-American and Latino men in bars who were constantly attacked and it was because of the struggles they underwent that Stonewall[12] even happened.

GLASSMAN: And don't forget the transgender people and the drag queens.

AUDIENCE MEMBER 6: The transgender and transvestite communities were not asked to be part of the organizing committee when the twenty-fifth anniversary of Stonewall was celebrated. It's kind of funny how the status hasn't moved very far. I'm old enough to remember ACT UP.[13] The gay and lesbian community used ACT UP opportunistically as a way to gain visibility.

ACT UP lent a sense of militancy to the Gay Pride parade.[14] Giuliani (Mayor Rudolph Giuliani) was furious and did everything in his power to try to blanket down the strength of the community. He stopped the parade at intersections for ten minutes at a time. People said that as the community got closer to mainstream, there would be

---

12. On June 29, 1969, a group of patrons outside the Stonewall Inn in New York City rioted against police harassment. The next evening, 1000 persons rioted in protest. Demonstrations continued over the next few days. As a result, gay advocacy groups such as the Gay Liberation Front were started.

13. AIDS Coalition to Unleash Power (ACT UP): An organization formed in 1987 to take action to end the AIDS crisis.

14. The first Gay Pride parade took place on June 28, 1970, to commemorate the Stonewall riots of June 28, 1969. Parades also took place in Chicago, San Francisco and Los Angeles.

costs. I go to the parade now and it's not the same. The militancy is not there.

I think that mainstreaming is dangerous. I'm wondering if the mainstreaming aspect is partly responsible for something like Proposition 8.[15] It doesn't make sense to me, that in 2008, our communities would allow a separation like that.

GLASSMAN: Let me take the last part about Proposition 8 first. There was a lot of editorializing immediately after Proposition 8 passed blaming the African-American community and the Hispanic community. As it turns out, it's not true; the issue was age difference. Seventy-six percent of people ages eighteen to thirty-five voted against Proposition 8. The issue is more about age, openness and receptivity. Young people seem to have many LGBT people in their lives—family members, kids in school, or co-workers.

Their life experience has been very different from that of their elders. Cutting across all demographic lines, the Proposition 8 issue was about age, which touches on the rest of your question: movements age; every civil rights movement ages. As a movement, we're in a different place now than we were back in 1969 and all through the '70s.

The bottom line is that there is room for every phase you mentioned in the contemporary movement. In fact, we need all of those aspects. The militancy of one segment allows other people to get inside and meet with legislators. ACT UP enabled the human rights campaign to meet with congresspeople, because the congresspeople said, "Well, we certainly don't want to meet with those folks. You who are dressed in shirts and ties, yeah, you look more reasonable. We'll let you in."

And that's exactly what happened. It happens in every movement. It happened in the African-American civil rights movement. Each of

15. Proposition 8 is a California ballot proposition and constitutional amendment passed in the November 2008 state elections. It provided that "only marriage between a man and a woman is valid or recognized in California." Following the June 26, 2013, decision of the U.S. Supreme Court declaring Section 3 of the Defense of Marriage Act to be unconstitutional, California's Ninth Circuit Court lifted its stay on same-sex marriages on June 28, enabling Governor Jerry Brown to order same-sex marriages to resume in California.

the civil rights movements builds on the lessons of the African-American civil rights movement—a great training ground. The bottom line is that if you try to make the movement into something it's not, then, not only is it inauthentic, it's going to be ineffective and won't last.

We've watched cyclical patterns of a militantly engaged activist generation followed by a quiet, almost apathetic, generation and then back to militancy. What we've seen in this last election cycle should give us great hope. This country is much more engaged in the political process, the electoral process and the activist process.

Three hundred simultaneous demonstrations were held nationwide in opposition to Proposition 8. Five thousand people in Philadelphia showed up spontaneously at City Hall. We didn't see that response to the other twenty-eight ballot initiatives that passed in the last election. This time there were only four ballot initiatives. Why, all of a sudden, were protests going on?

I think that the Obama campaign and presidency—the first African-American president in the White House, a brilliant orator who raised enormous amounts of money and engaged the country in the political process in a way that nobody else in recent memory has been able to do—has energized all the minority movements. Civil rights movements have been reactivated, reengaged in ways that allow the more active or militant groups as you might refer to them, inside the Beltway or the halls of Congress.

It's infused a new energy throughout society. I predict that in the next several years we'll see more ongoing action by groups who are struggling for equality and acceptance. It's not going to be a quiescent time. It will be a more participatory time; people of all ages will be engaged. I myself showed up at the Proposition 8 demonstration in Philadelphia at City Hall. If I had consulted with anyone, I probably would have received instructions not to show up, but that would not have stopped me.

The time in which we live is a celebratory time, a time infused with excitement and energy that we haven't seen in a long time. We have great opportunities ahead of us in the next four years. The fact that you showed up for this kind of talk tonight means that you were all engaged before you walked into this room. That's a healthy sign, for our democracy.

AUDIENCE MEMBER 7: What if you are a person who has trained and developed herself to be the risk-taker? What if you are a person who is comfortable with being uncomfortable, who would say something no one else would dare say? What do you say to the sea of onlookers who say, "Don't do that—stop, we can't take it, no more of that?" What kind of conversation or dialogue would you suggest to engage with that type of individual?

GLASSMAN: What you have is a great deal of personal power. It's clear just by the way you articulated your position. You're a natural leader, as far as I'm concerned. People simply need to be aware that you're willing to engage in dialogue. What often happens with very strong and empowered people who have a lot to share is that the oppression they've suffered has given them a need to stand up in a very bold way. What often happens is that others are afraid of or intimidated by you.

Evaluate how are you presenting yourself: How are those with whom I want to engage seeing me? How can I present my message in a way that allows people to enter into a dialogue? How can I avoid having them feel, 'She is so powerful and so strong that I could never match that presence; I can't even engage [with her]?' You may need to step back and see how you can convey the message in a way that allows others to get the beauty of you and the richness of your experience in a one-on-one dialogue.

AUDIENCE MEMBER 8: I'm curious about what the job of Commissioner of Human Relations entails?

GLASSMAN: As a Cabinet official in the governor's administration, I have the responsibility of running a state agency. It is the largest human relations agency in the United States. We provide employment, public accommodations, housing, credit, lending and educational services to minorities and women. Our mission—a very large task that may never be fully realized—is to eradicate discrimination and bias in the Commonwealth of Pennsylvania.

To achieve that goal we work in a variety of areas. In our agency, we accept investigation cases—at any given time we have approximately 12,000 cases being investigated by our staff members. We also offer legal services. We have a separate law firm in the agency of sixteen full-time civil rights attorneys who do precedent-setting law in a variety of areas. For example, we were the first agency in the United States to deal with disability discrimination at ATM machines and on buses and transportation.

All the law that exists in the United States having to do with disability rights emanated from Pennsylvania. Our agency made Pennsylvania the first state to desegregate schools in the United States. We are one of the oldest agencies as well as the largest. Back in the early 1950s, we established precedent-setting law particularly with regard to race relations, which transmuted over the years into dealing with women's issues, disabilities, age and other protected-class statuses.

We work with all the school districts and 1,217 police forces in Pennsylvania to ensure equality in advancement, testing and hiring procedures. Also under our purview is the way in which their duties are prosecuted with the general public. As a law enforcement agency we have a responsibility to work with all of those community service agencies. For example, I meet frequently with police chiefs, school superintendants and university professors to try to achieve educational equity for minorities and women in the state.

AUDIENCE MEMBER 9: What made you pursue a career in this field?

GLASSMAN: I didn't actually pursue this career. Things sometimes happen in surprising ways. I went to graduate school for architecture and practiced architecture professionally for about twenty-five years. At the same time I have always been engaged in civil rights work, protesting the war in Vietnam when I was in high school and working for causes that benefitted gay/lesbian/bisexual/transgender people. As a young man, anyone of minority status was on my radar screen.

Those interests gradually overtook my interest in architecture. I used architecture, essentially, to fund my ability to do volunteer work. Ultimately I became the head of a political organization in the state that was working to achieve equal rights in legislation for LGBT people. After a nearly seven-year struggle, we got a hate-crimes bill passed in Pennsylvania and I was working with the legislature on practically a full-time basis, probably not doing as much architecture as I probably should have.

At the time it was passed, it was the most inclusive hate crimes law

> ✒ *By listening to the voices of those with a different perspective and life experience, we can broaden our own understanding of what works in the world, how things can happen very differently and effectively in ways we've not yet explored.*

in the United States and received a lot of national attention. The governor's race was just ending at that time. So, a new governor was coming in, I was nominated, went for public hearings before the Senate and was approved. Sometimes, by happenstance, you get the most interesting opportunities in life.

AUDIENCE MEMBER 10: You are obviously well educated. But we've seen tuition costs rise at least 50 percent in many places. In Maryland, where I'm from, my university tuition went up at least 50 percent over the last five years, if not more. Especially with regard to minorities, how can we address giving them the opportunity to receive a higher education?

GLASSMAN: To begin with, we're in an extraordinarily challenging time because of the economic crisis. Credit markets are nearly frozen, which is affecting everyone regardless of which school they're attending. Until we overcome the challenge to education funding, it's difficult to take a long-range view.

I think there will be a paradigm shift in the distribution of money and how the government interacts with funding. At our agency, one thing we've advocated for with the Department of Education in Pennsylvania is for the government to get into the middle of the business of funding education instead of doing it through the banks, essentially a middleman. Government should provide the funding at much lower costs and interest rates.

There is a model for that in Pennsylvania, now a national model,

called the Pennsylvania Higher Education Assistance Agency, a funding agency for education with $60 billion in assets. Unfortunately,
because of the drop in the stock market and the crunch in the credit
markets, there's been a severance of monies emanating from PHEAA,
but that should improve as the economy improves. Our basic philosophy has been that if government is going to adequately serve the people, one of the things it must do is fund education and advancement
for our young people so that the society as a whole benefits.

This is one area where government can actually be more efficient
and effective than private enterprise, because government is not in
the business of making money. It's not a profit-making organization in
the way that banks are. And the government can sustain those loans
for a longer period of time, granting consideration when students are
taking fellowships, are unemployed or unable to pay back their loans.

It is still necessary to develop a comprehensive solution that doesn't
respond only to students of academic privilege, but also to students
coming from less advantaged backgrounds, minority students in particular. Scholarships in this country exist primarily for those who achieve
at the highest levels academically. The money that's really needed is
for students who have never had an equal educational opportunity.
These students need scholarship funding early in their education so
they can receive the opportunities that allow them to advance, achieve
academically and excel.

The funding stream must be evaluated differently than it has been
in the past. For those who achieve academically, there are plenty of
scholarships. But for those who have been deprived the opportunity to
even get in the game, money is very limited. This past year, we rewrote
a bill that was offered in our legislature by a very thoughtful legislator
who, nonetheless, did not understand these critical inequities.

This African-American legislator from Philadelphia offered a bill
to advance scholarship money based upon benchmarks having to do
with scholastic success, high levels of attendance, lack of disciplinary
problems, and so on. We explained to him that the money really needs
to go to schools and individuals who are caught up in a system that
is discriminatory in its very nature. If you look at and disaggregate the
data, you learn which students are being disciplined unfairly and out

of proportion to their population, which students are in classes twice the size of others, which are not getting the teachers with the best credentials and training, which students are not getting extra courses for advanced placement, art, music or even athletics. It's always the minority students, the poor students, and the ones in the lowest-performing schools. That's where the money needs to be directed, where resources need to be reallocated to give everyone a level playing field so they can achieve and advance.

AUDIENCE MEMBER 11: In a society like India where I come from, homosexual relationships are still illegal. When discrimination is so strong, how do you start talking about rights for the LGBT community?

GLASSMAN: There is an international organization run by a friend of mine, Paula Ettelbrick. It's called the International Gay and Lesbian Human Rights Commission, which works with the United Nations in countries around the world to promote dialogue in a safe way so that people aren't arrested or disallowed from their participation.

One challenging concept is that of cultural competency. It has to do with being able to effectively deal with and understand differences in religious beliefs, languages, traditions and heritages between other countries and cultures and one's own. Sensitivity awareness training is offered to people who are going to work with local community activists in other countries. They learn from one another and create a support system in countries where laws are even more restrictive than they are here.

Although I must say that in the United States we do not have the most inclusive or supportive laws for LGBT people. We have a patchwork of laws that are very strong in some places and absent in others. Some people are protected; some are not. However, in countries where there is a longstanding prohibition on homosexuality they are actually talking about behavior since there doesn't necessarily exist a concept of what culture might be for lesbian/gay/bisexual/transgender people.

In that case, we have to work from the foundation of their cultural traditions and find ways to identify principles of common ground between their society and the marginalized group. We need to identify ways to work on mutual projects or initiatives where trust and relationships can be built. More than anything, success in any minority community with regard to equal rights is based upon people knowing who people are as individuals and not stereotypes, not mythologizing them unfairly with misrepresentations or misinformation that have been handed down from generation to generation without any supporting facts.

As people get to know one another and establish personal relationships, barriers break down, assumptions are changed, people often open up and become more receptive to others they didn't understand simply because they didn't know them.

AUDIENCE MEMBER 12: Have you felt that your mission and motivation has been energized or has shifted with current times? With the election of President Obama, Proposition 8 and the hate crimes that have been occurring, with opportunities for change and the obstacles that are occurring now, is your mission going to change?

GLASSMAN: It gives me great hope that we have people as articulate as you in high school. Thank you for your question. My response is perhaps more subtle in nuance than you might expect. While obviously it's a tremendous gift to this country and to the world to have the first African-American president, Barack Obama is also a politician. The same issues that challenge the current president will challenge him. These issues are not going to disappear. In fact, we're going into an extraordinarily challenging time: getting ourselves out of two wars where we should never have been in the first place, getting ourselves out of an economic crisis that is deeper than any we've known in our lifetimes — no one sitting in this room, no matter how old, has ever experienced an economy with the depth of challenge we are currently experiencing.

We should be very careful not to set this president up for failure by having expectations that are too high, not thinking that within six months or a year he's going to solve everything. He will be working with a Congress that is perhaps more supportive of progressive initiatives than the current Congress, but it's still a Congress representing people and states from all over the country. There is an entrenched bureaucracy with government agencies doing their work in the way they have always done it.

Change takes time; it doesn't happen overnight. I have learned that one of the greatest challenges and gifts is the development of patience. It doesn't mean that you give up your integrity or your commitment to addressing issues that need to be changed, but you learn to prioritize. You learn to balance out what you're doing before doing the next thing, how to multi-task, and realizing that some initiatives will move forward rapidly. Others will take more time because you must build relationships with multiple people in order to get something passed.

That's exactly what President Obama is going to have to do. He's not going to be able to change "Don't Ask, Don't Tell" as rapidly as he and our community would like to. He's going to have to build relationships and alliances with the military brass at the head of every military agency before he can get that change to happen in a productive way.

When Harry Truman changed the way African-Americans were dealt with in the military,[16] creating equity for people of color in 1948, he did it after years of study. He began by integrating various aspects of the military in small ways before he made the big change. It took two long years, with a lot of resistance from within the military, until there was real equity. The military is the best place to do this because people are trained into a culture that obeys and follows orders.

It's actually easier to get people to do things in the military than it is in mainstream society. That's why it's important to wait until there is a consensus of support before moving ahead. If people feel that policy has been forced on them, they will secretly undermine it, doing things to hurt it more than help it. Consensus must be built through educating, training and creating sensitivity to these issues.

Statistics that have just been published for a poll done earlier this year by the Servicemembers Legal Defense Network, the national LGBT organization dealing with the "Don't Ask, Don't Tell" policy, show that, for the first time, a slight majority of soldiers, men and women now serving in the military, is in favor of abolishing "Don't

16. July 26, 1948: Executive Order 9981 signed into law by President Truman: "It is hereby declared to be the policy of the President that there shall be equality of treatment and opportunity for all persons in the armed services without regard to race, color, religion or national origin." (from: www.trumanlibrary.org)

Ask, Don't Tell." We have a better opportunity now than we've ever had before to overturn that policy.

With regard to the general basis of your question, we have to be careful to strike a balance between what we demand and expect of a new president and what is realistic for this most progressive and artic-ulate individual. Barack Obama is probably one of the greatest orators we've ever had in the history of this country. But even somebody who has a very compelling way of delivering the message has to have the support of people who are actually voting on these issues in order to get an agenda passed.

So in our community, the first thing we've laid out that we believe we can get passed in the first year or so is hate crimes legislation, a very important piece of legislation from a symbolic standpoint. It's also important in reality: what you won't read in the press is that federal hate crimes legislation only deals with federal crimes—only 10 percent of all of hate crimes.

Ninety percent of crimes that happen are either state or local crimes. So federal hate crimes legislation, while certainly laudable and useful, is actually not going to address that many crimes. What it's going to do is set up an elevated standard of expectation in this coun-try about what we have a right to demand with regard to equality and social justice.

That's a very good thing and will make it easier about a year later, probably, to get the Employment Non-Discrimination Act[17] passed in Congress. We hope to deal with housing and public accommodations law and "Don't Ask, Don't Tell" in the next several years. Finally, we need to undo the Defense of Marriage Act,[18] the most insidious piece of federal legislation passed in my lifetime.

But all these things are very difficult to do because they hit at the

---

17. The Employment Non-Discrimination Act has been introduced in almost every Congress since 1994. If passed, it will prohibit discrimination against employees on the basis of sexual orientation or gender identity.

18. The Defense of Marriage Act is a federal law that allows states to refuse to recognize same-sex marriages granted under the laws of other states. It did not prevent states from recognizing gay marriage, but it imposed constraints on the federal benefits received by all legally married gay couples. In United States v. Windsor (2013) the U.S. Supreme Court declared Section 3 of this act to be unconstitutional.

edge of the envelope with regard to social issues in this country, striking at the resistance of those who are desperately fighting to hold onto power and the status quo. The last act of the far right is to not allow LGBT people to enjoy the same kind of freedom and equality as others because it is often conflated with religion. So, from my perspective, this is an ideological stance, not a rational one.

It's about emotion, feeling and attachment to an old way of looking at things. It's not one that you can intellectually posit makes a great deal of sense. When you're fighting that kind of battle you must win over many different constituencies through logic, rational behavior and intellectual conversation so that people understand, point by point, the reality as opposed to the disinformation put out there by those opposed to advancing change.

AUDIENCE MEMBER 13: Who influenced you in your youthful days to become the courageous person you are today?

GLASSMAN: Thank you for that. I would say the most important influence in my life was my mother. I think parents and family can make a great deal of difference. It doesn't mean that you can't advance and create an opportunity by yourself, but the challenge is greater if you don't have role models from a very young age who embrace you, celebrate you and acknowledge every contribution you make. It's lucky to have parents who provide an emotional support system and offer you educational and social opportunities.

I had two parents who were very liberal politically. I participated in civil rights marches at the age of eight, carrying little picket signs against segregated restaurants and amusement parks. I also was fortunate enough to have had an extraordinary number of marvelous teachers from grade school through prep school, college and graduate school.

There were an inordinate number of extraordinarily sensitive, smart, engaging, critical-thinking people who challenged authority and the status quo, people who really engaged me in conversations that forced me to think outside of the box, not just repeat by rote what I was being taught. Critical thinking is the key to bringing vision and social change to society.

Programmatic responses, even done effectively, do not allow society to follow its natural urge to change and advance in ways that bring equality, justice and fairness to everyone. Society will function at its highest level when everyone has an equal opportunity to participate in a democratic way.

Although we like to talk about social justice and equality, we have many classes of people in our society. We like to look at our founding documents and quote them, but discrimination and bias were built into them – the disenfranchisement of an entire gender and for all those who didn't own land; anyone who was a person of color was only two-thirds of a person. These attitudes were built into the founding documents that we revere.

There are people who have to struggle to compete in a way that is unfair and which challenges them to do more in order to get to the same place as those who are automatically granted rights. The entitlements granted have nothing to do with achievement or accomplishment. They have only to do with skin color, gender and wealth.

AUDIENCE MEMBER 14: Most of us at this table, I believe, are leaders or have been leaders in our local communities. In Brooklyn, where I'm from, there are many parents and kids who, because of Barack Obama's election, are suddenly interested in politics, but the parents don't know how to begin nurturing the kids in that direction.

In the inner city, we know that if you want to be an NBA player, stay on the court; if you want to be a rapper, stay in the club. But when it comes to politics most parents don't have the mechanisms in place or even knowledge of the little things to get involved with. Since you grew up in this culture, I was wondering if you have any insight or anything we can share with the people in our community?

GLASSMAN: Sure. There are some critical things young people need to do if they want to get more engaged in politics. The first is to read many newspapers everyday, whether online or otherwise, to be informed, to keep up with what's going on all over the world. Now you can do it on the Internet. If you don't own a computer, you can use the ones at the library or in school labs.

In my position as a Cabinet member, I'm fortunate to get a news digest from the governor daily. It excerpts articles from papers all across the country. We sign up for subject areas so that we can see what's going on anywhere in the United States; we can sign up for foreign newspapers as well. I would certainly read the *New York Times, Washington Post* and *Los Angeles Times* to get various perspectives. There are many African-American newspapers that give a very different perspective on the world culturally. If you don't speak Spanish, there are Hispanic newspapers in English. I would start looking at some of those other voices so that you're not just reading a white cultural voice.

Although people are incredibly intimidated about this, young people can set up a meeting with any legislator. Legislators *love* young people but never get to see them. Just call up your state legislator, your state representative or Congressperson; they'll be *thrilled* to have you bring eight-year-old, ten-year-old, twelve-year-old kids into their office to learn about politics because most schools today don't teach civics or government.

The quickest way to get people engaged in politics is to actually meet and talk to people who are in elected or appointed office. Most offices would love to have young volunteers coming in after school for two or three hours a day. There are filing tasks and other mundane things to do, but in that environment they will meet people, hear about legislation and see people come in with advocacy efforts on particular issues. It's possible to learn more by being in the environment of a politician's office than anything studied in school.

The two items I just mentioned are free and simple to do. You will be welcomed because the younger you are, the less dangerous you seem. Those are two ways to get a young person started that nobody seems to do, but everybody can do without any cost.

AUDIENCE MEMBER 15: I've been thinking for a long time about what musicians and artists can do to contribute to a culture of peace. But I've been doing so much research on what's going on in the world: the economic crisis, climate change and international conflicts. I'm finding it rather difficult to find a place to start. It's easy to say, "Okay, I'm going to throw a benefit concert and call it 'Save Sudan,' " but I don't really feel like that's enough. Can you offer some specific advice for musicians and artists, so that they can be respected and can work with the movers and shakers in professional fields such as government and economics?

GLASSMAN: First of all, there is an organization, the Daniel Pearl Foundation, founded by Daniel Pearl's father, Judea. Daniel Pearl was a skilled musician. The foundation hosts concerts all around the world to bring a political message of understanding and moderate voices. Through music they help people learn about one another's cultures.

There are organizations you can Google. Quite a number of groups deal with political strife through the vehicle of music. There are also museums focused on this with exhibits that you can actually see that deal with political issues.

But I think it also makes sense to look at politicians who are musicians. Bill Clinton isn't the only one who played an instrument really well. One thing you might do is a survey of all the people in the New York State legislature. Ask them a series of questions about their musical education, if they play an instrument, if they go to concerts. You could develop an interesting survey from the perspective of being an artist and a musician that would tap into their own particular skills and interests. And then you could engage them once you have found that common ground.

It's always about finding commonality. Once you've found it, you can get a meeting with them and talk about how you can use music to effectuate a policy initiative you might be interested in, either in their district or statewide. Music is a very easy vehicle because most people can find some music that resonates with them. That way you can bring people together and, in a subtle way, transmit a message that uses the vehicle of music as the common binder.

A politician playing an instrument might give a talk that's not an ordinary political speech, but is more about how to bridge the gaps between us, how to build a culture of peace, a culture of understanding, a culture of dialogue—all the issues that you're all involved with here in the SGI.

AUDIENCE MEMBER 16: You mentioned that your biggest influence was your mother and discussed the importance of having a good parent. I was born and raised in India. There is a generation of women who are struggling to balance work and children; there's very little time that they can devote to their children. How can we become better parents? We should be able to give them an environment that makes them a good person. In my country, working women are being blamed for the collapse of the family structure, based on women having stepped out of the house, gotten an education and jobs. How do we deal with this?

GLASSMAN: Women in the United States are blamed for that, too. It is, unfortunately, a common way of avoiding responsibility and scapegoating others. But you're asking an incredibly difficult question that I don't have an immediate answer for, but I will take a little stab at it. One of the things that I think we do well at agencies like mine is to open up dialogue and introduce people to one another so that they encounter different mindsets, perspectives and philosophies.

People in decision-making positions—often a very limited number of elected officials—are the ones who need to be educated about a new way of understanding roles and responsibilities in the world. If they are introduced to people they can respect, to new ideas, there is at least an opportunity to begin a conversation about existing laws that limit the ability of women to advance.

We need more legislation that offers economic opportunities, childcare and support services for working women. Those things don't exist in most places and laws often block women from advancing. Nearly all elected officials have schooling they must complete. For example, judges have to attend, literally, judge school for several weeks before they're allowed to sit on the bench. Elected officials go through several days, sometimes a week, of training.

If you can get involved with in-service training opportunities with officials, whether elected or appointed, you have a real chance of sharing other ways of viewing the world, the people in it and their roles in society. You have to start somewhere and training is often the very best way to do it. The problems that you're talking about are age-old, very complex and layered.

One short answer isn't really going to get at the foundation of how to resolve a problem like this because you're talking about many aspects of society that must come together for a long period of time before the shift is apparent. But, it is quite surprising that a country like Iran, for example, in thirty years under the Shah—no matter how bad you may have thought that regime was—went from a country that was completely non-Western to a country that had the highest percentage of college-educated women of any country, including the United States.

That has drifted backwards since a religion-based government has taken over Iran, but it is possible in a short period of time for social change to offer completely different perceptions of what is acceptable and is embraced in a society. It depends on the vehicle used to do it. So it doesn't necessarily have to take hundreds of years; it's that it usually does because of resistance to change by those who are in positions of authority and power. I'm sorry I can't give you a better answer to such a layered, complex problem.

AUDIENCE MEMBER 17: What aspect of your job do you find most difficult? What kind of advice do you offer future leaders about public service?

GLASSMAN: The most difficult aspect of my job is not the job itself; it's some of the people with whom I have to work. I work with many different constituencies but one of the most important is the entire state legislature and our delegation of nineteen Congresspeople. Not all of them share my perspectives or point of view on the issues we're addressing tonight. A surprisingly large number do, but there are many who come from a politically restrictive and conservative place.

I do a lot of media: talk shows on television and radio, call-in shows where I answer questions or interviews in newspapers. The challenge is to never lose my control. I must never react emotionally. I have to retain my passion for the issue without getting out of control or reducing myself to the level of vitriol I sometimes receive in these phone calls. I'm very good at that. But it takes its toll on me internally. It's not an easy thing to do, sitting for three hours and receiving sixty-seven phone calls in a row, all of which are hate phone calls. I've had to do that.

The biggest challenge is retaining your commitment to the issues and to a process of dialogue that is restrained, thoughtful and sensitive to other people's needs. It's important to remember that everybody has the potential to grow and change and to be better educated. It's important to realize that you have something to offer to people and to do it in a way that is controlled, not allowing yourself to rise to the bait.

Regarding the second part of your question about getting into public service: Don't lose your commitment to your ideals. It is easy to see people in public office becoming co-opted and controlled by the temptations of power, economic incentives or other things that seem alluring at the moment, but are deceptive and will undercut any progress toward change that you have made. Hold onto your ideals, understanding that your commitment is to social justice, to improving the lives of those who are disadvantaged and need your help.

Commitment to your ideals is a sacred promise you make to yourself. It's not between you and anybody else. It's holding onto the ideals of your youth, the essence of what makes you a leader and someone who will leave a legacy in this world. Let your ideals drive your life rather than money, power or material things. That would be the best advice I could give you.

~ November 13, 2008
SGI-USA New York Culture of Peace Resource Center

Global Migration and the Challenge of Development

Ali Modarres

Associate Director,
Edmund G. "Pat" Brown Institute of Public Affairs

Ali Modarres is the associate director of the Edmund G. "Pat" Brown Institute of Public Affairs at California State University, Los Angeles, and a professor in the Department of Geography and Urban Analysis on the same campus. He specializes in urban geography; his primary research and publication interests are community development and planning. He has published in the areas of urban development, transportation planning, environmental equity, social geography, immigration, and race and ethnicity as they relate to the issues of access and the role of public policy in disadvantaged communities.

Dr. Modarres speaks compellingly of many topics included in the eight action areas in the 1999 United Nations Declaration and Programme of Action on a Culture of Peace, especially focusing on the second: promoting sustainable economic and social development; and the sixth: advancing understanding, tolerance and solidarity. As he says: "When we think about global patterns of immigration, it's a labor imbalance phenomenon, a global phenomenon. It's not one country's issue. It's a combination of demography, geography and labor dynamics: Labor surplus versus labor demand. We need to see immigration in any one country within a global context—how it compares to the rest of the world."

Global migration is an issue that is strongly connected to the concept of a culture of peace. It is not just an issue for the United States; it's an international issue—one that may become more controversial before it gets better. Global migration can be described with demography: pure numbers, graphs and charts and the reasons that people move, but there is also the human dimension. Every immigrant is a human being, so this can be a complex topic. Rather than a purely statistical perspective, a different, large-as-life perspective is required.

With that in mind, I would like to walk through a series of complex issues. The story of immigration is probably best explained with the story of immigration in one's own country. Therefore I would like to start with a view of the United States that you may already be familiar with. Let's put it into a long-term perspective. The United States sees itself as the original nation of immigrants. There are facts and fictions about that view, but we will leave that for a moment.

Economics and Global Migration

From my perspective, a significant level of global population movement is driven by economics. The years from 1880 to 1920 were an era in which immigration expanded rapidly. During this same era, the United States saw a fantastic expansion of its industrial base. It needed labor and the labor came. But the labor force came with attached identity issues: How do you deal with so many millions of people coming in? How do you get along?

In 1924, we passed a law called the Immigration Restriction Act that said, in effect, "We don't need you anymore. Don't come." That era was followed by the Great Depression. During the 1930s, immigrants stopped coming and actually started to leave. It was the first decade in which more people left the United States than came to it. That was a shocking fact. During World War II, the economy improved, economic growth began to expand and what happened? The labor force, in large numbers, began to come back.

People move because of jobs. They come here because in their country of birth or the country where they currently live, things are not looking up. They must leave and go somewhere else. There is a political dimension to immigration. For the most part, immigrants came to the United States because things were getting better here. Since the 1940s, our economy has basically been on a gradual upward path.

Now, over the last few months, as things have been getting worse, we are beginning to read in the newspapers that people are leaving. This is normal. This is what happens when people go elsewhere for economic betterment. If immigration is seen as a revolving door; if we appreciate the fact that labor moves about; we will not be so bothered by various issues. We would accept this as the dynamic of labor balancing.

Changes in the United States and Global Migration

Things are changing. Thirty-seven million people now living in the United States were born in another country; that's about 13 percent of our population. Over the last eight or nine years we see that people come to the United States—the numbers go up and down—but they don't always go where they used to go. The state of California has seen a decline in the number of immigrants; Los Angeles has seen an even larger decline than the state. But places like Georgia, Alabama, and Kentucky are seeing more immigrants. States like Florida and New York continue to receive immigrants, but if you look at Los Angeles County, there hasn't been much movement over the past three years.

Our immigrants are getting older and becoming more settled. If we have the revolving door conversation, you would see a different dynamic at play here. But overall, while the immigrant population of the United States has increased from 35.6 million to 38 million over the past three years, immigration in Los Angeles has increased very little. We are not attracting immigrants anymore. Our economy is not inviting and, therefore, things are not really working out. People put up with attitude as long as there is a bit of positive economy at the same time.

We can learn from the significant level of uneasiness in the United States before we look at the global level of immigration. Across years immigration varies, across regions of origin things begin to change, and immigrants don't always come from Mexico. In one year during the 1990s, the largest number of documented immigrants to the United States did not come from Mexico; they came from the Philippines.

Things changed in terms of origin and in terms of destination. Immigrants don't always come to California and they don't always come to the United States; they go to other places as well. Labor migration is a function of perceived opportunity. Therefore, whether real or imagined, as long as other immigrants say things are looking up in Los Angeles, people will come. Therefore, real or imagined change in the social, economic and political landscape can produce a pattern of migration. People begin to move around.

Labor Surplus vs. Labor Demand

There are many ways in which to discuss immigration. For example, we can talk about the unique history of the United States. But, every country can do that. Australians can say, "Hey, we are a nation of immigrants as well." New Zealanders can say the same thing. However, we need to discuss it in a more sophisticated manner.

We can complain about the flaws of immigration, the pros and cons of why we need immigration laws changed. We can talk about it as a cultural phenomenon: "Some cultures are more prone to migration than others." Well, that's not true. There are elements within the economy that we need to talk about. But more important, a lot of people think immigration is out of control, that "the sky is falling" and "this is the end of the world as we know it."

But as you will see from the numbers, it is not the end of the world. It's just the beginning of a wonderful, new way of thinking about immigration. When we think about global patterns of immigration, it's a labor imbalance phenomenon, a global phenomenon. It's not one country's issue. It's a combination of demography, geography and labor dynamics: Labor surplus versus labor demand. We need to see immigration in any one country within a global context—how it compares to the rest of the world.

Let's introduce some statistics: In 1965, there were about 75 million people who lived outside their country of birth. By 1990, the number was 120 million; at the beginning of this decade, it reached 175 million and by 2005, it was 190 million. So, if you put all of the foreign-born into one group, the population would be that of a sizable country.

Although these numbers are large, keep this statistic in mind: Globally, around 3 percent of people migrate and this has remained the same since World War II. So, as the population grows, more people move around, but the percentage remains at about 3 percent and it stays at that percentage because we have so many restrictive laws.

About 10 percent of global migration has to do with politics: people have problems in their countries; they are persecuted or threatened and forced to move around. In this case, they don't leave their country because they need a job. Currently the migrant population is growing at the rate of about five to ten million per year, roughly the same as the growth rate of the global population.

There are trends we need to be aware of. The flow and the volume may change. As the economic structure of the world begins to change, this economic problem will work itself out. Ireland was a country that produced mostly immigrants. Now Ireland is a country that receives immigrants.

Foreign-born Populations Around the World

Globally things are beginning to change. Therefore, we have to be dynamic in the way we think. Most migration tends to be regional. Most of these 190 million people don't travel across continents. Traditionally, more than half of international migrants have moved from one developing country to another developing country. That's the pattern of movement.

It was only during the 1990s that a country such as the United States could really say, "We've gotten the biggest share of global migration." That's an amazing story to look at: Even though we are a nation of immigrants, it is only since the 1990s that we have gotten a larger share of global migration. In the mid-1990s, for example, a total of 46 million international migrants were in the United States, France, Germany, Canada, Australia and the United Kingdom. In 2005, the top ten countries of destination have 52 percent of the international migrant population, and, as I mention their names, think about the ones that ten or even twenty years ago would not have been on the list: the United States, the Russian Federation, Germany, France, Saudi Arabia, Canada, India, the United Kingdom and Spain. These are now the top ten countries with the highest percentage of international migrants.

We may think of ourselves as a nation of immigrants, but the following statistics show the percentages of foreign-born people living in various countries. Here is the ranking, from highest percentage to lowest: In the United Arab Emirates, 71.4 percent of the population are foreign-born; in Kuwait, 62.1 percent; Singapore, 42.6 percent; Israel 39.6 percent; Jordan 39 percent, Saudi Arabia 25.9 percent; Oman 24.5 percent; Switzerland, 22.9 percent; Australia, 20.3 percent; Canada, 18.9 percent. Where is the United States on this list? Actually, only about 13 percent of our population is foreign-born, so we don't really fit on this list.

The Service Economy

In over seventy countries around the world, the foreign-born population constitutes more than ten percent of the population. This is becoming a global thing. It's not a matter of just a few countries; there are many in this category. The emerging patterns are very interesting. There are high rates of migrants moving from less developed countries to more developed countries, but what is interesting about this process is that, similar to what happened between 1880 and 1920 in the United States, we now have a world which functions around a service economy.

A service economy has two faces: the high-end, including finance and banking and the low end, including the home worker and people who take care of the elderly population. The attraction of the emerging low-skill service sector to more prosperous nations is a new pattern. More people are moving across the globe to take jobs in home care, cleaning, retail sales and the food industry. We call it home-based care and consumption services that don't produce a product. It's just a matter of people taking care of other people.

With economic growth in the Middle East and other regions around the globe, the demand for temporary migrant workers began to increase in 1970. For example, in Saudi Arabia, about one-quarter of the low-skilled workers are foreigners—those in the home care industry.

Looking for More

There are other concerns: Higher rates of middle-class immigrants are moving. These people are not just looking for jobs; they are looking for jobs that pay more compared to what they can earn in their home country.

This includes computer programmers, engineers and designers. Migration to service nodes is increasing.

Most of the countries I mentioned before are typically the kind of countries where many services are provided, so you can think of them as resorts. You can go to a resort where many people are employed but no one is producing anything; everyone is just helping each other out.

This type of economy doesn't produce gadgets, it produces comfort. And out of the production of comfort comes the need for migration of labor. So, migrants are helping improve the quality of life, even if they're not helping themselves. They may improve their lot through economics, but they actually help the country of destination as well.

The Feminization of Migration

Global migration to these particular service nodes—the Persian Gulf countries are among those—is gradually becoming more feminized. This is an interesting and missed opportunity in terms of thinking. When we use the word "immigrant," people typically think of young males. For the last twenty years, a typical immigrant would have been a slightly older female, not a young male.

When women are a component of migration, we need to be concerned about laws for protection and safety. You can't leave it to smugglers or human traffickers. There are many issues that have to be dealt with. And then, on the home front, who takes care of the children who are left behind?

With that in mind, we need to begin to think about laws differently. With the recent global economic trends, migratory patterns are beginning to change and they will continue to change. We need to think about certain issues of significant importance such as the demographic imbalance in certain countries, like Japan. Some countries are graying. Large numbers of young people are not being produced in those countries, so they will have to import their labor force.

Exporting Labor

We don't yet have this problem in the United States, but think about this statistic: In the United States over half of new labor growth comes from immigrants, not from the native population. Due to global economic ineq-uities, migration has been, and will continue to be, an important source of revenue for the countries of origin through remittances and also for the countries of destination because they create an economy in which they can survive. So countries like the Philippines will do really well for a while.

The majority of current immigration patterns are rooted in previ-ous labor and economic relationships. Countries that know each other, that have had relationships with each other, be it through war or through peace, have created a flow. So England, with its relationship with South Asia, is going to attract South Asian immigrants. Our relationships with the Philippines and other regions of the world have created the same sort of flows as well. We need to understand this point.

The logic of late capitalism, which is the kind of economy we have, is for certain nations to move beyond exporting their natural resources to exporting labor. This new dimension of migration has led to governments' increasing role in facilitating the migration process.

Since 1970, a number of countries, including the Philippines, have begun to realize that they must capitalize on the migration process. They recognized the need to provide structure to the process of sending people out to work elsewhere.

In terms of basic numbers, countries that send folks out typically have economies that do not produce a lot of comfort at home. The level of income is very low. For example, in India a large portion of the popula-tion lives on less than two dollars a day.

I usually talk more about Nigeria more than any other country; it's a country to watch. It's growing rapidly and it's very dysfunctional. It has oil but not enough for rapid growth. Nigeria must become a net exporter of population. We think we are going to see more and more immigration from Nigeria. For now, the West Coast hasn't seen it, but the Nigerian community on the East Coast is growing.

The Dynamics of Movement

When we look at the numbers in different countries, we realize that there are various dynamics of movement. For example, in countries such as the Philippines, there may not be a large number of people living on less than two dollars per day as in India. There is a higher level of education and a mismatch: too many people with college degrees and not enough jobs in the country. Therefore, the country needs to move them out and needs to control how they go about it.

In this case, it is not a matter of global migration. We think of one country as a net sender and another as a net receiver. In reality, the same country can be both a sender and receiver. The best examples of this are India and Pakistan. These countries produce a lot of outflow, but there is a lot of local movement within them as well. For example, a Nepalese may move to India to improve his or her economic standing. This is an economic balancing act. As long as there is a net economic improvement, population movement begins to happen.

As global processes begin to confine the opportunity structure, migration is channeled to just a few countries. What happens when many of these countries of opportunity place restrictions on immigration? If only three out of twenty countries of opportunity allow entry, then everyone is going to go to try to go to those three.

Sweden has experienced this. It had a liberal immigration policy for many years, but the Swedish unions, government and people began to say, "We can't do this anymore. The rest of Europe is not carrying their share. We are becoming the net recipient." So, just a few countries receive this massive concentration of population. In the case of India and Pakistan, we have seen this in terms of their population and the number of emigrants who leave those countries. This suggests that globalization may be moving toward a more rapid concentration of international migrants into a few countries.

What we really are coming down to is seven countries carrying a disproportionate share of migration. That creates agitation and blame about how things function.

The Rapid Growth of Global Migration

Let me give you a sense of the rapid growth of global migration. The Gulf Corporation Council, made up of the countries along the Persian Gulf, has an amazing rate of growth of migrant workers. For example, the United Arab Emirates had only 62 thousand international migrants in 1970; in 2000, it had 9.6 million. So, certain places are attracting a large number of migrant workers.

I am not talking about numbers; I am talking about human beings. These 9.6 million individuals have feelings for their home country. They arrive in a country that does not have laws to handle their situation. There is no implementation of a public policy for the social integration of this population. They are regarded as temporary workers who come in and then leave. However, they don't leave permanently. They leave and come back. They constantly recycle through the laws.

Although the level of growth is impressive, these countries become highly dependent. In the United Arab Emirates, 89.8 percent to 90 percent of its working population is foreign-born. Imagine if everyone left at once; the economy would come to a halt. Imagine 90 percent of the labor force leaving one morning. So, the receiving country has an interest that I want to emphasize.

An Unstoppable Trend

If there is one thing to be said about migration, it is that it is happening; we can't stop it. If we try to divert it, it goes to other places. And, if we try to force everyone to stay where they are, that will actually create more problems. I suggest that, in order for us to understand the nature of international migration, we need to go beyond this old-fashioned conversation about push-and-pull factors; we need to talk about how migration actually happens.

The Three Phases of Migration

There are three phases to migration: pre-migration, migration and post-migration. I must present the subject in this way because, from a policy perspective, each phase requires that different parties get involved, different laws be passed and different protections be put into place.

Migration is not a simple process. We must look for individual agency and begin to figure out which institutional structures need to be created. The "Immigration and Naturalization Services" of the world are not the way to handle immigration. Human beings must be facilitated, their rights protected and their jobs monitored in ways that will also help the country of origin. We can also develop mechanisms for the movement of populations and formulate policies to take care of them at every phase.

Let's talk about what's happening in a few places. The three major sources of global migration today are China, India and the Philippines. They have faced a demographic condition that has created a supply-side labor situation. Why does it happen? It has to do with the second stage of demographic transition.

As a country experiences a high birth rate, improved medical conditions reduce the death rate. As more people survive, there are more young people. With more young people, the country has to figure out how to avoid economic collapse. If they operate as usual, the unemployment rate can rise to thirty to forty percent. These countries have one relief valve and that is to send people out or create a situation where people leave.

Historically, China and India have done that, even without government involvement, but the brilliance of the Philippines is a bit different. When the 1970s produced a condition in which labor began to move, a policy, the 1974 Labor Code of the Philippines, was implemented. The text of this code is fascinating because it acknowledges the very things I've mentioned.

The code acknowledges the importance of contract labor migration as a mechanism for responding to the lack of local employment opportunities, increasing the level of foreign currency in the Philippines and examining development opportunities. In 1974, they understood that when someone leaves and works abroad, that person would send money home, a win-win situation. The unemployment rate is lowered, foreign currency comes into the country and that foreign currency is invested in the country. The receiving country has also gained the labor they need—a perfect situation.

The Philippines labor code is now called the 1982 Philippines Overseas Employment Administration. Many countries are now looking to the Philippines to learn from them. Thirty-five years ago, there might have been more countries thinking as the Philippines has done, but that is not now the case. So, there are issues that need to be discussed.

Just having a supply of labor doesn't mean that a good policy will emerge. It takes an active, not a passive, government to set up policies that support their labor force. By dividing migration into its three phases—pre-immigration, migration and post-migration—the responsibility is shared by the country of origin, the country of passing through and the receiving country. Everyone has a responsibility to everyone else. Each country is responsible for the human being who is passing through their border. Borders are important, but respect for human life is also important. The activity that will inevitably happen through smugglers and human trafficking should rather be done properly so everyone can win.

The Pre-Migration Phase

In the pre-migration phase, we need to consider how people emigrate: the availability of information about the global employment opportunity structure, means of travel, prospects for returning and reinvesting the surplus income, permissiveness of migration within the country of origin, border crossing and labor market entry in the country of destination and labor recruiters.

It's important to consider these dynamics, get involved in actual employment recruitments. The receiving country engages in the process of attracting folks to come and work; the country of origin makes sure there is a labor contract with the receiving country. The two governments stay in communication. With this example, we can say that countries with labor surplus need to consider these issues and get organized.

Labor surplus in countries such as India, China, Philippines, Indonesia, Malaysia and other Asian and African nations becomes a necessary component in this way of thinking. There are many countries that can participate in this process of supply-side labor.

Here are some facts using the example of the Philippines. In 2007, more than one million temporary migrant workers left the Philippines to work in 190 countries. There were few countries in the world that Filipinos would not go to. Think of all the languages spoken in those countries.

There was a unique element to the skills of the Filipinos: They spoke English. In the 1970s, even in the Middle Eastern countries, receiving countries recognized that the migrants working in their homes could be teaching English to their children. So, Filipinos went to many different countries. In 2007, about 1 million of them worked abroad. The Commission on Filipinos Overseas estimates that now nearly 8.7 million Filipinos live abroad and that half of them are temporary workers.

The Philippines does not disown this population of temporary workers. It owns them and says they will be returning. They are *cyclical* migrants.

And I want to introduce that word into our vocabulary. A cyclical migrant is one who goes to other countries to work but returns and then goes back out to work again, perhaps to a different country this time. We need to acknowledge their rights. They need not be forced to be a citizen of just one country. They should be helped to be citizens of the world, to function in the way they know how to function, to enable them, not disable them. This demonstrates how the entire process would be different. The Philippines is at least trying.

Importing Labor

Now, on the demand-side for labor are the countries with a high gross national product. These countries are typically facing a diminishing supply of labor. Importing labor is therefore unavoidable. These countries have gone through a very unique phase in trying to fix the labor problem: They have brought the female immigrant into the labor force.

During World War II, the United States was the first to have massive growth of the female labor force. For a few decades following the war, that did the job, but then even more labor was needed. As two-family incomes became more prevalent, more home workers and low-skill labor is needed to take care of the home front.

The following nine countries are those with the largest aging population: Greece, Germany, Japan, Sweden, Belgium, Spain, Bulgaria, Switzerland and Italy. In these countries, more than 20 percent of the population is over sixty years of age. So these countries must quickly figure out whom they will invite to support the health care industry, to take care of the retired population and their children.

All of these aspects of global migration are important parts of each country's economics. National survival is dependent on how we think about immigration. It's not about cultural encounter or conflict; it's about survival. Japan has been trying to deal with these issues and has its own stories but we won't go into detail here.

Right now, in the United States, the population is not rapidly aging, but we are on our way. Within a few decades, when the last of the Baby Boomers arrive at retirement, immigration will be the only major source of labor. To repeat the numbers once more, the immigration of skilled labor to the United States is about 10 percent, which is equivalent to

global levels. These are the engineers and nurses that we attract. Sixty-
one percent of our foreign-born population sixteen years of age and older
is employed—that's 17.3 million people. In the 1990s, new immigrants
contributed 47 percent to the labor force; between 2000 and 2003, they
passed the halfway mark; now more than half of all new labor growth in
the United States comes from immigration. In about three decades, the
native labor force will be much smaller than the foreign-born labor force.

If they are working and have income, they will be the people buying
houses, paying taxes and contributing to Social Security. So while these
people may just be coming to do housework, they're contributing to the
national economy as well.

There are other forces to consider about why people come from a particular country and go to another, such as religion, language and historical
affinity. But we also must consider international treaties, the relationships
between countries. We need to understand that subcontracting practices
produce ways of working together. For example, if our country does most
of the subcontracting with India, an Indian worker is going to say, "Wait a
minute, I can be a programmer in India and earn twenty thousand a year
or I can go to the United States and get a higher salary." In this example,
we can see that labor contracts cause movement.

Here is the irony: For decades, nearly a century, we have tolerated capital movement, but we haven't learned to tolerate labor movement. We
are okay when a corporation goes to Malaysia and invests, but we freak
out when Malaysians come our way. In some ways, this is actually a direction of capital flow. It's not just money going out, it creates relationships
in terms of movement.

Over the last few years I have dedicated a portion of my talks to the
feminization of immigration. The growth of the female emigration population brings with it serious concerns. We need to think about the subject
in two ways. The first element is that, globally, a large number of female
migrants serve in people's private homes and so they become invisible.
Therefore, we need to make sure that their rights are protected.

The second element is that not every female who comes to the United
States, Australia or New Zealand is a home worker. There are actually
many professionals. A large number of Chinese, Filipinas and professionals from other countries are coming here. We want to make sure that the
innate inequities of our own system, that is women being paid less than

men, do not produce problems for the immigrant population as well, because they will not be able to live up to their potential.

The numbers are quite startling. In the early part of this decade, 570,000 Sri Lankan women were reported to be working in the Middle East. Two-thirds of Filipina immigrants, about a half-million women, were employed in home-based service. To develop a full appreciation of the feminization of the migrant labor force, there are other numbers to consider. Among all Filipino emigrants, two-thirds are women. Not all of them are single; many are married. So, who takes care of the children, the family? Who is left behind? There is a series of responsibilities for the country of origin and a series of responsibilities for the country of destination. The responsibilities should be shared evenly between both countries.

If we need Filipina nurses, our responsibility goes beyond just getting them to come; we need to accommodate the population. And as the countries of destination receive populations from Korea, from India, from Pakistan and other countries, this has to be expanded beyond a single nationality.

There is a brain-drain function, and we benefit from it. These countries educate their population. Therefore any country that attracts an educated person from another country benefits from the money invested in that person.

Social Integration of the Migrant Population

This phenomenon has transformed itself into a new debate on the issues of structural integration. We need to discuss as follows: "So you're a nurse. Is that your whole life? There's more to it. You live here. You shop for groceries; you pay for things; you use public transportation; you drive a car." It's not as simple as just giving someone a good salary. We need to figure out how to encourage social integration without forcing people with a statement such as, "The only way we can help you is for you to become an American or an Australian." We need to put the human being first and the national imposition second. Without forcing it initially, how about allowing people to be multiple citizens? (Applause.) Thank you! I don't usually get applause; I usually get yelled at. This is a great audience!

If we are thinking through the development of labor migration, we need to think about the notion of contracts between different countries.

We need to talk about the middle class population as it begins to move around and about their relationships in terms of visiting relatives. How does immigration help the sending country – the remittances – the money sent home, how does it work?

Sending Money Home

Once people start leaving and sending enough money home, if things go well, the number of people who need to leave that country is reduced. And, the people of neighboring countries are actually attracted to that country. This has already happened in Greece and Spain. Money sent home is invested in the country of origin. Human capital transfer makes immigration an important component of envisioned development. The money sent home does a couple of things: As people leave, unemployment and all the economic problems that go with it are reduced. At the same time, money comes back into the country, so it's a win-win situation.

The receiving country does not have enough labor; once that labor arrives, the economy gets going. So, in fact migration is a positive, not a negative thing for everyone. Migration becomes a problem only when it is thought of as a nationalistic issue. Seeing others as being completely different from one becomes the source of the problem. In purely economic terms, migration is a win-win process that many countries have benefited from.

The Philippines is a great example, but the same is true for Mexico, India, Nigeria, Indonesia, Bangladesh and many other countries that have sent out their people. The Philippines' largest source of foreign currency is supplied through remittances of migrants. In 1999, it amounted to about $7 billion and helped defray 50 percent of the Philippines' trade deficit. So much money was sent back home that it could be counted toward the trade deficit.

While the exact figures of remittances are difficult to obtain, immigrants can be seen as important engines of economic development in particular areas. The money going home doesn't go to every Filipino or every Mexican. It goes to a specific family, a specific town and a specific city. It is not across-the-board development. One criticism that has been made of the Philippines program is that it has not developed a way to evenly distribute the money throughout the economy. Some money goes into the

Immigration and emigration are labor and economic issues driven by demographic, economic and political imbalances at the global level. But, in the end, it is important that we pay attention to change. We need to be ready for change.

construction industry or real estate or retail, but it is a trickle-down process. It helps, but it is not quite tailored to what it should be.

In contrast, in Mexico remittances are only 1.6 percent of its gross domestic product, not a huge number. In 2007, Filipinos sent home $14.5 billion in remittances, which helped increase private consumption and contributed to the country's 7.3 percent economic growth, a much higher expansion. We are talking about the economic growth of a country. A percentage of it comes from the migrants' money and this is expanded upon. What I suggest is that, over time, a beautiful interdependence of economies can develop. One country receives labor and grows its economy; the other country grows their economy by recapturing remittances. However, laws are needed to protect both sides.

There are many countries where a large portion of their gross domestic product comes from remittances. Jordan is one. This is not a country we often talk about, but it's important to look at it. In Jordan, 22.8 percent of their gross domestic product came from migration, a great economic boost. In terms of expansion, Lesotho shows a much larger percentage of gross domestic product at 26.2 percent. The net producers of migration are doing well, but other countries tend to have varying percentages.

Here are some interesting numbers: For 2008, estimated global remittances are $375 billion, a huge number. The share of this going to developing countries is $283 billion dollars. The difference between the figures – $375 billion and $283 billon – goes to developed countries. Americans working overseas send money home, too. So, when we look at remittances, we are looking at everyone sending money home, which means people of well-to-do nations benefit as well. Globally, that's what it looks like.

A geographer always has to show at least one map, so here's one that shows that the other areas with major remittances are China and South Asia. Mexico is the other country. You'll get a prize if you can tell me the country with high remittance rates in Europe: it's France. France has enough expats overseas that it gets quite a lot of remittances.

Some countries are beginning to understand the dynamics. Syria is one. It has begun to create a formal structure, the Ministry of Migrants, to track migrants' capital. They are thinking about how to invest in their migrants and how to create avenues for economic betterment, not only for individuals, but for the state also.

The economic activities of migrants will make countries of destination function as places of capital accumulation. In 2003, Saudi Arabia generated $15 billion in remittances, making it the largest source of remittances. Some countries distribute a lot of money by bringing migrants in and investing money in them. For the United Arab Emirates and others it ranges from $4 billion and more. Collectively, the Gulf countries produce $25 billon of the $387 billion-plus global total.

There are a few other things needed in the pre-migration phase. We need to pay special attention to mechanisms that lead to decisions regarding migration: inadequate jobs and the issues of specific economic sectors that are not functioning. More than anything, governments need to learn how to facilitate the movement of people between countries. We need to learn about it, love it, accept it, embrace it and move on without anger.

We also need to remain aware of the gender dimensions. In some countries, the majority of migrants are female. In the pre-migration phase, we need to consider that, to talk about it and plan for it so that migrants don't leave their countries and end up with problems. We need to take care of the problems before they happen.

Government Involvement in Global Migration

We need to think about social welfare systems so that if a migrant fails, it's not just their individual failure; the state is there to help them. And I'm not talking about the country of receiving, I'm talking about the country of origin that needs to think about social welfare systems to help this process, to create an equity process. Revisit punitive immigration laws forbidding people to leave. Let's get to a point where we can have people saying, "I can't get a good job here, I need to go somewhere else," and I say, "Great, what can we do?" Don't say, "You can't have a passport."

Overall, we must educate migrants. Give them a passport, but tell them, "Let's educate you about the laws of the countries you may be going to. Let's make sure you don't go blindly to a country and get abused. Here are the basic labor laws of the United States, in case that's where you're going. Here are the basic labor laws of England if you're going to England," and so on. The Philippines does some of that and other countries are beginning to do that as well. Migrants need to understand their political legal rights, the issues of cultural and social relationships and how to prepare for the destination country.

Countries need to assume specific responsibility for their expatriates. They need to monitor labor recruitment, not leave it to foreign agencies or some *ad hoc* person looking for labor in their country. They should arrange to be part of the negotiations so that when people sign contracts, they don't end up getting abused from the pay perspective, if nothing else. Then they won't be accepting contracts with a low-level pay, getting to the country of destination and then realizing that the income is inadequate to survive.

There are many things countries can do. The Philippines Overseas Employment Administration performs some of these functions. If the Filipinos knew how much I was promoting their country…

The Migration Phase

During the migration phase, the part that causes me the most concern is when people fall into the shadows of the law as they move between two countries. At that time, it is not clear whose law applies to you. We need to create secure passage; to ensure that travel fares are set fairly so that people are not left stranded; that they know how to navigate to their country of destination so that smugglers won't benefit. One of the greatest dangers in expansion and migration is smuggling. And the danger is not just along our border with Mexico. It's in Europe and in Asia; it's everywhere.

It's a global economy growing around the strange laws we have generated. This is the most stressful part of the process and we need to diminish that as much as possible. We need facilities for this part of the process. It is the most stressful part of the experience and we need to diminish that as much as possible.

The Post-Migration Phase

Of course, in the post-migration phase, the responsibility belongs to the country of destination. But, if we can have bilateral agreements on capital flow, why not have bilateral agreements on migration? We have laws about how Nike can go to Country X and invest, but then why isn't there a bilateral law that details how Country X's migrants will be treated when they arrive and what their rights are? Why can't we talk about multiple citizenships? Is it the end of the world if someone has five passports? I'm getting ridiculous so you can see my point.

We need to get over some of these issues so we can talk about the well-being of migrants, their families and our collective economies and to talk about a global economy, not one country over the other. It's a peaceful way of saying, "Let's see if we can figure out a way that your citizens and my citizens are seen as equal human beings, not that mine are better than yours."

Collaboration in the matters of immigration, which is indeed human capital exchange, needs to take into account the dignity of the human beings involved. Everything is not about dollars. It has to be about the dignity of the migrant who is going through the experience. Otherwise when economies go bad, we ignore migrants or we deport them.

Demographic, Economic and Political Imbalances

My final words are that immigration and emigration are labor and economic issues driven by demographic, economic and political imbalances at the global level. But, in the end, it is important that we pay attention to change. We need to be ready for change. The United States is not always the destination country and the Philippines or Mexico the country of origin.

During my talk I tried not to discuss Mexico because when we fixate on one country, we forget about the other two hundred-plus counties whose people are also moving around. India is a recipient of migrants, what about them having laws as well? It's not a matter of any particular country having more responsibility than others; it's a matter of sharing equal responsibility for the whole process.

We need to attempt to control the flow. But, if we try to control the flow of immigration without attention to issues of labor dynamics and human rights, then we will create nationalistic, self-serving laws. They will not be sustainable. Eventually we'll have to revise them, and then re-revise them. We should not oversimplify migration; we should embrace the complex issues and work through the complexity to create appropriate laws.

I've been told time after time, "But we don't have laws like that. " That's my point exactly. We need to create them. If we already had laws, I wouldn't be giving this talk. It would sound ridiculous. So, it's important is to say, "We are in territory we don't know much about. For many years we have seen everyone who doesn't come from our country as a potential problem. We have trained ourselves this way. It is time to say that we are all the same. If everyone is afraid of everyone else, no one will be moving anywhere. But, globally, 3 percent of our population is moving around. They are brave souls. They go everywhere; they do what they need to do. Some of them do well; some of them suffer. Wouldn't it be better if we loved them, hugged them, embraced them and said, "You're moving; we'll help you"?

The more we do this, the more ready we will be for the next phase. This process is not going to end. Whenever the United States sees a little swelling of immigration, it says, "OK, the problem is fixing itself." But the migrants are going elsewhere. It's a global issue and that's why the United Nations is involved, why other organizations are involved. The integration of immigrants is important. The humanity of the whole process cannot be forgotten. We help ourselves by having better laws, regulations, policies and better ways of thinking about this process and not in the hateful way as usually happens, not just in this country, but in a lot of countries.

Questions and Answers

AUDIENCE MEMBER 1: Beyond economic demands, what is the fundamental right of a person to go to another country? I am not talking

about the legality; I am talking about the fundamental or founda-
tional right.

MODARRES: From my perspective, the fundamental right belongs to everyone. Everyone should be allowed to move if they so wish; that's a personal perspective. It does create a bit of a problem and I want to confess
to that. Now let me get to the political side.

For the past two hundred years, we have drawn lines in the sand
and imagined that nations have the right to have these lines. I have
no problem with that or with the desire that these boundaries be
respected. The problem I have is that when a human being perceives
an opportunity for a life somewhere else (and I am emphasizing the
word "perceives," they don't need to prove it), it's their right to pursue
it. This is the earth as a shared concept.

If we are all under the same set of laws—in other words, equality
at the global, not national, level—everyone should be able to move.
That is not easy to say with two hundred-plus countries that are worried about who lives within their boundaries and the legal definition
of citizenship. It's a very difficult issue. Because of that, I would like
to return to the idea of circular migration, to allow people to move
through boundaries, through countries. If you don't force people to
stay where they are, to have a single nationality, people move.

On the average, most people would like to return to their home
country, stay a few months and then return to the country of destination to work—one year here, three years there and five years here.
Once you have gone to three or four countries and know how to move
around the globe, going to the fifth country is easier. The migrant is
the same way. As far as I am concerned, the right of movement is absolute. The problematic part is the mechanism of the movement. I can
say that everyone has the right to move wherever they want, but that's
not the way it is done. We have laws, elements that prevent movement.
We need to undo these elements, so the right to move can be restored.

When I talk about human rights, I include every aspect: the right
to earn a living, to services, to an attainable quality of life. Being an
immigrant or a migrant shouldn't mean that a person is not entitled to
the same rights as the citizens of the country they are going to. I have
also said that there is nothing wrong with people voting in multiple

countries. If you live in, pay taxes to and contribute to the economy of three countries, why do you only have a voice in one? How does that work? Where is the equity in that?

For example, there are American expatriates who go to their embassies or come home to vote. We are seeing more people from overseas coming here to lobby the expat community to vote for them. This means we are growing up and finally coming out of the toddler phase of migration. Gradually we are getting a bit more adult and learning that it is not such a bad thing.

AUDIENCE MEMBER 2: I understand you to say that remittances are generated through the collaboration between the countries that are exporting and receiving migrants. You called it "gross national product," but is it also considered taxable income in the Philippines, which therefore would go into the greater good so that a collaborative economic development plan can be created through the migrants' work?

MODARRES: Great question. We look at the dollars as a percentage. It doesn't mean that it directly contributes to the gross national product. So we look at the dollar amount of the remittance and the gross national product and see what the percentage is.

Now, some countries have ways of capturing those remittances, in other words taxation laws, but not every country has these. The reason they don't is that they haven't started to think about it as a way to actually distribute this wealth. That's why there is criticism for countries that tracked the process in the Philippines over a thirty-year period. They haven't figured out the double taxation problem. If a person has been taxed in the United States and then they are also taxed in the Philippines, they may not send money home. They are still trying to figure out this balance. It's something that is still being negotiated; the outcome is undecided.

Many researchers say that remittances actually create class problems in the country of origin, for example, certain regions in India. I once watched a colleague presenting a paper overseas. He showed pictures of a neighborhood saying that when you walk by these houses you can tell that the families have been able send someone overseas because they look so much better than the rest.

So, certain individuals and families in specific regions are helped, but not everyone. Within those towns where this happens, there is at least some local distribution and the construction industry thrives because of these monies. The origin of the money is not national, so a specific city or neighborhood benefits in a natural way and there is some trickle-down effect. But we are still a long way from what you are talking about. But, it is a great idea and I agree with it.

AUDIENCE MEMBER 3: Is any country handling global migration correctly? Here in America, of course, we have tremendous controversy about the Latin American issue of illegal and legal immigration. There is a lot of racist friction produced by that. What can America do? Is there a model in a foreign country that we can learn from? I know Germany has had Italian workers for many years; I believe France had Algerian workers for many years. Is there any country that is doing it right and is there a department in American government that could be developed to do it right?

MODARRES: In terms of which countries are doing it right, I think every country is experimenting. As I mentioned, the Syrians are experimenting with a department for migrant laborers. They are trying to create overseas labor rights, overseas jobs and the capturing of remittances.

There are some programs that are in their infancy. The United Nations has been trying to push this. There have been international treaties signed to talk about refugee rights. One hundred-fifteen-plus countries signed up. The United Nations has begun to talk about global migration and development. A significant portion of the problem is the sending country. This does not include India, China and the Philippines, a handful of countries that have gotten used to the idea of their people leaving. There are countries whose people have been leaving for more than twenty years that still haven't caught up with the notion. The models are still in the making, and it would be kind of difficult to say that a particular country is a great example that we can emulate. Every country is going to be different.

AUDIENCE MEMBER 3: Are you thinking about designing a model for global migration?

MODARRES: I am hoping to. When you talk about human rights issues, just looking at it from the perspective of one country does not create the dynamic you are talking about. The dynamic is international and I say that it can be done one country at a time. The United Nations can try to create a model, but it has no teeth to implement it. It's a tiger without teeth. We need to create the kind of culture that understands human rights as a global phenomenon—not the American way, the United Arab Emirates way or the Saudi way. Human rights are human rights, basic standards. In terms of labor rights and how labor is managed, further negotiation needs to take place.

In Belgium, about three years ago, there was a conference that dealt with this issue. Belgium is a major player in this arena. At this point we are in the development phase. The Migration Policy Institute has papers on circular migration. We are trying to get this defined better, so it creates a mechanism to, at least, go through phase one of policies on how to ease the process of movement between the sending and receiving countries. The rest will evolve.

~ December 13, 2008
SGI-USA Santa Monica Culture of Peace Resource Center

Into a New Era of Victory Over Violence

Lawrence Carter

Dean and Director of the Martin Luther King Jr. International Chapel, Morehouse College

Dr. Lawrence Carter became the first dean of the Martin Luther King Jr. International Chapel in 1979. He is a tenured professor of religion and College Curator at Morehouse College. He has appeared on radio and television and has spoken at institutions of higher learning and peace organizations all over the world. His expertise includes the psychology of religion, religion and ethics and the life and thought of Mohandas K. Gandhi and Martin Luther King Jr. This talk was given at the Thurston Chapel of Punahou School, President Barack Obama's alma mater, to commemorate the tenth anniversary of the youth-led Victory Over Violence initiative, which, since 1999, has collected over one million signatures from concerned citizens across the country, pledging their commitment to live nonviolent lives.

Dr. Carter addresses many of the eight action areas in the 1999 United Nations Declaration and Programme of Action on a Culture of Peace, most notably the third: promoting respect for all human rights. As he says: "I am here to invite you to emulate [President Barack Obama's] willingness to put himself in the shoes of persons who have been abused. If we are willing to practice empathy, if we can begin to feel the hurt, the anguish, the struggle, the difficulty of many less fortunate than we are, then the violence in Hawaii will stop."

I am delighted to be with you and pleased to bring you warm greetings
from Atlanta, Georgia. And those warm greetings are from the heart
because the temperature there is currently seventeen degrees. I am thrilled
to be in the greenest school in America; thrilled to be in the school with
the best sports program, having been chosen out of thirty-eight thousand
high schools by *Sports Illustrated*; a school that is distinguished for its
outstanding alumni and whose marching band will perform in Barack
Obama's presidential inauguration parade in Washington, D.C. And I'm
going to be there to see that.

It's a real pleasure to be here and, I must say, you are some of the most
mature high school students I've ever seen. I brought a high school talk
with me this evening and I am going to let all of the mature ones in the
house eavesdrop on what I am going to say to those who are young at heart.

Self-Evident Truths

I came here thinking about the need to affirm the dignity of all. So, let
me begin with one quote from history. On July 4, 1776, the Declaration
of Independence of the United States of America became a reality with
this pronouncement: "We hold these truths to be self evident, that all men
(and that includes women) are created equal, that they are endowed by
their Creator with certain inalienable Rights; that among these are Life,
Liberty and the pursuit of Happiness."

This ideal vision came closer to full realization of affirming the dignity
of all on November 4, 2008, at 11 p.m., eastern standard time, when United
Press International and the Associated Press chimed the news from coast to
coast and continent to continent that the American Civil War was finally
over, when a black man, Barack Hussein Obama, won enough electoral
votes to become the forty-fourth President of the United States.

There is no such thing as a self-made anything. Everyone is dependent on someone, some group, some family, some institution, to get us to
where we are tonight. Martin Luther King Jr., Barack Hussein Obama and

you are not exceptions to this rule. Because of the sacrifices and self-discipline of many who came before us on the Hawaiian Islands, this beautiful, sacred land, this moment was made possible – this local and international moment. This is a relay race, not a marathon. You have received a baton from someone; you are going to pass the baton to someone else; you will not run the entire race alone.

Defining a New National Character

Tonight, we are in a time of change, of transformation and renewal in America and in the world. We stand on the threshold of complete inclusion, full cooperation and realized equality throughout America. The only thing that is keeping us from actualizing Dr. King's dream fully is our love affair with violence. Unfortunately, in the last eight years, violence nearly became the definition of our national character. But this evening let me congratulate the Punahou School for appropriately focusing on the theme of Victory Over Violence.

It is helpful to the entire planet to be concerned about identifying and overcoming violent tendencies in ourselves and in our most interpersonal relationships, so we can enjoy peace in our daily lives, our relationships and in the world. I understand that your motivation for focusing on the need for victory over violence is the increase of gang-related violence that has plagued Hawaii's youth.

Practicing Empathy

Yesterday was Dr. King's eightieth birthday anniversary. On Monday, as you know, the entire nation will celebrate his federal holiday. I remind you of this because at the heart of Dr. King's dream for America was human dignity and his desire to create a society characterized by peace and justice, not just for black people, but for all.

Forty years after the dream of King and the vision of Robert Kennedy, the Punahou School gives the nation and the world Barack Obama, who has a dream that everyone will learn to practice empathy. If you don't remember anything else I say this evening, I want you to remember that. I didn't make that up. These are Barack Obama's own words that are now in print everywhere. He wants the nation and the world to learn to practice empathy. Barack said in his book *The Audacity of Hope*, that when he mistreated someone his mother would say to him, "Barack, how would you feel if you were in that person's shoes?" Mr. Obama has developed a deep and profound feeling for all people. He feels their hurt.

I am here this evening as a representative of Martin Luther King Jr.'s alma mater, Morehouse College, where it is my privilege to teach. I am here to pay tribute to him and to thank you for giving America and the world Barack Obama. He is not an accident, but an on-purpose, and I am here to invite you to emulate Barack's willingness to put himself in the shoes of persons who have been abused. If we are willing to practice empathy, if we can begin to feel the hurt, the anguish, the struggle, the difficulty of many less fortunate than we are, then the violence in Hawaii will radically drop.

The Spirit of Aloha

President Barack Obama is introducing to the nation and the world the spirit and ethic of inclusiveness, unity and harmony, the spirit of aloha that he learned in Hawaii. I am particularly overwhelmed by the affection, the compassion and the love that I have felt since I have been here. I have not sensed this in any other state, other than the "state" of the SGI. Whatever this spirit is, you must do everything you can to keep it alive because Hawaii may actually save the nation. With his leadership and the spirit of inclusiveness, Mr. Obama is changing the mood of the nation from one of cynicism and skepticism, to hope and optimism.

If you've been watching CNN, you'll have noticed that he had dinner a couple of nights ago with some of the most prominent Republican journalists. The liberal commentators were very jealous. Have you wondered, "What is it that is driving Mr. Obama to seek harmony in the life of a nation with so much diversity, so many different opinions and ideologies?" Have you wondered where his motivation is coming from? Well, his wife, Michelle, says, "In order to understand Barack Obama, you must understand Hawaii." Surprise! A core spirit of the islands is the ethic of *ho'oponopono*. It is the idea that we can work things out and isn't that exactly what we are witnessing Mr. Obama doing?

> ⤙ *We must build a society that has more than*
> *short-term profit as a goal. Most important is*
> *to respect oneself and live with dignity.*

Punahou, you must keep alive *ho'oponopono*. This is the only way you will have harmony amidst a great diversity of races and cultures. Barack believes that peace is the most important thing and that you can get there by respecting people, by affirming the dignity of all. Barack says in his second book that only a strong sense of communal values, a sense of mutual responsibility and social solidarity will help you experience victory over violence. Let me repeat that: communal values, a sense of mutual responsibility, and social solidarity.

You look far too comfortable; I'm doing all the work. Why don't you turn to your neighbors on the right and left and repeat after me? Say to your neighbor, "Are you working on yourself or is this all we're going to get?" Now, that's what it all comes down to. Are you the one who is participating, or should we look for another? Are you going to come out on the field and play the game of life responsibly, or are you going to sit in the dugout and look up, waiting for something good to fall out of the sky? We're all stunned that, out of nowhere, with the thinnest resumé, comes Barack Obama to claim the White House. How did this happen? There is hope for all of us.

War in Miniature

Barack tells us that school is a place to embrace diversity, to witness passions and to delve into history. Don't anticipate the negativity. Embrace the dignity of difference. Everybody can't be like you. But we must learn to affirm the humanity of everybody, even the people who are our oppressors. In dialogue we must learn to appeal to their conscience. This is what Dr. King did, and this is why there is a federal holiday in his honor. My friend and teacher, Daisaku Ikeda, a Buddhist, a member of the Japanese community who lives in Tokyo, said this last October: "Bullying is just war in miniature."

Bullying is what goes on in a lot of high schools, coming from people who do so because they think they can get away with it. So Dr. Ikeda says that bullying, picking on others, is just war in miniature. Pettiness, arrogance, jealousy and self-centeredness, all of those base and destructive emotions violate human rights. On a larger scale, he continues, they manifest as war and crime. Character is the foundation of human rights. We must build a society that has more than short-term profit as a goal. Most important is to respect oneself and live with dignity. When you put leis around the necks of your visitors, isn't that an affirmation of another's humanity and an attempt to live with dignity?

A Shift in Global Consciousness

A few months from now, a blue, white and silver Boeing 747, emblazoned with "The United States of America," will touch down on a tarmac somewhere in Europe or Egypt or Africa or South America. The door will open and down the stairs will come Barack and Michelle Obama. Their appearance will shift global consciousness to a more inclusive respect and dignity for all, because the world is still reeling from the fact that their skin is dark. The racial barrier has been shattered and that is why, not just Jesse Jackson, but youth were on their knees crying as the news was being chimed that the forty-fourth president was an African-American.

This happened because one man from Punahou School, one man, made a decision to be for peace—not against war, but for peace. He realizes that peace is not an outside job. It's an inside job. That's why I had to ask you a question. Are you working on yourself? Coming here is a wonderful thing for my ego. But if you don't leave here with the intention, the intentionality, to improve everything about life, beginning with yourselves, then your coming was in vain.

We must work on ourselves. If you go to school and you're not using your classes to work on yourself, you're not getting an education. Barack Obama worked on himself, realizing that you cannot have what you are not willing to be. He worked on himself by making himself an example of peace. When you do this you will always change the course of history. So be it, and so it is. Amen.

The Gift of Words

I've come here and gotten an education on how to pronounce the name of this school, so I'll leave just a little better. It has been my privilege, in collaboration with the Soka Gakkai International, to encourage educational institutions all over the world to work for peace. One of the things that we do is make contributions of books to school libraries—books by and about Gandhi, King and Daisaku Ikeda. I personally think that all three of these people, and they're not the only ones, as world teachers have left us wonderful footprints, maps, a compass, by which we can find our way.

So I'm going invite Punahou School to receive this gift. Our three world teachers—Gandhi, King, Ikeda—did all their activism, all their work, from an informed consciousness. They were all scholars. Gandhi's collected works filled over one hundred volumes, each volume averaging five hundred pages. If you saw Richard Attenborough's movie *Gandhi*, you didn't see Gandhi writing even one time. So, we need an addendum to that film. Filling one hundred volumes, every one with five hundred pages, makes you wonder what he did in his spare time.

Clayborne Carson at Stanford University is editing the collected papers of Martin Luther King. When those volumes are complete, there will be fourteen volumes, also averaging five hundred pages each. One evening Clayborne Carson called me in my office in Atlanta and said, "There is something I need to share with you, something I think you should know. When we have published all fourteen volumes of Dr. King's papers, it will only represent 2 percent of his work. And remember, he left us at age thirty-nine and led the movement for only twelve and a half years."

It's phenomenal how these men appreciated the use of time. The SGI exists as twelve million members in one hundred ninety countries and territories, with thirty languages spoken. When Dr. Ikeda became president in 1960, the Soka Gakkai only existed in Japan. How did this man build the Soka Gakkai across all those racial, cultural, national and economic boundaries? I think the Harvard School of Business needs to study his organizational skills. This is phenomenal!

He did it with the power of words. His own publications number over two hundred books. Over fifty of those are dialogues with scholars from all over the world on different subjects that affect our common humanity. So, he actually has demonstrated this "soft power" that he talks about, this dialogue that will bring peace to the world and increase understanding.

This is what Barack was saying when he said, "Yes, I will go and talk to our enemies." And he never backed down, even after he was attacked. I was so impressed and I said, "Others can't understand. What he said sounds so much like Jesus, who said he "must needs go through Samaria" (John 4:4). I am very pleased to present this listing of the books for the library and we hope that this will add to the Victory Over Violence movement here in Honolulu. And you'll notice I said "Honolulu"; I'm getting beyond the walls of Punahou School because we want this to spread.

~ January 16, 2009
SGI-USA Honolulu Culture of Peace Resource Center

Appendix A
Declaration on a Culture of Peace

United Nations Fifty-third Session Agenda Item 31: Resolutions Adopted by the General Assembly

The General Assembly,

Recalling the *Charter of the United Nations,* including the purposes and principles embodied therein,

Recalling also the *Constitution of the United Nations Educational, Scientific and Cultural Organization,* which states that "since wars begin in the minds of men, it is in the minds of men that the defences of peace must be constructed,"

Recalling further the *Universal Declaration of Human Rights*[1] and other relevant international instruments of the United Nations system,

Recognizing that peace not only is the absence of conflict, but also requires a positive, dynamic participatory process where dialogue is encouraged and conflicts are solved in a spirit of mutual understanding and cooperation,

Recognizing also that the end of the cold war has widened possibilities for strengthening a culture of peace,

Expressing deep concern about the persistence and proliferation of violence and conflict in various parts of the world,

Recognizing the need to eliminate all forms of discrimination and intolerance, including those based on race, colour, sex, language, religion, political or other opinion, national, ethnic or social origin, property, disability, birth or other status,

Recalling its *resolution 52/15* of 20 November 1997, by which it proclaimed the year 2000 as the "International Year for the Culture of Peace," and its *resolution 53/25* of 10 November 1998, by which it proclaimed the period

2001–2010 as the "International Decade for a Culture of Peace and Non-Violence for the Children of the World,"

Recognizing the important role that the United Nations Educational, Scientific and Cultural Organization continues to play in the promotion of a culture of peace,

Solemnly proclaims the present Declaration on a Culture of Peace to the end that Governments, international organizations and civil society may be guided in their activity by its provisions to promote and strengthen a culture of peace in the new millennium:

ARTICLE 1

A culture of peace is a set of values, attitudes, traditions and modes of behaviour and ways of life based on:

(*a*) Respect for life, ending of violence and promotion and practice of non-violence through education, dialogue and cooperation;

(*b*) Full respect for the principles of sovereignty, territorial integrity and political independence of States and non-intervention in matters which are essentially within the domestic jurisdiction of any State, in accordance with the Charter of the United Nations and international law;

(*c*) Full respect for and promotion of all human rights and fundamental freedoms;

(*d*) Commitment to peaceful settlement of conflicts;

(*e*) Efforts to meet the developmental and environmental needs of present and future generations;

(*f*) Respect for and promotion of the right to development;

(*g*) Respect for and promotion of equal rights and opportunities for women and men;

(*h*) Respect for and promotion of the right of everyone to freedom of expression, opinion and information;

(*i*) Adherence to the principles of freedom, justice, democracy, tolerance, solidarity, cooperation, pluralism, cultural diversity, dialogue and understanding at all levels of society and among nations; and fostered by an enabling national and international environment conducive to peace.

ARTICLE 2

Progress in the fuller development of a culture of peace comes about through values, attitudes, modes of behaviour and ways of life conducive to the promotion of peace among individuals, groups and nations.

ARTICLE 3

The fuller development of a culture of peace is integrally linked to:

(*a*) Promoting peaceful settlement of conflicts, mutual respect and understanding and international cooperation;

(*b*) Complying with international obligations under the Charter of the United Nations and international law;

(*c*) Promoting democracy, development and universal respect for and observance of all human rights and fundamental freedoms;

(*d*) Enabling people at all levels to develop skills of dialogue, negotiation, consensus-building and peaceful resolution of differences;

(*e*) Strengthening democratic institutions and ensuring full participation in the development process;

(*f*) Eradicating poverty and illiteracy and reducing inequalities within and among nations;

(*g*) Promoting sustainable economic and social development;

(*h*) Eliminating all forms of discrimination against women through their empowerment and equal representation at all levels of decision-making;

(*i*) Ensuring respect for and promotion and protection of the rights of children;

(*j*) Ensuring free flow of information at all levels and enhancing access thereto;

(*k*) Increasing transparency and accountability in governance;

(*l*) Eliminating all forms of racism, racial discrimination, xenophobia and related intolerance;

(*m*) Advancing understanding, tolerance and solidarity among all civilizations, peoples and cultures, including towards ethnic, religious and linguistic minorities;

(*n*) Realizing fully the right of all peoples, including those living under colonial or other forms of alien domination or foreign occupation, to self-determination enshrined in the Charter of the United Nations and embodied in the International Covenants on Human Rights,[2] as well as in the Declaration on the Granting of Independence to Colonial Countries and Peoples contained in General Assembly resolution 1514 (XV) of 14 December 1960.

ARTICLE 4

Education at all levels is one of the principal means to build a culture of peace. In this context, human rights education is of particular importance.

ARTICLE 5

Governments have an essential role in promoting and strengthening a culture of peace.

ARTICLE 6

Civil society needs to be fully engaged in fuller development of a culture of peace.

ARTICLE 7

The educative and informative role of the media contributes to the promotion of a culture of peace.

ARTICLE 8

A key role in the promotion of a culture of peace belongs to parents, teachers, politicians, journalists, religious bodies and groups, intellectuals, those engaged in scientific, philosophical and creative and artistic activities, health and humanitarian workers, social workers, managers at various levels as well as to non-governmental organizations.

ARTICLE 9

The United Nations should continue to play a critical role in the promotion and strengthening of a culture of peace worldwide.

107th plenary meeting
13 September 1999

1. Resolution 217A (III)
2. Resolution 2200A (XXI), annex.

Appendix B

Programme of Action on a Culture of Peace

United Nations Fifty-third Session Agenda Item 31

The General Assembly,

Bearing in mind the Declaration on a Culture of Peace adopted on 13 September 1999,

Recalling its *resolution 52/15* of 20 November 1997, by which it proclaimed the year 2000 as the "International Year for the Culture of Peace," and its *resolution 53/25* of 10 November 1998, by which it proclaimed the period 2001–2010 as the "International Decade for a Culture of Peace and Non-violence for the Children of the World";

Adopts the following Programme of Action on a Culture of Peace:

A. AIMS, STRATEGIES AND MAIN ACTORS

1. The Programme of Action should serve as the basis for the International Year for the Culture of Peace and the International Decade for a Culture of Peace and Non-violence for the Children of the World.

2. Member States are encouraged to take actions for promoting a culture of peace at the national level as well as at the regional and international levels.

3. Civil society should be involved at the local, regional and national levels to widen the scope of activities on a culture of peace.

4. The United Nations system should strengthen its ongoing efforts to promote a culture of peace.

5. The United Nations Educational, Scientific and Cultural Organization should continue to play its important role in and make major contributions to the promotion of a culture of peace.

6. Partnerships between and among the various actors as set out in the Declaration should be encouraged and strengthened for a global movement for a culture of peace.

7. A culture of peace could be promoted through sharing of information among actors on their initiatives in this regard.

8. Effective implementation of the Programme of Action requires mobilization of resources, including financial resources, by interested Governments, organizations and individuals.

B. STRENGTHENING ACTIONS AT THE NATIONAL, REGIONAL AND INTERNATIONAL LEVELS BY ALL RELEVANT ACTORS

9. Actions to foster a culture of peace through education:

   (a) Reinvigorate national efforts and international cooperation to promote the goals of education for all with a view to achieving human, social and economic development and for promoting a culture of peace;

   (b) Ensure that children, from an early age, benefit from education on the values, attitudes, modes of behaviour and ways of life to enable them to resolve any dispute peacefully and in a spirit of respect for human dignity and of tolerance and non-discrimination;

   (c) Involve children in activities designed to instill in them the values and goals of a culture of peace;

   (d) Ensure equality of access to education for women, especially girls;

   (e) Encourage revision of educational curricula, including textbooks, bearing in mind the 1995 Declaration and Integrated Framework of Action on Education for Peace, Human Rights and Democracy[1] for which technical cooperation should be provided by the United Nations Educational, Scientific and Cultural Organization upon request;

   (f) Encourage and strengthen efforts by actors as identified in the

Declaration, in particular the United Nations Educational, Scientific and Cultural Organization, aimed at developing values and skills conducive to a culture of peace, including education and training in promoting dialogue and consensus-building;

(g) Strengthen the ongoing efforts of the relevant entities of the United Nations system aimed at training and education, where appropriate, in the areas of conflict prevention and crisis management, peaceful settlement of disputes, as well as in post-conflict peace-building;

(h) Expand initiatives to promote a culture of peace undertaken by institutions of higher education in various parts of the world, including the United Nations University, the University for Peace and the project for twinning universities and the United Nations Educational, Scientific and Cultural Organization Chairs Programme.

10. Actions to promote sustainable economic and social development:

(a) Undertake comprehensive actions on the basis of appropriate strategies and agreed targets to eradicate poverty through national and international efforts, including through international cooperation;

(b) Strengthen the national capacity for implementation of policies and programmes designed to reduce economic and social inequalities within nations through, *inter alia*, international cooperation;

(c) Promote effective and equitable development-oriented and durable solutions to the external debt and debt-servicing problems of developing countries through, *inter alia*, debt relief;

(d) Reinforce actions at all levels to implement national strategies for sustainable food security, including the development of actions to mobilize and optimize the allocation and utilization of resources from all sources, including through international cooperation, such as resources coming from debt relief;

(e) Undertake further efforts to ensure that the development process is participatory and that development projects involve the full participation of all;

(f) Include a gender perspective and empowerment of women and girls as an integral part of the development process;

(g) Include in development strategies special measures focusing on needs of women and children as well as groups with special needs;

(h) Strengthen, through development assistance in post-conflict situations, rehabilitation, reintegration and reconciliation processes involving all engaged in conflicts;

(i) Incorporate capacity-building in development strategies and projects to ensure environmental sustainability, including preservation and regeneration of the natural resource base;

(j) Remove obstacles to the realization of the right of peoples to self-determination, in particular of peoples living under colonial or other forms of alien domination or foreign occupation, which adversely affect their social and economic development.

11. Actions to promote respect for all human rights:

(a) Full implementation of the Vienna Declaration and Programme of Action;[2]

(b) Encouragement of development of national plans of action for the promotion and protection of all human rights;

(c) Strengthening of national institutions and capacities in the field of human rights, including through national human rights institutions;

(d) Realization and implementation of the right to development, as established in the Declaration on the Right to Development[3] and the Vienna Declaration and Programme of Action;

(e) Achievement of the goals of the United Nations Decade for Human Rights Education (1995–2004);[4]

(*f*) Dissemination and promotion of the Universal Declaration of Human Rights at all levels;

(*g*) Further support to the activities of the United Nations High Commissioner for Human Rights in the fulfilment of her or his mandate as established in General Assembly resolution 48/141 of 20 December 1993, as well as the responsibilities set by subsequent resolutions and decisions.

12. Actions to ensure equality between women and men:

(*a*) Integration of a gender perspective into the implementation of all relevant international instruments;

(*b*) Further implementation of international instruments that promote equality between women and men;

(*c*) Implementation of the Beijing Platform for Action adopted at the Fourth World Conference on Women,[5] with adequate resources and political will, and through, *inter alia*, the elaboration, implementation and follow-up of the national plans of action;

(*d*) Promotion of equality between women and men in economic, social and political decision-making;

(*e*) Further strengthening of efforts by the relevant entities of the United Nations system for the elimination of all forms of discrimination and violence against women;

(*f*) Provision of support and assistance to women who have become victims of any forms of violence, including in the home, workplace and during armed conflicts.

13. Actions to foster democratic participation:

(*a*) Reinforcement of the full range of actions to promote democratic principles and practices;

(*b*) Special emphasis on democratic principles and practices at all levels of formal, informal and non-formal education;

(*c*) Establishment and strengthening of national institutions and processes that promote and sustain democracy through, *inter alia*, training and capacity-building of public officials;

(*d*) Strengthening of democratic participation through, inter alia, the provision of electoral assistance upon the request of States concerned and based on relevant United Nations guidelines;

(*e*) Combating of terrorism, organized crime, corruption as well as production, trafficking and consumption of illicit drugs and money laundering, as they undermine democracies and impede the fuller development of a culture of peace.

14. Actions to advance understanding, tolerance and solidarity:

(*a*) Implement the Declaration of Principles on Tolerance and the Follow-up Plan of Action for the United Nations Year for Tolerance[6] (1995);

(*b*) Support activities in the context of the United Nations Year of Dialogue among Civilizations in the year 2001;

(*c*) Study further the local or indigenous practices and traditions of dispute settlement and promotion of tolerance with the objective of learning from them;

(*d*) Support actions that foster understanding, tolerance and solidarity throughout society, in particular with vulnerable groups;

(*e*) Further support the attainment of the goals of the International Decade of the World's Indigenous People;

(*f*) Support actions that foster tolerance and solidarity with refugees and displaced persons, bearing in mind the objective of facilitating their voluntary return and social integration;

(*g*) Support actions that foster tolerance and solidarity with migrants;

(*h*) Promote increased understanding, tolerance and cooperation among all peoples through, inter alia, appropriate use of new technologies and dissemination of information;

(*i*) Support actions that foster understanding, tolerance, solidarity and cooperation among peoples and within and among nations.

15. Actions to support participatory communication and the free flow of information and knowledge:

   (*a*) Support the important role of the media in the promotion of a culture of peace;

   (*b*) Ensure freedom of the press and freedom of information and communication;

   (*c*) Make effective use of the media for advocacy and dissemination of information on a culture of peace involving, as appropriate, the United Nations and relevant regional, national and local mechanisms;

   (*d*) Promote mass communication that enables communities to express their needs and participate in decision-making;

   (*e*) Take measures to address the issue of violence in the media, including new communication technologies, *inter alia*, the Internet;

   (*f*) Increase efforts to promote the sharing of information on new information technologies, including the Internet.

16. Actions to promote international peace and security:

   (*a*) Promote general and complete disarmament under strict and effective international control, taking into account the priorities established by the United Nations in the field of disarmament;

   (*b*) Draw, where appropriate, on lessons conducive to a culture of peace learned from "military conversion" efforts as evidenced in some countries of the world;

   (*c*) Emphasize the inadmissibility of acquisition of territory by war and the need to work for a just and lasting peace in all parts of the world;

   (*d*) Encourage confidence-building measures and efforts for negotiating peaceful settlements;

   (*e*) Take measures to eliminate illicit production and traffic of small arms and light weapons;

(*f*) Support initiatives, at the national, regional and international levels, to address concrete problems arising from post-conflict situations, such as demobilization, reintegration of former combatants into society, as well as refugees and displaced persons, weapon collection programmes, exchange of information and confidence-building;

(*g*) Discourage the adoption of and refrain from any unilateral measure, not in accordance with international law and the Charter of the United Nations, that impedes the full achievement of economic and social development by the population of the affected countries, in particular women and children, that hinders their well-being, that creates obstacles to the full enjoyment of their human rights, including the right of everyone to a standard of living adequate for their health and well-being and their right to food, medical care and the necessary social services, while reaffirming that food and medicine must not be used as a tool for political pressure;

(*h*) Refrain from military, political, economic or any other form of coercion, not in accordance with international law and the Charter, aimed against the political independence or territorial integrity of any State;

(*i*) Recommend proper consideration for the issue of the humanitarian impact of sanctions, in particular on women and children, with a view to minimizing the humanitarian effects of sanctions;

(*j*) Promote greater involvement of women in prevention and resolution of conflicts and, in particular, in activities promoting a culture of peace in post-conflict situations;

(*k*) Promote initiatives in conflict situations such as days of tranquillity to carry out immunization and medicine distribution campaigns, corridors of peace to ensure delivery of humanitarian supplies and sanctuaries of peace to respect the central role of health and medical institutions such as hospitals and clinics;

(*l*) Encourage training in techniques for the understanding, prevention and resolution of conflict for the concerned staff of the United Nations, relevant regional organizations and Member States, upon request, where appropriate.

107th plenary meeting
13 September 1999

1. United Nations Educational, Scientific and Cultural Organization, *Records of the General Conference, Twenty-eighth Session, Paris, 25 October–16 November 1995*, vol. 1: Resolutions, resolution 5.4, annexes.
2. A/CONF.157/24 (Part I), chap. III.
3. Resolution 41/128, annex.
4. See A/49/261-E/1994/110/Add.1, annex.
5. *Report of the Fourth World Conference on Women, Beijing, 4–15 September 1995* (United Nations publication, Sales No. E.96.IV.13), chap. I, resolution 1, annex II.
6. A/51/201, appendix I.

Appendix C

United Nations Resolutions and Other Reference Documents on a Culture of Peace

A/RES/62/89   International Decade for a Culture of Peace and Non-Violence for the Children of the World, 2001–2010, Adopted 17 December 2007
www.un.org/Docs/journal/asp/ws.asp?m=A/RES/62/89

A/RES/61/45   same as above, Adopted 4 December 2006
www.un.org/Docs/journal/asp/ws.asp?m=A/RES/61/45

A/RES/59/143   same as above, Adopted 15 December 2004
www.un.org/Docs/journal/asp/ws.asp?m=A/RES/59/143

A/RES/58/11   same as above, Adopted 10 November 2003
www.un.org/Docs/journal/asp/ws.asp?m=A/RES/58/11

A/RES/57/6   same as above, Adopted 4 November 2002
www.un.org/Docs/journal/asp/ws.asp?m=A/RES/57/6

A/RES/56/5   same as above – start here, Adopted 5 November 2001
www.un.org/Docs/journal/asp/ws.asp?m=A/RES/56/5

A/RES/55/47   same as above, Adopted 29 November 2000
www.un.org/Docs/journal/asp/ws.asp?m=A/RES/55/47

A/RES/53/25   same as above, Adopted 10 November 1998
www.un.org/Docs/journal/asp/ws.asp?m=A/RES/53/25

A/RES/52/13   Culture of Peace, Adopted 20 November 1997
www.un.org/Docs/journal/asp/ws.asp?m=A/RES/52/13

E/1997/47   International Year for the Culture of Peace, 2000, Adopted 22 July 1997
ap.ohchr.org/documents/E/ECOSOC/resolutions/E-RES-1997-47.doc

OTHER REPORTS

A/62/97   International Decade for a Culture of Peace and Non-Violence for the Children of the World (2001–2010), Note by the Secretary-General, Issued 28 June 2007
www.un.org/Docs/journal/asp/ws.asp?m=A/62/97

A/61/175   Culture of Peace, Notes by the Secretary-General, Issued 24 July 2006
www.un.org/Docs/journal/asp/ws.asp?m=A/61/175

A/60/279   Midterm global review of the International Decade for a Culture of Peace and Non-Violence for the Children of the World, 2001-2010, Issued 19 August 2005
www.un.org/Docs/journal/asp/ws.asp?m=A/60/279

A/59/223   International Decade for a Culture of Peace and Non-Violence for the Children of the World (2001–2010), Note by the Secretary-General, Issued 10 August 2004
www.un.org/Docs/journal/asp/ws.asp?m=A/59/223

A/58/182   International Decade for a Culture of Peace and Non-Violence for the Children of the World (2001–2010), Note by the Secretary-General, Issued 24 July 2003
www.un.org/Docs/journal/asp/ws.asp?m=A/58/182

A/57/186   International Decade for a Culture of Peace and Non-Violence for the Children of the World, Implementation of General Assembly resolution 56/5, Note by the Secretary-General, Issued 2 July 2002
www.un.org/Docs/journal/asp/ws.asp?m=A/57/186

A/56/349   International Decade for a Culture of Peace and Non-Violence for the Children of the World, 2001–2010, Report of the Secretary-General, Issued 13 September 2001
www.un.org/Docs/journal/asp/ws.asp?m=A/56/349

A/55/377   International Decade for a Culture of Peace and Non-Violence for the Children of the World, 2001–2010, Report of the Secretary-General, Issued 12 September 2000
www.un.org/Docs/journal/asp/ws.asp?m=A/55/377

OTHER REFERENCE DOCUMENTS

World Report on the Culture of Peace

Civil Society report at midpoint of the Culture of Peace Decade,
Issued 2005
decade-culture-of-peace.org/report/wrcpx.pdf

Appendix D

About the SGI-USA Culture of Peace Resource Centers

The SGI-USA is involved in non-sectarian, public awareness activities to promote the values of peace, culture and education and works with other civil-society and non-governmental groups to develop youth programs, traveling exhibits, cultural events and symposia.

For more information, go to www.sgi-usa.org.

Santa Monica Culture of Peace Resource Center
SGI Plaza
606 Wilshire Boulevard, Santa Monica, CA 90401

Chicago Culture of Peace Resource Center
SGI-USA Chicago Culture Center
1455 South Wabash Avenue, Chicago, IL 60605

New York Culture of Peace Resource Center
SGI-USA New York Culture Center
7 East 15th Street, New York, NY 10003

Honolulu Culture of Peace Resource Center
SGI-USA Hawaii Culture Center
2729 Pali Highway, Honolulu, HI 96817

Washington D.C. Culture of Peace Resource Center
SGI-USA Washington D.C. Buddhist Culture Center
3417 Massachusetts Avenue, Washington, D.C. 20007

San Francisco Culture of Peace Resource Center
SGI-USA San Francisco Culture Center
2450 17th Street, San Francisco, CA 94110

Index